The Story Animal

Reflections on the Narrative &
its extraordinary power to inform,
persuade and enchant

David G. Wade

The Story Animal

© 2020 David G. Wade

ISBN 978-1-9163396-8-2

HERBARY
BOOKS

Published by Herbary Books
Caernarfon, Wales

www.herbarybooks.com

Contents

Prologue

Language and what it is to be Human

'*Humans' most important tool is language*'
DANIEL EVERETT

'*We shape our tools, and then our tools shape us*'
MARSHAL MCLUHAN

In the broad sweep of human social evolution it is possible to identify five major stages, each centred on language, that were responsible for dramatic transformations in our human understanding of the world and of our place in it. We might characterise these as cultural *phase-changes*. Physicists use the term phase-change to describe those particular and special physical transitions that take a substance from one state to another without affecting their chemical composition – from solid ice to liquid water to gaseous steam for instance; or from being non-magnetised to magnetised. A phase-change then, results in a complete transformation of the nature of the same basic matter into an entirely different state.

By analogy, something of this sort must have occurred with the acquisition of language by early hominids. Over time the ability to communicate in this novel, far more efficient way would have brought about radical changes in our ancestors lives. The possession of even rudimentary language skills will have opened up all manner of new possibilities and survival advantages. This development – which was the first phase of the 'language gap' between humans and all other species – was bound to have led to a cognitive revolution. From the evidence of their cultural remains, their use of symbols, and their extensive exploration of the planet, it is likely that this process really got under way with the pioneering hominids, *Homo erectus*. What we know of the tool-making skills and social arrangements of this species seem to indicate a great advance on those of earlier more ape-like hominids. They were in fact the first human species to walk fully upright and use a variety of tools. We may surmise that as a direct result of acquiring speech *Erectus* evolved to become fully self-conscious. And we know, from their remaining artefacts, that they possessed imagination – that magical ability to imagine beyond existing realities. Their language skills, such as they were, were certainly developed enough to facilitate their remarkable achievements – they were globe-trotters and travelled 'out-of-Africa' (as far as modern Indonesia) long before our species.

However, we also know from their fossil remains that the *Homo Erectus*' vocal structure simply would not have allowed the greater fluency of their successors *Homo Sapiens*; ourselves. *Sapiens* out-evolved *Erectus* and all other hominids, and the development of greater language skills must have played an important part in this. In fact the neurological, cultural and intellectual advances involved are now believed to have been responsible for a second, more advanced cognitive revolution. *Sapiens* could not only speak better than earlier human types, they/we were smarter, more intellectually adaptable and more culturally advanced. In fact all these things went together. This second cognitive stage, in which Sapiens hunter-gatherers not merely communicated with each other but freely exchanged both practical and abstract ideas, was the period that saw the construction of evolved stories that explained and made sense of their world – including tribal origins, the ancestors, the spirit-world, natural phenomena and so on – what we now describe as the age of Myths and Legends. During the early millennia of our species there must have been very many of these – and importantly, these narratives would have marked the beginnings of the complex human relationship with the Story.

A third critical phase-change came about with the invention of writing and the recording of previously orally-transmitted tales; in other words, the beginnings of Literature. This stage of human development is generally associated with the Neolithic Revolution, the transition from a hunter-gathering lifestyle to that of settlement and agriculture. These far-reaching changes in human behavioural patterns, with the beginnings of large-scale settlements, saw the recording of more ancient stories and poetry together with the compiling of so-called Wisdom literature. The Mesopotamian *Epic of Gilgamesh* and Homer's *Odyssey*, which are among the earliest surviving works of literature, are characteristic productions of this era. And there was no going back – the attainment of literate civilisation marked a non-reversible stage of human social evolution that was to endure for centuries. Literature and narratives of many kinds became more diverse and complex, as did the societies that produced them – and the Story became even more central to human experience. Importantly, such accounts eventually gave rise to the complex, elaborate texts that became the foundation of all the major Religions which were to endure for centuries.

The challenge to the forms of social order that ultimately drew their authority from sanctioned written texts only really came with advances in technology – and typically, this fourth stage was itself invoked by the use of language; this time by the invention of the *printed* word. The invention of movable type in the mid-15th century had very far-reaching consequences – essentially it ushered in most of the now-familiar features of the modern, industrialised world. The Canadian author Marshall McLuhan spelt these out in his famous 1962 book *The Gutenberg Galaxy*; McLuhan attributed not only the rise of democracy and individualism to the introduction of printing, but also of capitalism and nationalism. He emphasised the role that the introduction of new technologies (particularly those involved with language) had on human consciousness and outlook – and he foresaw the far-reaching effects that would inevitably follow the introduction of the new forms of electronic media, which had already begun to appear.

The advances in instant global communication, the advent of the Internet, social media and Information Technology (particularly in combination with the 'fourth-screen' technology of smart phones, tablets etc.) has indeed meant that at present we are all involved in another era of profound transformation – one that has already brought about enormous changes in the lifestyles of just about everybody on the planet, and which clearly has not yet run its course. These changes have not been all for the good of course. In common with the previous phase-changes (and humans being humans), there are negative aspects to this transition. Despite its unprecedented powers of communication, and the great hopes it offers for increased human understanding, electronic media has allowed old hatreds, demagoguery, deception and criminality to flourish in its wake.

There was nothing uniform in the roll-out of the phase-changes referred to above. In historical and geographical terms the earlier transitions were more gradual, whereas the most recent is rapidly changing the entire global outlook. However language was, and still is, deeply implicated in all of these transformations, precisely because it is one of the primary characteristics of Humans, and probably the most important. Certainly the possession of this faculty sets us apart from the rest of Nature. Our natural milieu is the socially-constructed world of language, culture and ideology – and because human nature is so completely conditioned by language, it affects the entire range of our behaviour, most importantly, our sense of identity. This, it turns out, is critical for us as the intensely social animals that we are. Our intelligence, like that of our primate forbears, is finely tuned to the minutiae of social interaction, and the notion of 'belonging' is essential for our sense of balanced well-being. It is also the principle way we establish our place in, and make sense of, the world. For most of us it seems perfectly natural to belong to and identify with a group, or rather, in our more complex societies, with a whole range of groupings. Language, together with its associated tendency to storification, is critical in this process. It provides the basis – the template – of our personal and cultural identities, of our moral sensibility. It is in this sense that we are the *Story Animal*.

Introduction

'Story is a basic principle of mind. Most of our experience, our knowledge, and our thinking is organised as stories'
MARK TURNER

Humans *love* stories – we love to hear them, to discuss them with others, and we like to believe in them. In fact our entire outlook is coloured by narratives of one kind or another, and always has been. Human culture, and there is no other kind, actually rests on stories. Even in this thoroughly digitised, technologically advanced 21st century we are swimming in a positive Sea of Stories. Just consider the sheer quantity of fiction that is regularly consumed, world-wide, on a daily basis – this formidable list would have to include countless soap operas, radio and TV dramas, the publication of thousands of novels and magazines every month, not to speak of all the movies, theatre plays and operas being produced. In fact our appetite for fiction seems unquenchable and it clearly fulfils an important need in many people's lives (particularly soap-operas). In addition there are the mass of quasi-factual accounts that are equally popular these days – news from the world of actors, sports personalities and other 'celebrities' in the burgeoning list of gossip-magazines and daytime TV programs.

And there are other, rather less benign narratives that have come to impinge on our daily lives – I refer, of course, not only to genuine News broadcasts, but also to the hydra-headed monsters of Fake News, Conspiracy theories and the general proliferation of malicious reports for some or other propaganda purpose. The 'Global Electronic Rumour Mill' has acquired enormous influence in the relatively short period since the digital world has come into being. Also, hardly a day goes by without news of a suicidal religious fanatic blowing themselves and others up in the name of some deluded, text-based, fundamentalist cause. Indeed, literalist interpretations of ancient texts have become one of the more insidious threats to modern civilised life. These are particularly destructive since the protagonists of these pre-modern texts seem perfectly willing to use all available modern technological means to impose their distorted interpretations and the programmes based on these. Biblical Creationists and Islamic 'Jihadists', for instance, appear to see no conflict in the patent contradictions between their fantasies and the realities of modern life that are supported by its science and technology.

Overall, we seem to be as enthralled and affected by Stories and their outcomes as ever we have been. This book, then, is an investigation into the place of the story in human thought and experience, but also into the ways in which our story-forming habits can lead us into so many of our less creditable forms of behaviour. We count ourselves as the most intelligent species on the planet but all too often it seems that the gift of Reason, that uniquely human attribute, actually gives us a permanent licence to act really stupidly. It is certainly the case that creatures of lesser brain-power than ourselves do not engage in mutually destructive wars, do not follow obviously psychotic leaders, do not allow themselves to believe clearly delusional doctrines, etc. But we humans do all of these, and similarly idiotic things, on a fairly continuous basis – and what is more, we usually feel that our actions are entirely justified and we are prepared to vigorously defend them. We are smart but stupid too – and unfortunately, much of the latter seems connected with the fact that we tend to frame our experience in stories.

The term Story is of course very broad. It can be a mere account of events, or tales, anecdotes and narratives across a whole spectrum of real or imagined events – but the contention here is that the story form is a far more important aspect of the human psyche than is generally realised. We not only enjoy stories and rely on them to buttress our sense of identity, but we use them to interpret and construct our realities. In a very real sense we are made of stories. It still does seem surprising, however, that implausible narratives are so often believed in favour of reasoned explanations of events, and that obviously misconceived notions manage to persist against a mass of evidence (and common-sense). Even in this age of mass media, instant communication and unprecedented access to every kind of information there seems to be a continuing fascination with improbable myths and unlikely events. Part of the reason for this seems to be that stories are a sort of currency. We all accumulate them, and they have an important role in our social transactions. We live our own story-line, which is part of a greater story, and weave the events of the 'outside' world into our own inner reality. In this way our existence is given narrative meaning and structure – but in common with a great deal of human behaviour, this process is not always reasonable or rational.

In certain pathological mental states, touched on later in the book, a sufferer can build highly complex, but entirely deluded, systems of thought that manage to incorporate all kinds of unrelated and unlikely events. The unfortunates who hold systematised delusions of this kind can be particularly disturbing to normal people precisely because they present extreme manifestations of common habits of thought. They make us uncomfortable because, in a sense, they give the game away. To a lesser extent we all participate in complicated, self-centred stories, often involving fantasy, retrospective falsification and the like. In fact, the usual and most comfortable state of being for humans is to feel that we are 'in the right', with a consistent, continuous, and above all consensual, explanation of events in the very different worlds we all inhabit. But this is illusory.

In reality our thought processes are rarely entirely rational, and our powers of perception are far from being as perfect as we imagine them to be. Our mind/brains are essentially creative and constructive, which means that we fill in the gaps in the information that we take in, and smooth out all the deficits, ambiguities and contradictions. We also tend to be highly selective in our memories and are past masters at reconstructing events in line with current prejudices. In short, we confabulate as a matter of course – all of which means that our view of the world is nothing like as reliable as we are inclined to believe. In addition to these perceptual shortfalls, we all appear to need a certain level of emotional stimulation in our lives. Novel, sensational and quirky topics will always be more appealing than the mundane and the familiar. New modes of thought, new fashions and new turns of phrase are particularly contagious for this reason.

Other factors are likely to influence our acceptance, or rejection, of any communicated account. Stories that support existing explanation are more likely to be given credence, since confirmation of one's basic beliefs is always welcome. This is also true of accounts, including gossip and rumour that come from a familiar source such as friends and acquaintances. Stories that contain an element of *schadenfreude*, i.e. those involving the harm or discomfort of others, are engaging because they appeal to those lower, vindictive, human instincts – and of course there is a perennial fascination with mystery, miracles and magic. Any tale that contains some element of either of these is likely to gain acceptance, and to be passed on.

Not that all stories are equally comprehensible. Although we have the advantage of historical hindsight, it often requires an effort of imagination to see past events and the framework of beliefs upon which they were enacted as the entirely coherent state of affairs that they must have presented at the time. Attitudes and actions that once were regarded as fitting and normal can now appear peculiarly distorted. But the fact is that there has never been a reliable touchstone to distinguish credible from erroneous suppositions – and it is really no easier now than at any time in the past to differentiate between reasonable propositions and those that are merely rationalising fantasies.

It is certainly the case that, in their own time and place, some of the strangest ideas have been held to be perfectly valid – and that this is as true now as it ever was. From a psychological point of view, this is precisely because humans are so adept in constructing a framework of justification for their beliefs and actions. The creative power of the human imagination has been responsible for all the marvels of civilisation, but this remarkable instrument is also perfectly capable of distorting perception and blinding us to any possible alternatives to current beliefs and modes of action. Man is not so much the 'rational animal' of Aristotle's definition, as the *rationalising* animal. The main consequence of this is that consensual explanations of events, or beliefs, or behaviour, are usually far more important to us than objective truths about these things. What we are always looking for, in any social setting, is a *convincing* account of 'what is going on'. In fact, this is a psychological necessity. Anomalies are uncomfortable – as

Aldous Huxley pointed out, it would be absolutely intolerable to live in a world that made no sense.

As culture-bound creatures, then, we have a pressing need for social reassurance. Surveying history, we can see that every society was supported by a system of belief that had its own articles of faith, its own modes of acceptable and appropriate behaviour, and its own back-stories that supported these convictions – and we can be sure that each group, and each individual within that group, felt that their particular take on reality was the proper and most convincing version. Cultural assumptions, by their very nature, are intended to evince confidence. Group identities of every kind are authenticated by their respective *weltanschauung*, and these are bound to appear consistent and complete. This could hardly be otherwise. Cultures do not have gaps in their outlook, any more than individuals have blank spaces in their perception of the world. For better, and sometimes for the worst, both rely on a seamless view of the world.

The astonishing thing is how little most people are aware of the narratives that rule all of our lives. It is resonant with the proverb that 'the last thing a fish would ever notice would be water'. We inhabit a storified world, but like the fish in water, are scarcely aware of the fact.

David Wade
Powys, Wales
2020

1. The Ape that Learned to Talk

'*Man acts as though he were the shaper and master of language, while in fact language remains the master of man*'
MARTIN HEIDEGGAR

'*Language shapes the way we think, and determines what we can think about*'
MARSHAL McLUHAN

'*Language is the Rubicon that divides man from beast*'
MAX MULLER

Evolutionary rocket fuel

It is unlikely that the origins of language – that is to say the precise details of its transmutation from the more limited communicative skills of our early hominid ancestors – will ever be fully determined. What is certain is that this adaptation was closely connected with the acquisition of a number of other characteristics, including culture and intelligence, developments that led to our dramatic separation from all of our near-relatives. The fossil evidence, patchy as it is, gives a clear overall picture of this progression. Two and a half million years ago our forebears had the same brain capacity as their ape-cousins, around 475 cubic centimetres. In the course of the next million years or so the proto-hominid brain size gradually doubled. Then, around a million and a half years ago the process of brain enlargement really began to gain momentum – there was a diversification of archaic hominid types, but overall, skulls (and brains) got much larger over time and, as far as can be determined, the proportion of the brain dedicated to language increased exponentially.

It seems likely that most 'proto-hominids' possessed some measure of 'proto-language', but somewhere around 300,000 years ago[1] *Homo Sapiens* appeared, with a brain three to four times larger than those of our ancestral great apes, and a capacity for advanced speech as fully developed as our own. The advances in hominid evolution, as indicated, occurred with great rapidity – and the adaptations for voice-based communication are likely to have been a central factor, if not the main catalyst in this process. As far as we humans were concerned, language was evolutionary rocket fuel. It provided the escape velocity that lifted our kind not merely away from the world of apes and monkeys, but completely out of the instinct-dominated existence of the rest of the animal kingdom. All the advanced skills that make humans unique – our technological capabilities (cooking, making clothes, building dwellings, navigating a whole variety of terrains etc.), together with a willingness to co-operate with non-relatives, ultimately derive from our ability to communicate and share information in this new, highly efficient way.

There were of course, other, more basic, developments that marked the original hominid departure from its simian ancestry, such as bipedalism and extensive tool-use. It is the case that the rudiments of both of these abilities are found among apes, and that they too have complex systems of vocal communication. But true linguistic skills seem to have been a purely hominid adaptation. Hominids appear to have been natural and prolific

---

[1] There is currently much debate about this, but recent fossil discoveries have greatly extended the time-lines and complexity of hominid evolution

tool-users from the word go, but language itself was their tool *par excellence*. And *Homo Sapiens* became the best at it.

That *Homo Sapiens* is particularly well adapted for language is evident in every part of our anatomy that involves speech production. The human larynx, lips, teeth, tongue and respiratory system have important functions that we share with other animals, but each has been greatly modified to create the special sounds required for speech. That this facility, to varying degrees, compromises the original functions is a sure indication of its evolutionary importance. Our teeth, for instance, are upright and meet evenly; this is not a particularly efficient method of chomping food, but is essential for the production of certain sounds. Similarly, our lips are far more sensitive and adaptable than is strictly necessary for eating and drinking, and so are our tongues. All of these have a dual functionality, but their role in articulating an extensive range of sounds is of primary importance. The larynx is perhaps the best measure of evolutionary selection for speech production in our species. Unlike other primates our larynx contains a 'voice box' that allows air to pass freely through. This enables us to talk clearly and continuously, but since it also makes us vulnerable to choking on our food we pay a rather high price for this. Apes and monkeys don't have this problem, they never choke on their food, but our evolutionary trajectory has obviously deemed that the risks of this adaptation were well worth taking.

A remarkable skill

The extraordinary proliferation of hominid species after the breakaway from the main body of primates, and the comparatively rapid speech-related physiological changes that resulted, provide the clearest indication of the evolutionary value of speech. This was a remarkable skill, and was undoubtedly the single most important adaptive feature in hominid evolution. It is fairly obvious why. For an animal that had a high level of social organisation the ability to communicate complicated signals would clearly be useful in a whole range of situations – allowing a rapid response to unforeseen contingencies, facilitating forward collective planning and, most importantly, enabling learned skills to be passed on to future generations. In short, it allowed a release from purely instinctive reactions and immediate concerns. As a result language facilitated, and was completely bound up with, the development of culture and of higher intelligence. It is clear from the fossil record that hominid brains and minds grew larger in tandem with the various anatomical adaptations that controlled speech. It is also extremely likely, although not apparent from ancient remains, that radical neurological rewiring must have occurred. As we became more adept at language we gradually became brainier and more like the creatures of Culture that we are today. In addition, the ability to talk to others of one's kind, almost of necessity, fostered the magical capability of abstract thought.

It is now broadly accepted that *Homo Sapiens* has an innate propensity for language. We not only have the physical ability to articulate speech, but we have been endowed with the mental equipment to deal with the intellectual demands of language. In other words, *languages* themselves are many, diverse and have to be learned, but the *disposition to use language* is innate and universal among humans. Current theories tend to go against older views that there are specific areas of the brain that are exclusively dedicated to language – the consensus now is that of an integrated functional system which co-opts a range of different areas of the brain to perform this complex faculty. That is to say that we use a range of brain functions for speech just as we use a range of anatomical features to articulate the necessary sounds (this sort of evolutionary re-use of functions is known as *exaptation*).

Critical-period learning

It has been proposed that the basic elements of human speech derive from a set of discrete sounds called phonemes (Aah, Ber, Ker, Dah etc.), which we assemble to form words and sentences. In this view all languages have their own distinct variants of these 'speech sounds' – English has around 44, divided between 'vowel' and 'consonant' phonemes – but like language itself, these elements are highly variable (and their precise inherited nature is still a matter of conjecture). The capacity and inclination to form these sounds are believed to be universal, hardwired in the human brain from birth, but they tend to be language/culture specific, to the 7000-plus distinct languages – each of which is governed by its own complex rules and intonations. Moreover, it appears to be the case that although well-equipped to learn any one of these languages, we have to do this within a relatively short time-frame – specifically, within the first few years of life. After the onset of adolescence the brain seems to lose its plasticity in this regard; languages can still be learned, but they are unlikely to be accent-free (in Japanese some sounds have to be learned in early infancy, but this is an extreme example). Generally speaking, to be spoken 'perfectly', a language has to be acquired before the ages of 12-13. Additionally, in order to speak any language properly one must hear others speak it early on – which in turn implies that culture itself has a determining role in brain development.

The unfortunate examples of language deprivation in various sad cases of severely neglected and 'feral' children provide some of the strongest evidence for the inter-connectedness of our linguistic, intellectual and cultural skills. There are many accounts, from both historical and modern sources, of abandoned or seriously maltreated children somehow surviving – but they are invariably socially and intellectually, as well as speech, impaired. It is clear that the lack of exposure to language and socialisation in the early years of life leaves such unfortunate children with permanent difficulties in mastering language – *and* with severe intellectual and emotional deficits. It is now generally recognised that there is a critical period for learning languages that has a natural cut-off around the years 13-14. As indicated earlier, relatively few people are able to acquire an additional, accent-free, language after this age, but it is also the case that children who have experienced serious social deprivation before the years of 12-14 are not only linguistically disadvantaged but are also in danger of losing their ability to attach and bond to others – and as a result are unable to fully realise their intellectual potential. In the past, feral children were a source of fascination to those who believed that they might represent an example of 'unspoiled' humanity, but the harsh reality, then and now, is that children who have been isolated at this critical early age usually require close care and attention for the rest of their lives.

Autonomous signing & Idioglossias

The employment of sign languages provides one of the most striking demonstrations of the compelling human need to acquire language *by any means* – particularly among young children. The use of signed languages by the deaf is not in fact a modern phenomenon; the practice was mentioned as early as Classical times. And interestingly, signing is not restricted to the deaf; there are many instances where, for one reason or another, this form of communication has been adopted by those with full hearing. In tribal societies it has provided a means of overcoming speech taboos (Australia); it has also been used as a means of inter-tribal exchanges where there was no common language (North America); and was employed extensively in medieval monasteries that had adopted a rule of silence (Europe).

What is perhaps even more remarkable is a famous instance of 'autonomous', that is to say, self-created sign language that occurred in Nicaragua in the 1980s. During this chaotic period of revolution and civil war many deaf Nicaraguan children were placed in an institution but left very much to their own devices. In these difficult circumstances they gradually invented a sign language of their own, a system that was rapidly taken to successive levels of sophistication with the introduction of younger children to this community. Within a surprisingly short time this invented form of signing became a fully-fledged means of communication for the youngsters, who became adept in every kind of social exchange; it is now known as N.S.L. (Nicaraguan Sign Language).

The linguist Steven Pinker sees this unique occurrence as a 'language being created out of thin air' – an extraordinary piece of evidence for the existence of an innate instinctual drive, not only to language itself but to its essential socialising role.

Languages are 'created out of thin air' in another, rather different, context. *Idioglossias* are idiosyncratic, private languages that are produced by otherwise normal young children. The most common form of this phenomenon are the *cryptophasias* of twins. There are some notable examples of so-called 'Twin-talk'[2], but in each of these cases there seems to have been an initial isolating trauma that turned the twins inward, as it were, into their own privately-created world. Despite being of normal intelligence it would seem that their natural linguistic creativity was dominated by their relationship with each other – which tended to lead to even greater social isolation. An incidental aspect of cryptophasia is the tendency of those involved to mirror each other's mannerisms and body-language. Unfortunately, the outcome in these cases is not usually good for the mental development

---

[2] Two of the most studied cases are those of June and Jennifer Gibbons of Cardiff, U.K., and Grace and Virginia Kennedy of Columbus, Ohio, U.S.A.

of the twins involved since they tend to miss out on normal acculturation.

An almost opposite cause of *idioglossia* can occur among children who are culturally over-exposed. If a child grows up hearing a whole range of different languages and is not strongly directed towards any of these this may cause a sort of linguistic confusion that is resolved by the creation of their own 'mash-up' version of the sounds they hear. But in these cases the private languages generally give way, in time, to just one or two of the languages available.

FOXP2

An important recent development in the evolutionary origins of speech in humans was the discovery of a suite of 116 genes, controlled by a 'master-switch' gene named Forkhead Box Protein (*FOXP2*). Initially uncovered during investigations into a family that had speech difficulties as a result of a deficit in these genes, *FOXP2* was found to be critical to speech and language development. The genes involved are associated with control of the face and mouth and responsible for fluent articulation.

FOXP2 is a subtly altered version of a gene that is found in apes and is believed to have acquired its present function with the advent of modern humans. Its discovery in the 1990s has led to extensive and ongoing further research. Originally dubbed 'the language gene' (by non-specialists), the consensus among geneticists now is that there is much more to uncover in the field of genes and language acquisition in our species.

Interestingly, DNA samples taken from Neanderthals indicates that they too possessed the *FOXP2* gene, and that their version is similar to those of modern humans, but that it was regulated somewhat differently (with effects that are almost impossible to gauge).

Speech and Culture

The most fundamental, determining aspect of the physiology of speech and language lays in the human brain's *functional asymmetry*. This relates to the way our nervous systems are wired, an arrangement that means that the right half of the brain controls the left side of our bodies and vice-versa. This scheme is found in all animals with backbone, but is far more pronounced in humans than any other creatures, including apes. Indeed, in humans the left side of the brain controls the right side of the body *and of speech*. Conventionally, the left hemisphere has always been regarded as the 'dominant' partner in this arrangement which means that speech-based comprehension has a primacy over other forms of understanding – a fact that bears strongly on the notions predicated in this book. Left-brain dominance is also associated with 'handedness', our tendency to favour the right (or left) hand, which itself is associated with tool use, that other great human attribute.

Many different parts of the human brain are in fact involved in speech, and no other animal has this feature. The full range of *Homo Sapiens* suite of intellectual skills are certainly impressive. As well as being able to talk, we are intuitively numerate; we use tools for just about everything; are capable of abstract thought, and are able to carry a sense of our own history (both personal and cultural). Wherever we happen to live we create a cultural milieu, and become socialised within it. Most cultures have their own art and music as well as their own narrative traditions. It is unlikely that even those hominins that were our most recent predecessor had anything like the human facility for developed, articulated speech or, by extension, any of those other advanced faculties that seem to have developed alongside it.

Obviously, language itself would have had a complex evolutionary history, and there have been many interesting speculations on its origins and intermediary stages. However, since the subtleties of behaviour do not themselves fossilise, any such theory is beset by the problem of the lack of direct evidence (but see below). It is certainly the case that attempts to teach language to apes has met with a singular lack of success – our closest primate relations appear to lack both the hardware and software to manage this skill. By contrast, it would appear that even newborn human babies are sensitive to the sound patterns of human language, and that by the ages of 3-4 most children will have learned thousands of words and have mastered a basic understanding of the rules of language. Toddlers can ask questions (many), communicate quite complex ideas to adults and, importantly, understand and enjoy quite involved stories – and it is very important that they do so to become fully developed, fully accultured human beings.

Origin of Language theories

As indicated above, despite the evidential difficulties there have been many speculations on the origins of language. It has been proposed, for instance, that the various components of grammar common to all modern languages were assembled incrementally, in an evolutionary progression, beginning with much simpler word-orders[3]. In these speculations earlier protolanguages might have been comparable to the vocabulary of very young children. The early hominid *Homo Erectus* has been put forward as a candidate for this kind of partially-

---

[3] The first appearance of true language is at the present time a matter of some controversy. Some scholars question whether *Homo Sapiens* themselves were originally endowed with the capacity for developed speech and propose that this only appeared with the period of 'behavioural modernity', towards the end of the Middle Paleolithic, around 50,000 years ago. Others firmly believe that even earlier hominids possessed some linguistic capabilities, even a rudimentary 'language'.

formed speech[4]. Others dispute this model and are inclined to see all the advanced capabilities for speech arriving complete and simultaneously via one specific genetic mutation[5]. There are also leading theories that see speech deriving from, respectively, the use of Gesture[6], of Mime[7] and of Music[8]. Each of these latter conjectures are plausible and interesting and have a resonance with observable practice today. Most people gesticulate to some extent for instance (although this is notoriously culture-variable), and of course Mime and Music have had long, well-established roles throughout human history and pre-history.

Gestural theory: This proposes that language was first developed as a system of gesture, and only subsequently morphed into vocal speech. The evidence supporting this is from two sources. Firstly, that whereas apes cannot adopt speech in any meaningful sense, they can learn and use a great range of gestures. Secondly, that in modern humans, meaningful gestures use similar neural systems to that of vocalisation. And

---

[4] *Homo Erectus* were tool-makers (famous for their 'Achulean' all-purpose hand axe), and they were great travellers. But since their tools seemed to have remained unchanged for millennia it is suspected that they did not possess anything like the intellectual or linguistic flexibility of *Homo Sapiens*

[5] Noam Chomsky: Language and Problems of Knowledge, Cambridge, MA:MIT Press, 1998

[6] Michael C. Corballis: From Hand to Mouth, Princeton University Press, 2002; Michael Arbib: How the Brain got Language, Oxford University Press, 2012

[7] Giacomo Rizzolatti and Giovanni Buccino: The mirror-neuron system and its role in imitation and language in From monkey brain to human brain, Cambridge, Massachusetts: MIT Press, 2004

[8] Charles Darwin: The Descent of Man and Selection in Relation to Sex, 1871; Steve Brown: The 'Musilanguage' Model of Music Evolution, in The Origins of Music, MIT, 2000

the fact that the sign languages used by deaf communities are as complex and sophisticated as oral languages confirms the utility of this method. Ordinary gestures accompanying vocal conversation are certainly 'readable', even across language barriers. The signs for 'come here', 'over there' and 'go away' for instance are fairly universal – and there are many others. The problem for the Gestural theory as the precursor of human languages, however, is that it is hard to believe that our hominid precursors would have ever completely abandoned the medium of sound transmission that was adopted by most animals, on land and in the sea, from their very beginnings[9].

Mimesis: As a sort of extension of the Gestural theory this is perhaps more credible as a language precursor, particularly since the relatively recent discovery of the 'mirror-neuron' system. The particular brain circuitry involved in this system is situated close to those used for language and appears to be responsible for making a strong link between perception and action in the individual – which accounts for our ability to instinctively simulate perceived actions. The theory associated with this discovery is that language proper evolved from an earlier gesture/mimicry system of communication. Interestingly, the mirror-neuron effect is not limited to external appearances, but extends to the intentions and emotion underlying physical actions. This is paralleled in the way that children learn words and develop speech patterns by a seemingly unconscious echoing of the speech of others.

Musical Protolanguage: The notion that music and speech, both of which are universal human faculties, may have

---

[9] Daniel Everett, in his account of his experiences with an Amazonian tribe (*Don't Sleep, There are Snakes*), tells of an interesting extension of gesture, namely the use of whistling during hunting expeditions to convey basic directives

evolved together, goes all the way back to Charles Darwin, who suggested that sexual selection may have been involved in both. In his *The Descent of Man and Selection in Relation to Sex* he argued for an initial stage of improvement in general intelligence, followed by an increase in vocal control and the subsequent development of singing skills, to which 'meaning' was then gradually attached – the whole process driven by sexual selection. Attractive as it is, the problem with this theory from a modern standpoint is that it assumes the precedent of complex vocalisations before the ability to convey complex meanings and intentionality. It now seems more likely that these skills would have evolved in parallel.

*

It is abundantly clear then, that Language is so involved with the human psyche and the whole range of human cultures, that it can scarcely be considered in isolation but is rather part of an entire range of basic abilities. However, language in particular is deeply associated with our capacity for abstract thought, from which we derive our ability to contemplate past, future, and even imagined events. Other animals are intelligent, but only humans have such a developed degree of intellectual curiosity, sense of fantasy and the capacity for introspection – and it is precisely this advanced awareness of space and time and of our place in it that leads us, inevitably, to create and inhabit the reconstructed worlds of Stories. We are not dumb animals, we are imaginative animals: *Story animals.*

2. Our Narrative Selves

'A man is always a teller of tales, he lives surrounded by his stories, he sees everything that happens to him through them; and he tries to live his life as if he were recounting it'
JEAN-PAUL SARTRE

'The limits of our language mark the limits of our world'
LUDWIG WITTGENSTEIN

The Story Animal

So what again are the factors that make humans so different from all other animals? Let's recapitulate – unlike all other creatures we are perfectly self-aware and able to reason; we seek explanations for events, have imagination, can fantasise and are able to predict and rehearse future happenings. In other, paralleled, developments we came to use tools extensively, wear clothes, managed to domesticate fire and cook our food – and, of course, we seem always to have lived within a cultural setting that is way in advance of those of any other social animal. But could we do any of these things without language?

Probably not. As a skill, language is key to all of the above and is so completely integrated into the human psyche, so entirely connected with our sense of self-awareness and so involved in our interactions with the greater world, that it is questionable whether we could even hold meaningful thoughts without the allied ability to utter meaningful words. And although language is clearly the most distinctive of human traits it is clear that this ability is not an isolated one. A positive cascade of other specialised talents flow from our capacity for fluent speech, and it is really this complex set of skills taken together that have made *Homo Sapiens* so unique. Indeed the act of thinking itself has clear linguistic qualities[10].

Allied to this specialised repertoire of skills is our capacity for intellectual flexibility, and this too is entirely bound up with language. Animal communication, by comparison, is limited in scope, generally relating to a specific time and place and almost invariably prompted by stimuli, whereas humans can talk about *anything at all*, whether prompted or not. We can refer to past events, the present, or an imagined future, and can deal equally well with mundane facts or entirely fantastic ones. This means, in our speech and in our lives, that we are no longer completely tied to immediate, instinctual concerns. From the beginning, the ability to talk must have greatly facilitated communal cooperation, including the possibilities of planning ahead and working out new solutions to problems. Above all, these skills were also bound up with the acquisition of an advanced 'Theory of Mind', that extraordinary capability that allows us to understand that others have minds and, importantly, to intuit what is going on in them. The combined

---

[10] The proposition that our normal thought processes involve a constant 'inner dialogue' has attracted a great deal of research in recent times. It would seem that the mental functioning involved in this process allows us to compare different points of view and different perspectives in order to clarify our own intuitions. This *dialogic thinking*, a term coined by Charles Fernyhough, is thoroughly examined in his book *The Voices Within*, Profile Books, 2016

advantages of all these adaptations are obvious – in broad terms, language enabled us to share complicated information and to pass it on to future generations. Over time, this was bound to have led to the accumulation of reserves of knowledge, in other words, it endowed us with culture. Culture and language greatly enhanced group coherence and personal identity, which in turn bestowed a greater depth of meaning to human experience in general – and, since we are such a dominant species, has obviously conferred enormous evolutionary advantage.

In fact language is such an important and central feature of human existence that it has become a functional necessity – and it also meant that our social and personal identities have come to be based on self-defining mythalities. That is to say, having acquired language, notions of self and of group loyalty would, ever after, be framed in accordance with particular, exclusive cultural narratives. These narrative forms, in all their great variety, would inevitably have influenced our explanations of events – and they still do. They allow us to interpret reality by organising information into plausible sequences and scenarios – which, in turn, provide existential order and meaning. Indeed, an individual's self-image only really makes sense with this knowledge of a 'located' personal history. Memory, and consciousness itself, are tightly woven into the fabric of these narratives – without them a developed culture would be inconceivable, and without a cultural frame we would not, as individuals, be capable of intellectual development. As Dr. Johnson put it 'Culture is Life'; he might equally have said 'Culture is Language'. Cultural parameters themselves are defined, above all, by the particular language that they adopt; these are 'the archaeology of human experience'. National identities, for instance, are usually associated with a particular geographical location, but they are generally language-centred as well. To be English, French or German one has to *speak* English, French or German. Language is the primary cultural marker.[11]

To summarise: we always operate from within, or at the very least are mindful of, a particular narrative tradition; this is the root of self-awareness and provides the template for much of our behaviour. It could, in fact, be said that we are our narratives. We simply would not be 'ourselves' without the group – or more exactly, the group's collective consciousness, its characteristic story-lines or *mythality*. We are not merely *Homo Sapiens*, the thinking hominid, but perhaps more exactly *Homo Narrens*, the walking, talking, story-telling, narrative-bound hominid.

Languages and stories

The narrative form is in fact an inevitable outcome of language. Stories of all kinds not only involve grammar, but in some sense are a natural consequence of it. Although individual words may be practically meaningless in isolation, the very structures of speech (and beneath this our instinctual aptitude for grammar), dispose towards an ordered, narrative interpretation of events. At the very basic level a sentence, with its subjects, verbs and objects, is usually a mini-story – and the simple act of recalling events in sequence, and placing them in a particular time-frame, in a specific location, tends to organise events into a narrative form. Moreover, just as grammar provides a structure to what we want to say, narratives impose a framework on what we are able to understand. In other words, language shapes the mind/brain. As a result, there is a strong tendency, almost an imperative, for

---

[11] As the world's most widespread language, English is of course a special case. Its dominant position as a lingua franca in the fields of technology, computing, business and journalism – not to speak of the entertainment industry and in youth culture – means that there are in fact many forms of English.

us to interpret the world according to particular storylines, or in Sartre's phrase, to 'live our lives as if we were recounting a story'. The use of metaphor, which is fairly ubiquitous, underlies the extent to which we understand ideas and concepts in terms of other ideas and concepts. As a result, we habitually compare narratives (see below).

These narrative frameworks however, are infinitely variable. As indicated earlier, there are many thousands of languages on the planet, each of which is complex in itself, and each associated with a distinct and complex 'way of being'. Different languages have different rules, and so do different social systems – both of which are effortlessly absorbed at an early age. But the sense of identity that we derive from this bargain ensures that everyone tends to regard their own cultural outlook as the most proper and appropriate, a bench mark from which to judge all others. This disguises the fact that 'normality', of any kind, is actually a highly involved function, in which language-structure and cultural identity are thoroughly implicated. Language can be seen as a cultural invention, but culture is equally a linguistic invention. Our collective and personal pasts tend to be described and structured by the images thrown up by a particular language/culture and its sense of itself.

In short, groups and individuals are defined and differentiated by the stories they tell and believe about themselves – and this affects every aspect of our experience in infinitely subtle and often subliminal ways. All belief-systems – cultural, sub-cultural and individual – are formed on this basis. Our personal story-lines, and those of the groups to which we belong are, naturally, entirely convincing to us, they are indeed the most solid aspects of our reality. But these defining social narratives are at the same time unifying and divisive – unifying within a particular group, but rendering it distinct and separate from others. They may even rely on mutual opposition; 'we' are not like 'them'. This particular dynamic is, in fact, very pervasive.

National identities, for instance, are often formed in a clear contradistinction with those of a rival nation; 'we' are seen as the *opposite* of 'them' in so many ways. In the same way, the political Right and the political Left, have their own justifying myths, as do ruling and subordinate classes, squares and hipsters, and for that matter the Police and criminals. The younger generation everywhere also develop their own modes of speech, which are naturally resistant to attempts by oldies to emulate (at risk of extreme embarrassment). There are always cultural, and sub-cultural, pressures to establish this excluding aspect of a language. Ultimately, cultural diversity is promoted by the drive towards distinctiveness.

Social and role identities are of course a universal human preoccupation; it is a basic human need to have a secure sense of social location. Majority groups enjoy the comfort of a hegemonic narrative, lesser groups, and even out-groups create their own authenticating counter stories. Orthodox views are firmly set within established verities, whereas unorthodox or heretical groups tend to base their identities on a new narrative or, more often, a rectified version of an older text. These narrative constructs, which both demonstrate and maintain group membership, are a key part of human life. They are adopted, and strongly identified with, by all members of the group, and in this way become the basis of social conventions, and part of every individual's make-up. They become an essential part of the natural and normal way of things; effectively, they create a super-organism – again, with obvious evolutionary advantages. But precisely because the human condition practically requires us to be culturally embedded, our knowledge of the world tends to be far more contingent on cultural expectations than we generally realise.

The narratives that we create for ourselves naturally justify all our actions, reasonable and unreasonable. They make every perception, and every action based on them, appear to be part of a consistent, seamless whole – they establish our credentials and create a responsive format with which to deal with the world. This is what humans are *really* good at; we are myth-makers and myth-believers, and for the most part we are far more concerned with maintaining the narrative matrix of our existence than with questioning any part of it. In fact this derives from one of the most important functions of the mind/brain, namely, to provide constancy. Our minds take in information to the extent that there is a developed format ready to receive it; data that doesn't fit tends to be overlooked. In addition, we consistently seek reasons for events and if there are difficulties in arriving at one we tend to generate explanatory, even exculpatory, hypotheses. In most situations a *coherent* format is sought, whether it is straightforward or elaborate, plausible or implausible – one way or another, a satisfactory story has to be constructed.

Memory, Consciousness & the Autobiographical Self

Memory, which supports our individual sense of self, is a constructive activity – and is derived in large part from our conscious musings. Much of this capability is an inheritance from our primate ancestors, whose relatively large brains were necessary for their survival in an environment in which social interactions formed a prominent part. To survive and flourish in their social world requires a high degree of social intelligence (and large brains). For humans (with an even larger brain capacity), our enhanced social intelligence allows us to organise the knowledge of past interactions and to rehearse future ones in a far more extended way. Our imaginations greatly extend this capability, allowing us to reconstruct past and posit future events *of all kinds*, and to weave these into a self-orientated continuity. Individually, 'we' are the sum of these recollections and can never entirely suspend the habit of belief in them, however accurate or not they may be. This notion, of an internal 'autobiographical self', underpins all our actions and intentions; consciousness itself is a narrative.

However, not all memory is the same; it has been revealed as a highly complex function with quite distinct components. In 1972 the psychologist and cognitive neuroscientist Endel Tulving published an account that distinguished between remembering and knowing[12]. In this now widely accepted view, *Episodic* memory relies on previous, personal experience to recall particular events and experiences. It is this that enables us to relive earlier experiences and to plan and ponder future ones. By contrast, 'knowing' draws on *Semantic* memory, involving that which is commonly referred to as 'general knowledge', i.e. conventional ideas, concepts and facts, which are not necessarily drawn from personal experience (names of colours, countries, capital cities etc.). In addition to these two forms of memory, Tulving proposed an entirely other kind of long-term function that he described as *Procedural*. He saw Procedural Memory as 'automatic' and entirely concerned with motor skills – such as tying shoelaces, riding a bicycle or playing tennis.

Recursion: Packaging language – thought – identity

There are obviously no narratives without people to make them, but the reverse is equally true. According to Roland Barthes 'There does not exist, and has never existed, a people without narratives'; one might even say that people are created by their narratives. As we have seen, storylines are essential; they structure our thoughts and organise our knowledge – and as well as helping us to make sense of the world, they enable us to engage with others. In short, everything we do is influenced by the complex of interconnected narratives that underlie our cultures – and from these we draw all our beliefs, identity and

---

[12] Endel Tulving: *Episodic and Semantic memory* in *Organisation of Memory*, Academic Press, 1972

aspirations. But these 'storylines' are not to be imagined as a series of La Fontaine fables - it is all infinitely more subtle than that. A more useful metaphor sees our sustaining narratives as *recursive*, that is to say, recurrent and self-reflecting, to a very high degree – a modality that is an essential feature not only of narrative but of language itself, and indeed is the primary feature of our capacity for abstract thought.

Recursion, which implies embeddedness and self-similarity, is a term that has rather different applications in different disciplinary contexts. In maths and computer science *recursive* describes a data structure that is composed of other similar structures – in the way that a tree diagram can contain other, smaller trees (as in fractal geometry, where this process can be infinite). But in linguistics and grammar the term *recursion* applies to the function that allows the concertina-ing of phrases and concepts. For instance, the sentence 'John is walking down the road carrying a stick' compresses the distinct notions of 'John walking down the road' and 'John carrying a stick'. Trivial as this example may seem, practically all languages use this technique – and most theorists agree that the facility of packaging and presenting one's thoughts in this way indicates a high level of linguistic sophistication. It is clear that this approach greatly extends the possibilities of expression – but for the eminent linguist Noam Chomsky, recursion is itself the defining feature of human language. It is the product of a mind capable of projecting beyond itself, of organising narrative in sequential form and of juxtaposing disparate notional elements within sentences. Recursion allows the maintenance of a complex storyline which uses memory to create an identity, of oneself and others, and of the relationship between both[13]. By extension, human society is

---

[13] Chomsky's ideas on Recursion are linked to his notion of an innate 'universal grammar'. But since there are exceptions to this rule, i.e. languages that appear not to use recursion in their grammar, this has become a controversial topic in linguistics. Daniel Everett discusses this in his marvellous account of the Amazonian Pirahâs *Don't Sleep, There are Snakes*, 2009

based on narrative, and mind and consciousness are as much a collective, cultural product as a personal one. The pioneering linguist Edward Sapir went so far as to say that 'The worlds in which different societies live are distinct worlds'.[14]

Minds and Metaphors

In their 1980 book *Metaphors We Live By* the American cognitive linguists George P. Lakoff and Mark Johnson introduced a theory on the use of metaphors, claiming this usage as an absolutely essential component of language. Their argument runs along these lines – to conceptualise intangible, abstract notions such as *time* or *mind* or *thought*, we have to tie them in to more tangible, directly perceptible, phenomena such as *place*, *distance* or *size*; in other words, to describe one thing in terms of another. The authors claim that the communication of abstract thought, and even the thoughts themselves, would be impossible without this. In their book the authors present a set of linkages that they see as common conceptual metaphors; these include – 'Life is a Journey', 'Argument is War', 'Time is money'. In respect of the latter they quote such usages as – 'I don't have the time to *spare*'; 'You're *wasting* my time'; 'I've *invested* a lot of time in this project' etc. They argue that all language is thoroughly permeated with metaphor in this way, and that this exemplifies the qualities that make human thought and mode of communication unique.[15]

---

[14] The so-called 'Sapir-Whorf hypothesis', sometimes disparagingly referred to as 'linguistic determinism', proposes that a cultures world-view is entirely bound up, and influenced by, its form of language. Developed by the founders of American linguistics Edward Sapir and Benjamin Lee Whorf this theory, although controversial, still has a currency in the field.

[15] More controversially, Lakoff and Johnson have suggested that because the same sort of metaphors are common to many different languages the 'mappings' between conceptual domains correspond to neural mappings in the human brain.

To do their thing, i.e. to relate an event or process in terms of another, metaphors employ analogy. This requires the sort of imaginative and creative insight that humans also exercise with their 'Theory of Mind' (referred to earlier) – and it is interesting that the right cerebral hemisphere (on which, more later), is believed to be involved in both functions. Metaphors enliven language, lifting it up from mere literalism, by providing graphic imagery and by invoking complex webs of associations; language is given greater emotional depth.[16] In this way metaphors are able to reflect, but also frame, our multi-layered views of the world. And we use them all the time, mostly without even realising it.

But metaphors gradually lose their potency. When we say 'I see', meaning 'I understand', we are deploying a conceptual metaphor that equates vision with comprehension, but this has become worn out through extended usage, it has become routine. It seems that a great deal of ordinary language is comprised of these shadow metaphors, and many reflect conventional attitudes as a sort of 'cultural baggage'. Whereas a freshly minted metaphor enlivens language and thought and can provide new insights, tired metaphors are part of stock usage and clichéd thinking.

---

[16] It is sadly the case that those on the Autistic spectrum (A.S.D.), who typically have difficulties with communication and socialisation, also have problems in comprehending metaphors.

3. The Story-weaving Mind

*'After nourishment, shelter and companionship, stories are the
thing we need most in the world'*
PHILIP PULLMAN

*'Our personal narrative is a bit fictional, like the idea that we are
in control of our behaviour'*
MICHAEL S. GAZZANIGA

The Storification of Experience

Unlike other animals we humans are not tied to immediacy. We
do not respond instinctively to every situation as they do, and
because of this we are not the hard-core realists that they have
to be. Rather, as we have seen, we tend to view and comprehend
the world according to learned values, that is to say, through
a particular cultural lens – and most of our responses are
conditioned accordingly. Essentially, acculturation, without
which we are less than completely human, involves 'emplotment'.
This means that we live our lives, to a greater extent than we
tend to realise, in accordance with a story-line, or rather, to a
highly evolved compound of narratives. These cultural narratives

sustain our existence and give meaning to every aspect of our lives - but they can also be misleading. In fact, although we rely on them, our storylines almost inevitably have their own inconsistencies and contradictions. The extraordinary capacity of humans to adapt to, explore and exploit their environments is always associated with a high degree of social complicity, but to the extent that these beliefs may be based on unreliable evidence they can be susceptible to the vagaries of individual or collective delusion.

Above all, as reasoning creatures, we rely on *satisfactory* explanations of events: in fact this is one of the most important functions of the brain and mind. We seek explanations, and if there are difficulties in acquiring them we generate hypotheses. In any situation a coherent interpretation is sought, whether it is straightforward or elaborate, plausible or implausible – one way or another, an appropriate narrative *has* to be constructed. It is now believed that this essential function, the weaving of the elaborate hypotheses that we need to sustain our outlook on the world, takes place in the left hemisphere of our brains.

The Creature with Two Brains

It is perhaps not surprising to learn that just as human perception is rather more involved than that of all other animals, our minds/brains have a more complicated operating system. Notably, as mentioned in Chapter 1, our brains have a greater degree of *functional asymmetry* than all other species. The origins of this 'two-track', functionally-divided, mind/brain system actually go a long way back in vertebrate evolution. Fish, reptiles and birds all have elementary forms of brain asymmetry, for instance, but this feature is far more pronounced in mammals. In very general terms, the left part of the brains of most creatures specialises in routine activities and the right deals with more unusual and unexpected events.

It is also the case that wherever this anatomical arrangement appears the separate brain-areas involved are strongly cross-wired; this is an additional functional necessity. Just as the overall bi-lateral morphology of all creatures with backbones relies on partially-independent but strongly co-ordinated limbs to negotiate space, their brains employ partially-independent but strongly-coordinated brain halves to deal with the cerebral challenges presented by the complex environments that they inhabit. It would seem that a two-brain system is better than one in a complex and potentially dangerous world.

However, as indicated, humans have taken brain-asymmetry much further altogether. The two halves of our brains (the cerebral hemispheres) are far more specialised in their modus operandi than those of any other animal.[17] In humans the left cerebral hemisphere takes particular responsibility for speech and logic for instance, and the right has its own specialisations, to do with spatial orientation, recognition and association. This asymmetrical arrangement is connected with 'handedness', our tendency to be right- or left-handed – an evolutionary development that is believed to be connected with the increasing use of tools by earlier hominins (it would appear that handedness is less important in non-tool using primates). That the use of tools and language should have developed in tandem among our predecessors is perhaps unsurprising because, of course, language itself is a tool. In fact it proved to be the most useful tool of all. But, tellingly, the left cerebral hemisphere is not only responsible for language – for *Homo Sapiens* it became the site where our personal narratives are created. This area, which has long been described as the

---

[17] Observations of split-brain patients (where the connection between the cerebral hemispheres have been severed) indicate that this drastic surgery creates a high degree of 'self-separation', with each side having its own determinations, moods and capabilities. In broad terms, the left hemisphere has limitations in perceptual function, the right in cognitive function

dominant side of the brain, is the seat of our consciousness, of our vocally communicative and 'theory of mind' abilities, and the repository of all our tool-using and story-telling skills. It is where explanations of events, as a sort of a continuous running narrative, are generated. The left, dominant side of our brains then, is where our personalised story-weaving takes place.

This narrative construction is based on information derived from all our senses and will already have been filtered through the specialised processes of both hemispheres; but the left is firmly in charge of this material. Famously, the cognitive neuroscientist Michael Gazzaniga[18] has described the left-brain role as 'The Interpreter'.[19] The left-brain Interpreter continuously supplies explanations and generates hypotheses to create an integrated and convincing account of the real, 'outside' world. It not only coordinates this information but has a creative role, attributing causes and predicting effects. We rely on this incredibly sophisticated process to form an integrated and unified picture of the world. It is this that creates our notion of selfhood and gives us the sense that we are in control of our behaviour; in other words, it endows us with conscious self-awareness. The Interpreter's primary objective then is to convey a coherent and comprehensible account of a complex world, and it generally performs this function extremely well – unfortunately, when the system fails, it can lead to perceptions of the real world that *seem* entirely convincing, but which actually are delusory (see below).

---

[18] Michael S. Gazzaniga (b. 1939) is a leading, and pioneering cognitive neuroscientist and the author of several books on the brain sciences that are intended for a more general readership

[19] 'The Interpreter constantly establishes a running narrative of our actions, emotions, thoughts and dreams. It is the glue that unifies our story and creates our sense of being a whole, rational agent.' From *The Minds Past*, M. Gazzaniga, 1998

Confabulation: Weaving a personal reality

Our mind/brain is the most complicated piece of apparatus on the planet. The ways in which it constantly absorbs vast amounts of information, continuously edits all of this into a coherent, on-going account, and prompts actions on the basis of this narrative, is quite miraculous – even though we take it completely for granted. But it is not perfect. We have all experienced trivial visual misperceptions, misinterpreting an arrangement of objects for instance, before realising our mistake and correcting it. Most of us will also have had mild temporary amnesia while telling a story; 'losing the thread' as a result of some small distraction, before picking up the gist of whatever it was that we were talking about. And we are all more prone than we generally realise to *retrospective falsification* – muddling up what we remember of events with what we imagine to have happened. These minor system-failures are common – such lapses are rapidly corrected and scarcely impinge on the endless parade of certainties presented by our mind/brains. But more serious deficits in a mind/brain system can present far greater challenge to our life-time dependence on sensory reliability.

Confabulation, the unwitting filling of gaps in memory with fabricated (but fully believed in) facts and experiences, is associated with various neurological deficits, usually those involving damage to the temporal lobes of the brain.[20] Typically, patients with these pathologies tend to fill the gaps caused by memory loss with elaborate accounts that can be entirely convincing to themselves, but unconvincing, (and even patently absurd) to others. Because memory is central to our personal sense of being, its loss can be extremely disconcerting, and when serious failure occurs, there is a powerful drive to

---

[20] Including Korsakoff's syndrome; Capgras' and Anton's syndromes; Alzheimer's disease and other dementias; and certain aneurysms. It can also be a symptom of Schizophrenia

fill the memory-gaps that are left – that is to say, to create a complete account of where and who you are, and what is going on around you.

Those who suffer such devastating memory losses fall back on the creative power of their imagination to weave a story out of their new circumstances. So these patients, despite all evidence to the contrary, may cheerfully claim that they are not in hospital but at home; that they are in good health; insist that they are fully engaged in projects; that they are enjoying a cruise on an ocean liner; that they have been in touch with long-dead relatives etc. etc. – and are perfectly willing to expound on their stories. Such fabrications are not intentional deceptions in any way. The abiding characteristic of clinical confabulation is that these patients fully *believe* what they are saying.

In his best-selling book *The Man Who Mistook His Wife for a Hat*, the neurologist Oliver Sacks describes the persistent confabulations of a patient with Korsakoff's syndrome.[21] Mr. Thompson, who had been a shopkeeper, was quite unable to retain any recent memories and did not know from one moment to the next to whom he was talking. But although he had no insight into the seriousness of his condition he seemed quite unfazed by it, and was able to improvise explanations for any situation that presented itself. Those coming into ward were greeted as customers and engaged in conventional small-talk. Sacks himself, wearing his doctor's white coat, would be mistaken for an old friend, a local butcher. The mental confusion that might be expected, induced by his extreme memory loss, was masked by a compulsive, ever adaptive, narrative continuity. In this way Mr. Thompson was able, to his own satisfaction at least, create a sense of normality.

---

[21] Sergei Korsakoff described this condition in the late 1880s, as a form of serious memory deficit resulting from sustained alcohol abuse. Patients have poor recollection of recent events, but fill the memory-gaps with a stream of stories, ranging from the plausible to the entirely fantastic

The neurological complexity that is indicated by the mechanisms of clinical confabulation makes it of great interest to neurologists and philosophers alike. There is a clear contrast between the reduced ability of confabulating patients to comprehend what is *really* happening to them, and their ability of reconciling their new situations with the retained memories of their past experiences, albeit in fictitious narratives. Typically, those with confabulatory disorders seem unaware of the deficits in memory-function that are affecting them, and the narratives they create can range from mild distortions of reality to florid, exaggerated accounts. If inconsistencies in their stories are pointed out they usually try to fudge the issue, and soon loose interest in the matter. There seem to be two broad aspects to this condition, namely, the production of ill-grounded thoughts and beliefs, together with a failure to subject these constructions to any sort of reality-check. Stories are effortlessly produced, but the normal, correcting 'censor' function (the 'how will this sound to others' response), just doesn't seem to be operating. In confabulation all manner of unconformities and fantasies are readily woven in with those more realistic memories that are retained; fantasy and reality are completely combined.

Apart from those with compromised brain-function, confabulation can be found in two other groups, namely, in children under five and in some hypnotised subjects. Young children between three and a half and five years old find it difficult to distinguish between reality and fiction in any case, so it is not surprising that they should mingle the two in their stories, especially when prompted – and they quickly learn to tell stories that please or entertain adults, even about subjects that they are completely ignorant. It is also well known that some people are particularly susceptible to hypnotic suggestion and that they are prone to confabulate when in a hypnotic trance. In these cases, in which memory and sense-of-self are subverted by a practised hypnotist, the subject is induced to accept uncritically the narrative put forward by the hypnotist. While in this hypnotised state they fully experience the suggested version of events, and can be prompted to make their own confabulated embellishments based on these commands. It is a staple of stage-hypnotism to make the subject complicit in these suggested fantasies, to the great amusement of the audience. During this performance the subject is usually oblivious to the actual surroundings, and the constructed story that he has been given, fleshed out by his own imagination, completely eclipses his sense of everyday reality. These effects are so strong in some individuals that there is a real danger that they may extend post-hypnotically, i.e. into their later, waking experience. The implantation of false memories can occur in much the same way.

The mechanism of confabulation, whether prompted by memory loss, hypnotic suggestion or in the imagination of children, has an obvious relevance to the ordinary workings of our minds. In fact it has a strong bearing on the very nature of memory and perception. At the very basic level it is the case that we do not experience sensations in a pure, unmodified way – a great deal of neural activity is required to turn the complexities of sensory data into a meaningful, perceived reality. Perception requires more than a simple absorption of data; we hypothesise as part of normal brain function. And in fact, almost everything we experience has to have a *meaning* of some sort ascribed to it – that is to say that 'things' have to be incorporated into an established neural scheme. Memory itself is always a reconstructive process, and is usually far less reliable than we realise.[22] As part of our normal existence then, we habitually construct stories to make sense of the world, and our personal identity derives from the stories we tell ourselves

---

[22] The term *retrospective falsification* is applied to the effects on memory of pre-existent trains of imagery that can lead to confusion between what is remembered and what is imagined

and others. The narratives that sustain our identity and sense of common identity rely on the way we organise our memories. In other words, there is a sense in which most of us confabulate most of the time – with the same degree of confidence shown by clinical confabulators – the 'story-function' is thus woven into the human psyche at the very deepest level.

The Origin of Language and Psychosis

As we have seen in Chapter 1, there are a number of speculations on the origin of human language, but that the timing and the nature of the first appearance of true language is still keenly debated. There is even a lack of agreement as to whether hominids earlier than *Homo Sapiens* may have possessed some limited measure of linguistic ability. The range of opinion among scholars on the first appearance divides between those favouring 'Continuity' (that there was a gradual evolution towards speech), and 'Discontinuity' (the so-called linguistic 'Big Bang'). The latter includes the notion that language appeared as a result of a single mutation, relatively late in *Homo Sapiens'* development, a theory that is associated with the linguist Noam Chomsky – but this has been strongly contested (and it has to be said that such consequential evolutionary advances are rarely quite so dramatic).

Among the profusion of conjectures around this subject, and of particular relevance to the thesis of this book, are those of Timothy J. Crow, who has proposed that our highly developed capacity for language and social interaction had a high evolutionary price, namely, the human susceptibility to schizophrenia. The primary evidence that Crow offers for the connection between linguistic capabilities and schizophrenia is that the latter occurs in all human populations, at roughly the same age and with similar sex-specific ratios – additionally, that there is no evidence for schizophrenia in any non-human primates. According to Crow the connection between language and schizophrenia, which he believes has a genetic basis, is associated with the functional asymmetry of the brains of modern humans. In this view, the anomalous symptoms of schizophrenia are due to confusion between thoughts/understandings and perceived speech due to a failure of left-hemispherical dominance.[23] On the face of it, this strong linkage between human origins, language and psychosis does seem entirely convincing.

Impaired minds, Fractured narratives

It certainly appears to be the case that 'meaning', that uniquely human value which is deeply associated with language, is firmly linked to 'balance of mind'.[24] For an individual in a hyper-mental state *everything* is over-charged with meaning and significance, whereas, in the state of severe depression, *nothing* has any meaning or significance to the sufferer. The requirements of a stable, well-balanced state of mind would appear to require both a healthy supply of unimpaired, imaginative energy, together with the support and moderating influence of a consensual social narrative. In other words, for much of the time our shared stories help to keep us in our right minds.

This is a gross simplification of course – the human mind is extremely complicated and there are an infinite number of ways

---

[23] Tim Crow has conducted many investigations, and has published many articles, that associate the origin of psychotic symptoms with genetic deviations in the subtle asymmetries of brain cortex (causing confusion between thought and speech). He has also made the link between the genetic changes responsible for these effects with the emergence of *Homo Sapiens* as a species. See *Nuclear Schizophrenic Symptoms as the key to the Evolution of the Human Brain*; T.J.Crow, 2007

[24] Brain scans of schizophrenic patients have indicated that their 'inner voices' stimulated those parts of the Broca's area that are associated with articulated language

that it can go wrong. It is also true that other creatures (without language) can suffer 'mental' distress. But language, and the reliance on narrative forms, is so central to the human psyche that these are bound to be implicated in psychological disorders of many kinds. Patients' narratives will obviously follow their symptoms. Mania is frequently expressed in delusions of grandiosity; depression in delusions of guilt or doom; the 'inner voices' of schizophrenics indicate the broader fragmentation of their intellectual and social selves. In many conditions it can appear that the 'story' (or stories) are running the show – the minds of those suffering from *monothematic delusion*, for instance, tend to be dominated by one particular topic, those with *polythematic delusions* have a range of fixations.

The present consensus on the 'inner voices' of schizophrenics, which these patients believe to have an external origin, is that they are in fact self-generated. In other words the 'voices' are misinterpretations of inner thoughts, and in a heightened psychotic state these, along with other sense impressions, are interpreted as being far more significant than they really are. It would seem that schizophrenics have difficulty in screening out irrelevant stimuli (in the way that a normal mind does as a matter of course). So the delusions they hold that, for instance, people are discussing and possibly seeking to control or harm them, are actually misplaced over-readings of the entirely innocent actions of others. But the paranoid thoughts of schizophrenics, the sometimes florid and fantastic accounts that are created, and the associated delusional systems that support these ideas, usually have their own (albeit highly distorted) inner coherence. Their stories are seriously fractured, but they are still stories.

The obsessive/paranoiac patient can often be extraordinarily ingenious in incorporating all manner of stray references and coincidences into their convoluted systems – and occasionally these structured, delusional beliefs may be transferred from one individual to another, or indeed to a whole group of others.

Folie à deux is an unusual psychiatric condition in which a set of highly-developed delusions can be shared between two people in a personalised belief-system of their own construction. When this occurs it is often the case that these irrational beliefs have originated in the disturbed mind of a dominant partner, who has then convinced another of their validity – but sometimes a couple can mutually develop delusional fantasies, and reinforce each other's views.[25] When a larger number of people become irrationally fixated on some outlandish idea the 'clinical' diagnosis somehow seems less appropriate and tends to fall into the category of *mass hysteria*. *Folie à deux* and related psychotic disorders are intriguing because they present a distorted-mirror version of ordinary habits of belief and mutuality.[26] In fact, precisely because of this, there have been difficulties in classifying this spectrum of conditions as mental illnesses at all. If enough otherwise rational people come to hold a set of seemingly irrational beliefs (no matter how objectively peculiar they appear to others), then they are more likely to be regarded as a cult rather than a certifiable delusion.[27] The distinction here, as in many cases of improbable narratives, can be a fine one however…

Pseudologia Phantastica: Out of control storifying

The notion of pathological mental conditions as a distorted reflection of some or other aspect of ordinary habits of

---

[25] *Folie à deux* exists in a bewildering variety of sub-classes, including *Folie imposée* (in which a dominant personality develops his/her fixated ideas and draws another into them); and *Folie simultanée* (where both parties contribute and influence each other in their shared delusions)

[26] There is also a *Folie à trois*, *Folie à quatre*, *Folie en famille* – and the vaguer *Folie à plusiers* (group madness)

[27] Interestingly, the DSM-IV (the standard classification of mental disorders in the U.S.) does not recognise a person as being delusional if their belief is shared by sufficient other members of their culture (or sub-culture)

thought are particularly appropriate in the case of *Pseudologia phantastica*, more commonly known as compulsive lying[28] – indeed the degree to which compulsive fantasists should be regarded as mentally ill at all is a matter of some contention. We all exaggerate and fantasize a little, but some individuals seem to get completely carried away with their stories and become habitual fantasists – they are not, however, 'mad' in any generally accepted sense of the term (although there has been considerable debate over the degree of their self-awareness).[29]

Compulsive liars, as the term indicates, repeatedly and compulsively tell false stories, mostly involving themselves and their achievements. These can range from mild exaggeration to completely improbable adventures in which facts are thoroughly interwoven with fantasy. These imaginary tales are always presented as true accounts, and there is invariably an ego-boosting aspect to them. These *pseudologues* frequently portray themselves in a favourable light – as wealthy, brave, famous or important in some way or other.[30] Topics that come up in conversation are seized on and wildly elaborated. Their stories often have some element of truth that makes them superficially, and temporarily, convincing, but apart from a need to impress or seek attention there doesn't seem to be any element of calculation to any of this. In fact the entire charade can seem unnecessary and rather pointless.

---

[28] *Pseudologia phantastica* (or *fantastica* in the U.S.) was first used by the German physician Dr. Delbrueck in 1891. The condition is also known as *mythomania, pathological lying, compulsive lying* and *morbid lying*. In fact there is no consensus on the distinctions between these terms, or whether they refer to the same syndrome. As is the case in many mental disorders there is something of a spectrum of presentations

[29] The condition does present problems to the legal profession however, on the matter of personal responsibility. Do *pseudologues* (pathological liars) recognise their stories as false or real? Is the lying wilful and intentional, or simply beyond his or her control? If the latter, can their mental state be cited in legal defence? Is, indeed, a pathological liar competent to stand trial at all?

[30] Pseudologia phantastica occurs equally among men and women

It is a feature of this syndrome that those involved can come to believe their own fantasies, and the habit of relating them to become a sort of lifestyle, an end in itself – they often appear to have difficulty in providing a straightforward, truthful account of anything at all. But material reward is rarely the motive; the impulse driving this behaviour is to do with their internal psychology. The stories they relate are often spontaneous, clearly unplanned and, ironically, they can seem somewhat oblivious to the impression that they are creating. If their stories are challenged (and many of these tales are patently improbable or easily disproved), they tend to add further details and elaborations. If this fails to satisfy the doubter they may try to make light of the matter, or change stories, or otherwise try to wriggle out of the situation. Those possessed of this personality trait appear not to recognise the normal moral reprehension against lying, but otherwise appear to be perfectly sane. Interestingly, the level of intelligence is not a factor; some *pseudologues* are highly intelligent, others rather stupid.

Although it has long been known to psychiatry there are no generally accepted, definitive explanations for *Pseudologia phantastica*. This is partly because, as a relatively mild personality disorder, it has attracted less interest than more serious forms of mental illness. It has, however, been linked with psychopathic behaviour. Psychopaths themselves are usually pathological liars, are prone to grandiosity, and have a notorious disregard for the moral feelings of others. There is also a commonality with *pseudologues* in their need for stimulation.[31] Both categories become somewhat 'addicted' to their respective use of untruthful and manipulative behaviour. For the compulsive liar in particular their behaviour has some of the aspects of other addictions such as substance abuse or gambling – and it has the same basic function, i.e. of blotting out reality. A feature that does not

---

[31] All psychopaths are pathological liars, but the reverse is not true. However, pathological lying is linked to many other delinquencies

seem to be shared with classic psychopathic behaviour however is the apparent 'double-consciousness' of many pseudologues, in which the boundaries between fantasy and reality are blurred, but is accompanied by a degree of comprehension of both. This effect is also found in the fantasies that are prompted whilst subjects are in a state of hypnotic trance – a sort of semi-detached awareness of what is going on.

One of the more intriguing aspects of this condition is that it can affect individuals that are prominent in the public eye; particularly, it would seem, authors. There are obvious comparisons to be made between those who habitually produce fictive, fantasised accounts of events in their own lives, and those involved in creative writing, but for a few writers the fertile imagination that inspires their literary work seems to spill over, and even dominate, their lives. Carlos Castenada, Jeffrey Archer and Laurens Van der Post, all highly successful writers in their different ways, fall into this category.

It is perhaps less surprising to encounter the *Pseudologia phantastica* tendency in the whole criminal tribe of conmen, hoaxers, and imposters. For these it is a small step from fantasising that one is a doctor, lawyer, airline pilot or whatever, and attempting to act out, and to use these fantasies to exploit others. Many in the criminal subculture are in fact highly delusional, and their inflated ideas of their own worth, combined with a disregard for others, means that they can be remorseless in the use of their constructed stories to cheat and manipulate others (there are obvious parallels with certain demagogic politicians). But there is always a personal cost for such conscienceless behaviour; those who use false narratives to prey on people are very prone to become imprisoned by these same stories. To betray consensual beliefs with false ones is to isolate oneself from society; the conman's first and last victim is himself. Typically, *pseudologues* have difficulty in forming lasting friendships or indeed in maintaining human relationships of any kind (even though some of them manage to sell millions of copies of their books, or convince millions of followers of the veracity of their misrepresentations). Perhaps the moral of all this though is that although the story-telling impulse is deeply engrained in the human psyche, it can be dangerous to lose control of it.

Unusual Syndromes/Strange beliefs/Convoluted narratives

We have seen above how a range of neurological deficits can lead those affected by them into the construction of evolved, often quite fantastic, accounts of their experiences, convincing only to themselves. In *Capgras syndrome* the delusion takes the form of an unshakeable belief that their nearest relatives and/or friends have been replaced by an imposter or *doppelganger*. Whatever neurological deficit is initially responsible for this delusion, it is usually the case that the patient builds an elaborate narrative to rationalise their distorted observations. Sometimes these accounts can involve other complicated, grandiose or paranoid scenarios. The related *Cotard's syndrome* involves the profound conviction on the part of those afflicted that they have already died, with the expectation that others will recognise this fact and act accordingly.

Erotomania is a mental condition that takes the form of a belief that a desired person, usually of a higher social rank, is madly in love with the subject, and is conveying their feelings through a whole range of hidden signals (apparent only to those suffering from this disorder). The individuals caught up in this delusion are rarely convinced by the denial of any interest whatsoever on the part of the originator of these illusory advances, and usually persist with their obsessive claims. This is a notoriously difficult delusion to overcome.

In *Munchhausen syndrome* the subject will fake, or greatly exaggerate, an illness to get attention – sometimes paying great attention to the details of symptoms. Some with this syndrome can spend years travelling from hospital to hospital, and when suspected may abruptly leave hospital only to resume their activities in another location. In extreme cases the Munchausen subject can manipulate hospital staff into performing serious, often painful, and completely unnecessary medical procedures. This condition is also notoriously difficult to deal with – the subjects are completely caught up with their deceptions, it is central to their lives – they are genuinely mentally ill, but are in denial and will usually only admit to their assumed physical illness.

False memory syndrome: In this condition the sufferer has genuine beliefs that fictitious events involving themselves, including quite preposterous actions, have taken place. Psychologists have long known that memories are easily embellished and that some people are more open to suggestion than usual. As a milder expression of false memory it would appear that it is a relatively common effect for some people to take in the accounts of others' experiences and come to adopt them as their own. But this syndrome has a fraught recent history by its association with many cases of so-called 'recovered memories' of childhood sexual abuse, which were later judged to be *iatrogenic* (i.e. induced by the suggestions of Freudian 'therapists' involved). Since the questionable techniques of the practitioners involved in 'Recovered Memory Therapy' were prone to give rise to entirely confabulated accounts of childhood trauma, it is now regarded with a great deal of scepticism by mainstream practitioners. Unfortunately the treatment methods involved (intense analysis, hypnosis, sedatives etc.) were in many cases all too effective in planting spurious, but enduring, memories.

Perhaps the most striking aspect of all of these conditions, however mentally or socially disabling, is that they are over-ridden as it were, by the minds capacity to explain, configure and accommodate to their strange situations. But this is the basic point of *The Story Animal*. The continuous, retrospective validation of one's actions is a basic function of everyone's autobiographical memory – we all tend to recreate experiences with reference to present emotional needs.

4. Did you hear about... ?

'Language evolved to facilitate the bonding of social group, and it mainly achieves this aim by permitting the exchange of socially relevant information'
ROBIN DUNBAR

'Language is a social energy'
HENRY HITCHINGS

Gossip and Banter

One only has to itemise some of the habitual activities involving narrative lines to realise how important and central this function is to everyday human existence. Gossip, together with the familiar back and forth exchanges of male banter (which of course is not gossip), probably head the list. But there are other common features of speech that tend to be organised into some sort of narrative structure such as jokes, rumours, reminiscences, poetry, prayers etc. – not to speak of less benign exchanges involving slander, deception and propaganda. The appetite for stories also lies behind such insidious forms as Fake News and Conspiracy Theories – and of course the audiences for all of the above have been vastly extended with the advent of cyber space (see below). These days social media outlets such as Facebook, Twitter and the rest allow a positive torrent of gossip and rumours, together with all sorts of spurious disinformation and 'conspiratorial' revelations.

But on- or off-line it is still very much the case that stories constitute a sort of common currency within a community. This derives from the dual character of language – both as a means of communication and as a carrier of culture. The complex of narratives that create familiar cognitive frameworks have always been an essentially collective process – one of the outcomes of which is that narratives, once they gain currency, tend to persist within a given cultural milieu. Words and stories have the potential to intensify social exchanges, and in some circumstances they can be imbued with a particular resonance. Mere words can make the unreasonable appear acceptable, untruths to appear authentic and the harmful to seem beneficial. In fact, well-intended story-telling was only ever part of the picture where humans are involved. As we know, not all human behaviour is intended to make the world a better place, and stories are implicated in practically every kind of nefarious activity. These days the internet tends to be the favoured venue for cheaters and crooks to spin their storylines, just as they have throughout history and pre-history (and even pre-hominid, since our primate cousins apparently engage in deceit for their own selfish purposes). Even more ominously, would-be demagogues and other ill-intentioned individuals, who have always used the power of words and stories, are now able to use the hugely extended possibilities offered by the electronic media to further their narcissistic, morally imbecilic agendas.

Primate grooming and Human small-talk

To judge by the amount of time we spend on it, gossip (or to use the recent, more respectful term, networking) is important not simply for the value of the information itself, but as a mode of social exchange, a participation in shared streams of thought. However, 'small-talk' certainly occupies a high proportion of these exchanges – various studies have estimated that it constitutes a high percentage of all conversations (between 60% – 90% in fact).[32] Perhaps more surprisingly, it has been suggested that chit-chat may actually have had an important role in human evolution. In the 1990s the anthropologist Robin Dunbar made particularly high claims for gossip/networking, suggesting that it was implicated in the very origins of language. According to his theory, gossip is an advanced form of grooming.[33] The essentials of this idea are based on the observation that the higher primates spend a great deal of their time in mutual 'grooming' (i.e. cleaning and examining each others' fur for parasites etc.), far more, in fact, than could ever be warranted for purely hygienic reasons.

Clearly, there must be some compelling reason for this activity. Dunbar and others have advanced the idea that grooming is in fact an important way of building social cohesion in primate groups – which absolutely depend on strong group bonds for their survival. Further, ape brains are manifestly larger than they need be for the general range of their activities – from which it has been posited that their large brains evolved *primarily* to deal with others of their kind in the jostling, intensely hierarchical, social world that they inhabit. Taken together, these propositions seem entirely convincing. It is easy to imagine that in this setting one's life could depend on friendships, alliances and a well-tuned awareness of others' intentions within the group. The regular physical contact involved in grooming would clearly assist this essential social sensitivity.

---

[32] Robin Dunbar, in *Human Nature*, 1997 thought that 65% of conversation could be labelled as gossip, but a Netherlands group, headed by Profs. Beersma and Van Kleef (who published their results in the journal *Social Psychological and Personality Science* put the figure at closer to 90%

[33] Dunbar: 1996

Dunbar has extended these insights into considerations of the linkage between social development and language, observing that primate neocortices (the part of the brain associated with intelligence and speech in humans) are proportionate to group size.[34] He interpreted these changes as a response to the increasing need for ever more efficient forms of grooming/ social bonding as primate groups became larger and their social interactions more complex. Language, which enables *multiple* 'grooming', was the ultimate solution to this problem, and interestingly, the statistics seem to bear this out. The maximum size of non-human primates groups is around 55; those of humans (and presumably of earlier hominids) are much larger.[35] To summarise, it would seem that the shared narratives of gossip and small-talk have a critical role in holding our complex human societies together. Further, that this group-bonding aspect of interpersonal grooming/chatter is likely to have been an important element in the very origins of language and human social evolution.

However, the ability to communicate in this way will always have had its drawbacks (which are still with us). They include unreliability in the relating of accounts (the tendency towards exaggeration and embroidery), together with an inherent susceptibility to 'contagious' narratives (those stories that convince, but shouldn't). Our reliance on narrative also opened up many new possibilities for the less attractive aspects of human nature – particularly the tendency to manipulate and deceive (on which, more below). And, as already mentioned,

---

[34] The size of the neocortex relative to the size of the rest of the brain is known as the *Neocortical ratio*; as one might expect, this is highest in humans. Since Dunbar first put forward his theory there has been a growing body of evidence to support the correlation between brain capacity, intelligence, and the size of social group

[35] Dunbar went on to develop the 'Dunbar number' (150), which he proposes as the optimum unit-size for modern human groups – a number that does indeed seem to crop up across a whole range of social groups

the whole field of human verbal exchanges, both positive and negative, were dramatically expanded with the introduction of writing and, more recently, of the internet and social media.

Gossip and Rumour

It is perhaps worth differentiating here between gossip and rumour, on- or off-line. Traditionally, they tended to come from the same familiar sources, that is to say friends or acquaintances, but there is an essential distinction. Gossip is concerned with more local, immediate and personal matters (and may have an element of self-disclosure), whereas rumour usually refers to events or people at some removed from ourselves – and the latter is, almost by definition, far less reliable. Interestingly (and despite denials), men *do* gossip, but generally not when women are present, and it would seem that a great deal of the content of gossip, for both sexes, is about particular, known individuals. As a result it is to a large extent self-correcting – if particular points of a dialogue turn out to be untrue the whole exchange becomes debased. But this all means that gossip breeds familiarity and, to some extent, acts as a 'trustworthiness' test. Rumours, by contrast, can spread either (a) because they are true and relevant, or (b) simply because they are appealing in some other way. In narrative terms the 'factoid' snippets of information that are passed on in gossip and rumours are generally fairly minimal.[36] However, rumours may possess a greater nucleic potential, and can form the basis of far more elaborate accounts – one cannot imagine mere gossip fuelling social unrest, but rumours have a sorry history of achieving just that (see below).

---

[36] The term *factoid* was originally coined by the American writer Norman Mailer as a disparaging term to denote a dubious 'fact' that had become widely believed through repetition, particularly in the media. But the term evolved through common usage to mean a brief, usually trivial, item of information

Both are the products of a narrative imperative which manifest the greatest of human abilities and of our greatest weakness. Rumours in particular are frequently trivial and inconsequential, but in certain circumstances, particularly at times of heightened emotional tension, can have frightening persuasive influence. They frequently arise in response to unusual events or behaviours, often filling gaps in knowledge of events and providing missing meaning.[37] They also have a habit of becoming identified with and incorporated into the teller's persona and such stories can be subtly reinforced by personal association. This also occurs in Conspiracy Theories, and in Urban Legends (those 'it happened to a friend of a friend' anecdotes). To question the veracity of any of these passed-on anecdotes can amount to questioning the moral integrity of the teller. Such accounts usually circulate precisely because both sides gain from the telling. There is usually a certain cachet for being the source of information (and who doesn't enjoy captivating an audience?), and of entertainment value for the listener (even if the tale is not entirely believed). A good story, particularly if it involves 'special knowledge', can produce a bonding effect.

Rumours and Panics

Rumour is an important factor in most forms of epidemic panic (such as 'moral' panics, financial panics and other collective enthusiasms that can break out from time to time). Movements of this kind can take various forms, depending on which primary emotion is brought to the fore by the prevailing rumours. A general mood of anxiety is the usual background to these outbreaks, but this can be modified by a range of other

---

[37] The *interpreting* role of rumour has long been formulated according to a Basic Law, which holds that the amount of rumour in circulation varies with the importance of the subject multiplied by its cognitive ambiguity. Gordon Allport and Leo Postman, *Psychology of Rumor*, NY, 1947

collective emotions, including feelings of hostility, or sorrow, or greed – but epidemics of exaggerated fear are the most common expression, particularly if the context is perceived as threatening or perilous.

The classic example in the field is 'The Great Fear of France'. In the late summer of 1789, on the basis of reports about the extraordinary revolutionary activity in Paris, vast swathes of rural France became gripped by a general but unspecified sense of apprehension. Rumours of aristocratic conspiracies and of invasion by bloodthirsty foreign invaders multiplied and spread like wildfire. These usually followed the same pattern. Riders would appear in a village in an agitated state declaring that brigands had descended on their own (neighbouring) village and were slaughtering everyone they could find. The villagers rarely waited for confirmation – after all, this was just what they had been expecting. An alarm was rung on the church bells; women and children were bundled off to hiding places, money was quickly buried, the men would arm themselves with anything resembling a weapon – and someone was sent off to the next village, ensuring that the panic spread further. Many sought sanctuary in the great cathedrals, spending days there in a state of terror. In these conditions of heightened susceptibility the dominant image – in this case of brutal, bloodthirsty brigands – drove out any more reasoned responses. But the 'brigands' never did appear, to the great relief of many (and the bafflement of quite a few), and life was gradually restored to normality.

Rumours, then, are instrumental in mass-contagions because they provide 'explanations' and add 'meaning' where such is required – and they do this in graphic, plausible terms. They are particularly likely to arise at times of stress – during wars, riots or civil crises. Calamitous financial events, such as the Weimar 'Great Inflation' of the early 1920's, the Wall Street Crash of 1929, and the more recent collapse of the market of 2008, were accompanied at every stage by rumour. Ultimately, the value of capital relies on a general confidence that is dependent on a supporting narrative. Rumour can seriously erode this ideality and can lead to irrational, 'herding' behaviour and panics in markets – with disastrous results.

Memes

In 1976 the biologist Richard Dawkins coined the term 'meme' to describe the broad area of notions that carry from one mind to another – regardless of their plausibility, or whether they are particularly useful to their hosts. Using the analogy of gene transference and Darwinian selection, Dawkins postulated that those memes which replicated most successfully had the best chance of survival, rather than those that conveyed the greatest benefit to the recipient. That is to say, the ideas, stories, rumours etc. that, for whatever intricate reasons, exerted the greatest general appeal, were bound to spread faster and further, and endure longer. The analogy between memes and genes was taken further by other thinkers; memes were seen not merely to survive and spread, but to evolve, compete and mutate.

Organised religious belief was one area that Richard Dawkins proposed as 'memetic' (in a later book *The God Delusion* he went so far as to describe religious memes as 'mind viruses'). This description seems more appropriate to some aspects of religion than others, but it is certainly the case that those religions that actively proselytise tend to gain more adherents over time. It is also true that many of the customs and habits of mind associated with religious practices are culturally-inspired accretions. Food taboos can be taken as an example of 'memes' that seem to work principally as 'identifying markers' – cultural preferences which have no rational basis, but which are extraordinary resistant to change.

The concept of memes caught on (actually becoming a meme in its own right). But as the theory developed it gave rise to controversies; different interpretations of meme-replicators were made, some taking the theory more seriously than others – and there was confusion and controversy over their precise nature. For many, Dawkins' definition of memes as 'self-replicating units of cultural information' was simply too vague for the subject to be dealt with in any serious scientific way. It was a useful metaphor, but not much more than this. The philosopher Mary Midgely is one of those who have been highly critical of the entire notion of memes, as over-reductionist – seeing it as an entirely inappropriate atomisation of cultural attitudes and movements which, in her view, simply can't be broken down into distinct units.

Predictably, the emergence of the internet and social media opened up a whole new arena for 'memetic' activity, with its own forms of 'internet-meme', that greatly extended the original notion to include the now familiar viral video-clips. Interestingly, Richard Dawkins has declared this a hijacking of the original idea – which, since they are intentional, should not be considered as 'true' memes (which still lack a broadly accepted definition).

The Narrative Imperative and Social Media

In view of the primary role of language in human interactions, it is hardly surprising that the advent of social media has been one of the most extraordinary successes of the new digital age. Although it only really got under way around the turn of the century, the social media giant Facebook, at the time of writing, has well in advance of 2.45 *billion* followers and several other networking sites now count their users in the hundreds of millions.[38] People all over the world took to gossip/chat/ network on social media like ducks to water, although the

---

[38] The Facebook group alone includes Whatsapp (300 million users); Instagram (111 million users); and Messenger (70 million users)

function of social networking, i.e. to connect with, befriend and influence others, is hardly new – it is simply that it has acquired an extraordinary new cyber-momentum. According to recent official statistics over 80% of U.S. adults now use social networking sites, and the global figure is already around 40% and is bound to rise. Although usage is weighted towards younger users there are no notable differences between racial or ethnic groups – and interestingly, men and women use social media at similar rates. It should be added that it is hard to keep up with social media statistics – the changes though, worldwide, generally reflect a massive increase in usage.

There are, of course, some notoriously negative aspects of the increased use of the new media - notoriously, the rise in postings of insidious comments and gossip that have become known as 'trolling'. There is nothing new about the 'poison pen' and malicious gossip of course, but the relative anonymity of the internet has given a free range to those inadequate individuals inclined towards cyber-bullying or making provocative, inflammatory statements. When this occurs in the arena of political discussion, with the 'echo-chamber' effect amplifying reactionary ideological views into a hateful spiral, the results can be even more socially harmful. 'Fake News', even the most preposterous, has had serious real-life consequences – as when the deluded Edgar Maddison Welch burst into a Washington restaurant with a rifle, firing three shots into the ceiling. His actions were in response to a mad, completely fictitious, hostage conspiracy theory that had grown out-of-control online.[39] The early trickle of fake news turned into a torrent in mid-2016 when huge numbers of them were found to be emanating from the small town of Veles in Macedonia (of all places). It turned out that a group of young men in that obscure backwater had

---

[39] Welch later told police he had read online that the Comet restaurant was harbouring child sex slaves, part of a paedophile conspiracy involving the Democrat candidate Hilary Clinton

discovered that during the 2016 U.S. elections there was money to be made, through Facebook advertising, by concocting unlikely sensationalist stories (often lifted from right-wing American websites). This wave of regressive misinformation undoubtedly had some effect on the result of the elections.

At present it looks as if we will have to learn to live with these less salubrious aspects of the digital revolution; the social rules have already been rewritten and are likely to undergo further changes. If we take seriously the earlier quote by Marshall McLuhan ('We shape our tools and then our tools shape us') the new digital technology, of which social media is an integral part, will not only radically change our world, but is likely to lead to a rewiring of our brains to adapt to these changes.

The Global Electronic Rumour Mill

Conspiracy Theories of all kinds, together with 'urban' or 'contemporary' legends (and much else in the way of non-credible fables) have made an almost complete transition to the internet – and have themselves been transformed in the process. The obscure publications and pamphlets of the former, and the word-of-mouth transmission of the latter, have been replaced by the internet as the medium of choice. Social media, websites and email between them offer an unprecedented means of disseminating stories and ideas to vast audiences, and ensure that their contents are distributed around the world in hours or minutes rather than months or years. The power of the internet to transform society has already been amply demonstrated, but it seems likely that the full ramifications of a completely-connected world have yet to be fully worked through. Among other effects, it has meant that wild rumours, conspiracy theories and the like are far more prevalent now than in the past – fortunately there is also a counter-balance, in the form of sceptical debunking sites such as snopes.com, and discussion groups like Usenet.

Ironically, the major shift in public consciousness brought about by the emergence of the internet is historically associated with genuine conspiratorial threats. The appalling 9/11 attacks on the Twin Towers in New York will always act as a convenient marker of the new realities of globalism and technology, just as the Islamist jihadist/terror movement ISIS has repeatedly demonstrated the shocking efficiency of the internet's persuasive powers.

The globally-interconnected nature of the internet means that genuine news are transmitted more rapidly than in the pre-cyber past, but the same is true of rumour, conspiracy theories and extreme political/religious propaganda. Social networks in particular spread information (often of dubious veracity) extremely efficiently – which, among other things, has meant that conspiracy theorists with different agendas are brought into contact and cross-fertilise each other in unlikely ways. Unfortunately, the sharing of unmediated opinion and hateful and inciteful views can bolster these extreme outlooks, a process that is facilitated by the anonymity offered by this medium.

However, this new way of sharing information has also worked in helping to organise protest and revolt – particularly in countries with repressive regimes. The effectiveness of cyber-protest can be measured by the alarmed responses of the authoritarian governments at which it has been directed (both Saudi Arabia and Iran have threatened the death penalty for those who spread 'anti-government rumours' for instance, and China has detained hundreds of bloggers – there are many more examples). The value of social media in such regimes, and its capacity to affect lasting and positive change, is still hotly debated – but there is little doubt that, for better or worse, it is an extremely powerful instrument – which 'fourth-screen' technology (smartphones, tablets etc.) can only intensify.

Incredible Tales

Why is it that implausible stories are so often believed in favour of reasoned explanations of events, and why do so many obviously misconceived notions persist, sometimes for centuries? Even in this age of social media, instant communication and unprecedented access to every kind of information there seems to be a continuing fascination with improbable myths and unlikely events. Part of the reason is that humans appear to be inherently sensitive to suggestion, particularly where it supports existing prejudices. And just as we humans are naturally creative in our own story-weaving we also have a fascination with unusual and sensational stories that we come across - some people more than others it has to be said. But, paradoxically, it is precisely this essentially creative impulse that makes us vulnerable to deceit, hoaxes and superstitious beliefs – and in the more recent past, to urban legends and conspiracy theories. Some aspects of the Internet may have helped to dispel myths and conspiracy theories, but overall it has encouraged them enormously. These days urban legends have mutated into *cyberlegends*, and dubious stories such as those involving vanishing hitch-hikers, or dead grannies rolled up in carpets on car roof-racks, or poodles fried in microwave ovens, or of sports-cars filled with concrete by angry husbands, now have a world-wide audience, and are distributed at the speed of the World Wide Web – where there are plenty to choose from.

Our fascination with unusual and sensational stories has, of course, always been part of our make-up, but the heyday of modern urban legends seems to have been from around the middle to end of the 20th century (the term itself was coined by Harold Brunvand in 1968)[40].

---

[40] Harold Brunvand, a professor of English at the University of Utah, published his *The Vanishing Hitch-hiker* in 1981, the first of a popular series of books on the subject – showing that myth and legend were, at the time, alive and flourishing in modern urban culture

The characteristic features of the urban (or contemporary) legend are that it is usually presented as coming from 'a friend of a friend', and that they tend to have cautionary, and often macabre, aspects. The personal association with these tales – not too close, but not remote - enabled them to be related as unusual, but plausible, stories. They are also entertaining - an aspect that allows them to override a lack of specific details - and they are contagious.[41] An 'evolutionary' process of selection operates here, with those stories that get repeated most often generally addressing the most deep-seated of fears and anxieties – particularly those concerning aspects of modern life. This credulity is not, in itself, so surprising since it is the case that, in terms of evolutionary survival, it pays to be credulous. Nature has ruled that it is far better to be over-aware of potential dangers than to dismiss them (mistaking a clump of grass for a lion may make you jump, but mistaking a lion for a clump of grass will kill you).

The compilations of urban legends that began in the late 80s and 90s of the last century brought this hitherto invisible folklore to the notice of a wider public – although in its 'outing' the genre undoubtedly lost some of its mystique. The coming of the internet and the transference, *en masse*, of these tales to that medium seems to have led to a further loss of authenticity. The more static versions of legends that are passed these days (in emails, blogs etc.) seem to lack the vitality and constantly adaptive nature that they had in the oral tradition. To compound the issue, there have been many cinematic and televisual adaptations of urban legends in recent years (usually originating

---

[41] The author Chip Heath has identified a number essential features of 'contemporary legends', namely - that they should be in story format; that they act as a kind of mental flight stimulator; that they should engage emotional responses, and include elements of unexpectedness, which generates interest and a curiosity that upsets expectations; they should also present images and messages that respond to existing emotional responses (particularly those connected with fears and desires; they need to be credible, containing convincing, and striking, details, and above all, they should be both simple and profound (Heath and Heath: 2007)

in the popular collections). As a result the original mystique of these tales has, to a large extent, given way to familiarity.

Conspiracy!

By contrast, that other form of over-imaginative narrative, the conspiracy theory, has been hugely encouraged by the transition to cyber-space – indeed the internet has become the primary source of unusual and sensational stories of every kind (not to mention hoaxes and scams). These have flourished since the 2001 9/11 attacks on the World Trade Centre in New York, and there is a whole sub-genre dedicated to uncovering the 'true' purpose of that atrocity – without much consensus, it should be said, other than that it is widely believed that there was US federal government involvement.

The author David Aaronovich attributes these conspiratorial accounts, in the first place, to the human compulsion to create stories, but their ostensible aim is serious: 'Most conspiracy theories try to unmask a powerful, dangerous all-appropriating elite who seek nothing less than unilateral rule and a presumed nefarious regimentation of the populace that includes slavery of mind and spirit' (Aaronovitch:2009). Unfortunately most of these theories are notoriously resistant to any attempts at confutation, since the presentation of evidence that contradicts them can easily be construed as part of the grand conspiracy – never mind that there is generally no substantive proof for their exorbitant claims in the first place.

In essence, conspiracy theories are an attempt to explain events (they frequently appear after notorious, highly traumatic incidents), and to regain a sense of control over them. Naturally, the narratives that are formed will tend to validate existing suspicions and prejudices – which are in turn reinforced by these accounts. Most conspiracy theorists would subscribe to the essentially simple notion that world events have long been directed by shadowy powerful elites (although their actual identity varies in different times and places). It is usually imagined that the agents responsible for specific conspiracies are able to enlist powerful allies to further their plots and, of course, that their intentions are entirely malicious and self-serving. The implicit aim of conspiracy theorists then, is to expose and excise this powerful group.

The most obvious rebuttal to all of this is that such elaborate conspiracies that are claimed to exist would, in reality, be far beyond the capacity of any agency, governmental or otherwise, to control as comprehensively as the theorists suggest. In reality the main impulse to ascribe evil-intentions to a secretive elite is a form of psychological *projection* – which involves attributing blame to others while denying it in oneself. This is an expression of *dis*empowerment and is associated with personal or public crisis (or often both). These speculations then have more in common with the emotional, age-old demonisation of 'the other' than of any rational analysis of events. Not that this affects their popularity. Outlets for conspiracy theories, in common with those promoting extremism of all kinds (but particularly racist, sectarian, fundamentalist religious and other bigoted views), measure their visitors by the millions – the appeal of these narratives is immense. Reasoned analysis hardly gets a look in by comparison.

5. Inner Fictions:
Dreams, daydreams, fantasies & fiction

'*We are such stuff as dreams are made on*'
WILLIAM SHAKESPEARE

What are Dreams for?

Living as we do in a world of constant change, it is essential that we update our relation to it on a fairly continuous basis. In fact the continuity of our self-awareness relies on this constant process of re-construction and re-ordering of the narratives of our life experiences, an undertaking that is conducted by our subconscious minds. Since they give order and meaning to our lives, these personal stories are absolutely essential for our psychic well-being. An individual without a sustaining narrative is impaired indeed, and a society without the support of a narrative frame is inconceivable. However, in dreams we all experience alternate states of being that can go well beyond the constraints of experience and conventional social order (which is what makes them so interesting). The poet Gérard de Nerval declared that 'Our dreams are another life'– perhaps not, but they certainly are other *stories*. In dreams the irrational can become real and we can find ourselves struggling to accommodate the bizarre events and surroundings that we encounter – and there is often a mysterious unfamiliarity accompanying these experiences. How is it, considering that they must be the product of our own psychic processes, that we can be surprised, shocked, even terrified, by the events in our dreams and nightmares? It is as if the story-telling department in our heads is working overtime when everyone else has gone home. And how is it that the dream world, with which we were so entirely involved, can completely evaporate on waking? Dream events unfold as sequentially as those in our waking experience, but we seem to have far less control over events. Why is it that they can be so puzzling and confusing even though we usually retain a strong sense of self? Where *do* these dream-narratives come from?

Dreams frequently incorporate recent events, very often to those experienced earlier in the day (a fact that was observed by the Greek historian Herodotus). However, these evocations are never a simple replay - disparate elements, from different occasions, some invented, can be pieced together, often in incongruous ways. But even when dreams are entirely implausible they usually have some sort of internal coherence. It is also the case that many of our dreams are pervaded with elements of anxiety and other negative emotions – but why? 'Who writes this stuff?'

There have been many theories on the purpose and function of dreams, but the broad consensus these days is that they are associated with the mental reprocessing that goes on while we are asleep. During this essential 'systems maintenance' our various recent memories are consolidated, and this newly acquired information is integrated and cross-referenced with past experience. As may be imagined, a great deal of neuronal activity is involved in this process – which has led some investigators to propose that dreams are a mere 'epiphenomenon', that is to say, that they are an essentially meaningless side effect of this activity. Other researchers draw parallels between the mind and computers and argue that dreams operate as a 'clean-up' function, getting rid of the equivalent of unused files and unwanted settings. These theories actually reflect earlier ideas on dreams, which included the notions that they enabled memories to be worked into a more personally consistent narrative – that they developed and/or suppressed memories (which was the basis of Freud's ideas on the subject) – or that they operated in a sort of self-healing, therapeutic capacity. In fact the most likely explanation, in common with so many other features of the mind/brain, is that they may do all of these things and more; that the dream-process is highly complex and multifunctional.[42] Interestingly, MRI scans taken while subjects were experiencing particularly vivid dreams showed that these were associated with the amygdala and hippocampus – areas of the brain that are linked, respectively, to the processing of emotional reactions and their consolidation in long-term memory. From the perspective of this book it is also clear that our, sometimes bizarre, night-time experiences are woven into a narrative that seems to draw on our innate story-telling skills. In fact dreams, if nothing else, show that we are all endowed with this remarkable creative facility – that our minds are natural story-telling machines.

---

[42] For instance, it has been discovered that dreams occur during non-REM as well as REM- sleep, but are different in character – they are relatively sketchy in the former. Curious too, that MRI scans of dreamers made up to the present appear to indicate that there are no patterns of brain activity that relate specifically to dreaming

Putting reality on hold: daydreams

On the basis of the above we might construe consciousness itself as a form of self-narration and dreams as a shadow version of this faculty – hindered both by the hefty demands of overnight neural sorting operations – and by the lack of the steadying influence of reality-feedback. But what of *daydreaming*? Daydreams, the drifting off into mild, generally pleasant, fantasies are usually seen as occupying a quite different category to dreams proper. For a start we are awake when we daydream, and these waking reveries are on a rather more voluntary basis; we direct our daydreams in a way that is not usually possible in dreams (except in lucid dreams[43]). Daydreams involve a certain gentle detachment from mundane reality, which have, of course, given them a bad press – they have tended to be regarded as mere idle fantasies, and daydreamers themselves as Mittyesque fantasists.[44] But it turns out, as a result of older PET and more recent fMRI studies[45], that there is more to 'spacing-out' than hitherto realised. Daydreaming, it seems, is a very important function too.

Unlike computers, our brains are never on 'standby'; there is a huge amount of activity taking place in our brains even when they are not occupied with specific tasks. In 1997 a

---

[43] The term 'Lucid Dream' applies to any dream in which the dreamer is aware that they are dreaming and are able to direct events. In contrast to normal REM dreaming however there appears to be a higher level of activity in brain regions associated with attention and higher cognitive processes

[44] Walter Mitty is the eponymous anti-hero of James Thurber's short story *The Secret Life of Walter Mitty* (*The New Yorker*, 1939). The hen-pecked Walter dedicates a great deal of his time to repetitive daydreams – in which he invariably plays a leading, heroic role. Because the story was made into a movie he became Thurber's best-known comic creation

[45] PET is Positron emission topography; fMRI is Functional magnetic resonance imaging

group of neuroscientists using PET scans on conscious subjects discovered a previously unsuspected neural network that they described as a 'default mode'.[46] This default activity seemed to swing into action when there was not much else going on – and was all to do with evaluating memories from a purely personal perspective. This perpetual rehearsal of past events, it transpired, was usually accompanied by speculations on future prospects – indicating that we daydream for good evolutionary reasons. These musings amount to a running survey of possible choices and actions, preparing us for what might happen in the near future – and naturally, this stream-of-semi-consciousness has a storyline of hoped-for outcomes – and as a result it can be very constructive. Many creative people get inspired while daydreaming about their projects; ideas can come 'out of the blue' at such times.

The brain resorts to this default neural network whenever it can, notably in the down-time between more or less conscious activities – but it has also been found to operate during the early stages of sleep. It would appear that in this role it takes on the important job of sorting the accumulation of undifferentiated memories and intervenes to prevent a build up of irrelevant material. The selection criteria in this tuning-up process are naturally based on the accumulated data that is judged to be the most compatible with our existing story-line.

So the primary function of dreams, and of daydreams, perhaps ironically, is to reinforce our sense of our selves, to maintain mental fitness, and to keep us in secure touch with reality. Sadly, this is not always the case in those with more fragile psyches...

---

[46] See *A Default Mode of Brain Function*, Marcus E. Raichie et al, Mallinckrodt Institute of Radiology and Departments of Neurology and Psychiatry, Washington University School of Medicine, 2000

Psychosis, Fantasy & Delusion

Fantasy, as we have seen, is a common and beneficial experience in normal and healthy individuals – by contrast, the delusions of serious mental illnesses are symptomatic of a general disconnection from reality. The distinction between the two, between simple fantasy and outright, psychotic delusions and hallucinations, is that those engaged in the former are well aware of the fact that they are in a fantasy, whereas those in a psychotic state experience their intrusive thoughts as a part of reality, even though they may be terribly disorientating and debilitating. There are intermediary conditions. Some fantasists become over-involved in their make-believe worlds and can experience withdrawal symptoms of regret and frustration when compelled to come back to reality. In the end, however, these people generally retain the ability to distinguish between their fantasies and reality. Full-blown psychosis, on the other hand, involves a complete break with reality; highly irrational beliefs, unrealistic interpretations of events and paranoia are the classic symptom of this state. We might say that in the former the story-line controls are relaxed – habitual fantasists usually cherish their reveries; they offer a refuge from the tedium of mundane reality. But for those suffering psychotic delusions the experienced story-line can be distorted, fractured and utterly confusing. With their lack of rational comprehension comparisons are often drawn between these states and those of dreams or nightmares. In other words, these are story-lines that have gotten seriously out of control (see below).

Hardly surprising, in these circumstances, psychotic episodes are frequently characterised by confusion of thought and lack of personal insight. It is symptomatic of the obsessive paranoiac that they can freely integrate all manner of stray thoughts into their consciousness. The natural, human story-telling imperative means that these jumbled thoughts and interpretations can lead to the assembling of highly convoluted delusions – that one is rich and powerful, for instance, or possessed of special insights and knowledge. There is no end to the imaginative power of these disordered constructions; sufferers frequently develop their explanatory narratives to an extraordinary degree. In addition, the sense of dislocation, together with a fluid association of ideas and disturbed trains of thought, is often accompanied by paranoia, with the resulting suspicions also being woven into their personal narrative. The overarching symptoms indicate a severely reduced ability to differentiate between fantasy and reality. In their disorientated state the psychotic patient may be strongly attached to their own deluded interpretation of events, sticking to these accounts and interpretation of events even when evidence is presented that exposes it as misconceived. In such cases the personal narrative, which in normal circumstances hold the psyche together, works here to perpetuate a disorganised state of mind. The normal reasoning faculty has little part to play in these states.

Dreams, Psychosis & Cognitive Bizarreness

There are a number of similarities between the state of dreaming and that of psychosis, to the extent that dreaming has been considered as a useful model for psychotic conditions. The individual's experiences of both the dream-state and of psychic conditions are, of course, unique to the individual, but there are common phenomena – not least that of cognitive bizarreness. As is the case in nightmares, psychotic delusions can be incredibly frightening. And just as we accept the realities of our bad dreams when we are having them, a disturbed individual gives full credence to their distorted experiences – the difference being that one does not wake up and return to normality so easily from a distressed mental condition. In dreams we lack the capacity of normal reflective thought and this inclines us to take incongruous situations for granted. There are obvious parallels with the hallucinations and irrational beliefs of the psychotic experience. Also, there is a tendency to confabulate in dreams – to conflate different people and places and to find oneself involved in incomprehensible and incongruous activities – effects that are compounded by a lack of the ordinary self-awareness of normal consciousness. These sequelae are also typical symptoms of psychotic conditions.

It has been suggested that schizophrenia develops in particularly susceptible individuals as a result of the failure of their REM sleep discharge mechanism. This manifests as an inability to distinguish between waking reality and the 'metaphorical' reality of the dream state – whose primary function is precisely to generate such hallucinatory narratives. This would explain why the delusions and hallucinations associated with highly psychotic states are comparable to those experienced at times by all of us in dreams.[47] The further corollary of this theory is that schizophrenic thinking is subsequently driven by the right hemisphere, displacing the more analytical functions of the left hemisphere. This usurpation of the 'Interpreter' role (see Chapter 3), disturbs the brains natural bi-lateral functioning, which may account for the common psychotic experience of 'hearing voices' and also be responsible for the streams of unintelligible speech known as 'word-salad'. In an apparent confirmation of this theory, neuroscientists have found that similar neuronal pathways are activated during the dreams of normal subjects and by those experiencing psychotic episodes.

There have been various attempts to measure and compare the degree of 'cognitive bizarreness' experienced in dreams and psychosis. Comparisons between reports of the dreams of the mentally sound and the mental states of psychotic patients using

---

[47] See *Dreams and Psychosis: A New Look at an Old Hypothesis*, Charles McCreery, DPhil Formerly Lecturer in Experimental Psychology, Magdalen College, Oxford OXFORD FORUM Psychological Paper No. 2008-1

the T.A.T. assessment did indeed reveal many similarities.[48] The conclusion drawn from these particular trials was that, under these controlled conditions at least, the dream-state *was* a useful model for psychosis.

Dreams and Fiction

In purely evolutionary terms it is not at all clear why humans should engage with fiction to the extent that they do. It is hard to imagine any other animal that would gain a pleasurable experience by snuggling away on a rainy day to have their imagination taken for a ride by reading a novel, or watching an episode of a soap-opera. It's easy for us to understand that a person should be able to enjoy these or similar experiences, since we all do – but it not so easy to fathom in an objective sense why this should be the case. Why do we enjoy reading accounts of the lives of entirely imaginary people, or imaginary animals come to that? What exactly is the pay-off? There are obvious connections between this activity and those other, apparently non-essential, pursuits that occupy so much time of humans everywhere – art, music and dance for instance – each of which, as it happens, can be highly culturally-specific. But imagined stories are a special case; they can hold us in thrall on very personal level – and, of course, they are readily communicable.

To enjoy fiction we adopt an attitude involving the 'willing suspension of disbelief', a relinquishing of our critical faculties that allows us to accept imaginary and even nonsensical experiences as having validity – a function that seems also to happen automatically in dreams. In a sense then, fiction

---

[48] The Thematic Apperception Test, (T.A.T.), which was originally developed in the U.S. in the 1930s, is a rather old-fashioned form of personality assessment. It comprises a series of cards depicting ambiguous images that are intended to engender a response, from which a profile of the subject's subconscious may be drawn. The high degree of subjectivity in these tests naturally limits their reliability as measures of personality – or of cognitive bizarreness

permits a sort of synthetic, controllable mode of dreaming – and through it we exercise our minds in a somewhat similar way – the important difference being that we can always stop reading the book, or turn off the TV, or leave the cinema. By contrast, there is no exit door in dreams or nightmares.

The ability to pretend seems to be an aspect of our capacity for Recursive Thinking, referred to earlier, in Chapter 2, which allows our mind to project beyond itself and to modulate sequential thought. By dint of this we are able to de-couple our imaginative faculty from the more rational, organising functions of our mind/ brains. Pretending, or acting-through possible future events in our imagination, has an obvious value in evolutionary terms. It allows us to rehearse our responses to possible scenarios and to use our imaginations to come up with flexible solutions – and we do this from a very young age. Children do not have to be told about pretending and play-acting; it comes naturally to them. As children or as adults, through our daytime fantasying, in our dreams, and in fiction, we are able to practice these contingency skills. The evolutionary advantage that this delivers would chiefly operate *within* our social environments – and that is the underlying reason for the human fascination with fiction.

It is easy to draw comparisons between the worlds of dreams and fiction - in our night-time repose we are all accomplished fiction writers – and there are many famous works of fiction that draw directly from the dream experience. Lewis Carroll's *Alice* stories for instance, Robert Louis Stevenson's *Dr. Jekyll and Mr. Hyde* and Mary Shelley's hauntingly phantasmagoric *Frankenstein*. All of these are tales that had enormous initial impact and lasting influence, and each of them were drawn from, or inspired by, dreams.[49]

---

[49] Many writers have also drawn on their experiences of psychosis, to a greater or lesser degree of fictionalisation. Virginia Woolf famously declared that 'As an experience, madness is terrific... and in its lava I still find most of the things I write about'. August Strindberg, in his *Inferno*, made good

Dreams and cultural background

The character and *modus* of dreams are inevitably reflective of the dreamer's cultural setting. Obviously, the dreams of hunter-gatherer tribes-people would have been substantively different from those of a modern city-dweller, and Chinese, Indian and African dreams are bound to reflect their own, distinctive cultural realities.

In the aeons of our tribal past dreams and dream-interpretation would have been interwoven with the myths that ruled their lives and defined their continuing relationship with the spirit-world. As is the case with tribal people today, there would have been a greater porosity between the dreaming and waking state and because of this, dreams would have played a greater role in the continuities of their existence; they were a continuation of waking experience. We can only surmise about the dreams of pre-*linguistic* hominids, but it would seem very likely that they *did* dream (since most higher animals appear to) but being unable to vocalise their experiences these could not have contributed to a collective, cultural narrative.

The later radical cultural phase-changes (mentioned in the Prologue) were also bound to be reflected in the patterns of their respective dream-states. The transition from a hunter-gathering lifestyle to that of settlement and agriculture (the Neolithic Revolution) would have changed every aspect of social life, and these changes were bound to have been reflected in their patterns of dreaming – particularly as one of the radical innovations that marked this transition was the emergence of a literature. One might surmise that *literate* dreams date from this period.

---

use of his own psychotic episode to explore his esoteric obsessions. Similarly, Evelyn Waugh drew on his physical and mental breakdown in his novel *The Ordeal of Gilbert Pinfold*. Barbara O'Brien's harrowing, hallucinatory *Operator's and Things: The inner Life of a Schizophrenic* is perhaps one of the most graphic inside accounts of the experience of madness

Dreams are certainly mentioned in the very earliest recorded narratives, those of the Sumerians – from which it appears that they featured in rituals involving divination and prophesy. The interconnectivity between the dream and mythical literature is also evident in one of the most famous extended epics from this early period, *The Dream of Dumuzid*, which actually begins with the hero Dumuzid relating a frightening dream that he has just had (he is later dragged to the underworld by demons, where he is forced to stay for half of every year – thus creating the cycle of the seasons). The early Mesopotamian city-based religions developed a complex pantheon of local gods, each with their own cosmological narratives, and this was accompanied by the developing idea of an individual human soul. The later Sumerians came to believe that dreams were the result of the soul moving out of the body and visiting places and people, and possibly gods – a process that was sometimes aided by a 'god of dreams'.

The notions of divine beings (who led a separate, elevated existence) and that of a human soul (which might pass on to a life hereafter) were basic assumptions of other early ancient civilisations – and dreams were often seen as the means of understanding these matters. The Ancient Egyptians believed that they could contact their (many) gods through dreams, and that the secret knowledge thus acquired would allow them to predict the future. This came to mean that those individuals who experienced particularly intense dreams were regarded as being endowed with special powers. It was believed that dream journeys could extend to the stars, particularly to Sirius, which for Egyptians was the paradisiacal 'moist land', the home of the gods and source of higher consciousness. In time the whole procedure of receiving dreams and interpreting them became thoroughly ritualised, and those seeking divine revelations, or healing, or simply comfort, from one or other of their gods, would go to sanctuaries specifically provided with 'dream beds' for this purpose. Much of this is known because accounts of important dreams and attitudes towards them were frequently recorded on papyrus. The most famous surviving example of these 'dream books' dates from the reign of Rameses II (13th century B.C.). This collection lists no less than 108 types of dream, with corresponding interpretations – the papyrus itself seems to have been carefully preserved through many generations and was clearly a highly valued heirloom – essentially a holy scripture. In later periods the priests who specialised in dream interpretation (and in dreaming itself) were known as the Learned Ones of the Magic Library.

The Ancient Greeks, who had a high regard for Egyptian civilization, came to share many of its beliefs regarding the meaning and purpose of dreams. They too institutionalised the practice of sleeping in holy sanctuaries for the purpose of receiving messages from divine sources. Many temples had rooms that were dedicated to this form of ritual sleep – and they also referred to 'dream books' to guide the process. Dreams themselves were categorised according to their importance, with a distinction made between the mundane, the result of indigestion or anxiety, and those with spiritual significance. There is a great deal of evidence of the Greek preoccupation with dreams, both from written sources and on inscriptions at holy sites. In fact their literature abounds with references to dreams (usually as a literary device that is loaded with symbolic meaning). For most Greeks of this Classical period the notion of dreams as a conduit to the other, divine world would have been unquestioned and the appearance of a god in a dream as perfectly feasible. When people had a medical condition that required intervention, for instance, they would often pray for a visitation from *Asclepius*, the healing god, for diagnoses or cures. At sites dedicated to this god thankful inscriptions can still be found relating the effects of these curative dreams. There was also a general assumption in ancient Greece of the notion that dreams could predict future events. This is a constant theme from the *Iliad* and *Odyssey* onwards, but it is also found in nonfictional works – in Herodotus' *Histories* for instance.

The ways in which dreams are interpreted are, naturally, influenced by the prevailing belief systems of different regions – and these may reflect very different cultural attitudes. China provides a good example, where throughout its long history there was a continuing tradition of the value of dreams in matters concerning the spirit world. The seriousness which this civilisation regarded dreams is indicated by their inclusion in the Confucian classic, the *Rites of Zhou* (which dates from the 2nd century B.C.). This work is mainly directed towards the proper ordering of the State, but has an extended section on *Auspicious and Inauspicious Dreams*, a compendium that went on to become the authoritative guide to dream interpretation in China for hundreds of years. It divided dreams into six distinct categories, and presents hundreds of interpretations of specific examples. The collection remained popular over the centuries, was enlarged in later centuries and, remarkably, is still well known and consulted to this day.

Another great Chinese spiritual tradition, Taoism, frequently used the subject of dreams in its parables. One of the most famous, Taoist-tinged, stories in Chinese literature is the tale of *The Governor of Nanke*, in which a disgraced, once powerful, army officer embarks on an extended series of adventures in a fantastic new world, only to realise, on awakening, that all of his multifarious experiences were illusory, a mere dream. From this he draws the moral that life itself is full of illusions – and goes on to renounce the materialistic world to become a Taoist monk. The dream as an analogy of impermanence and illusion was in fact a common theme in Taoist literature. Another famous tale, *The Story in a Pillow*, concerns a young man who has failed his civil service examinations. This has a similar, time-warping narrative – again involving a dream of an alternative existence

– which, when revealed as illusory, acts as a consolation for the protagonists thwarted ambition. The moral, as in many of these tales, is that the acquisition of status and material gains that are commonly lauded have, in the end, little more substance than dreams.

In China generally, dreams were seen not simply as products of an individual mind, but as a possible channel to worlds beyond ordinary experience. It was believed that while much of the soul remained within the body during sleep, part of it was free to travel to these alternative worlds. Ultimately though, the worlds of dreams and reality were seen as more or less interchangeable.

As well as those mentioned above one could safely say that dreams and their interpretations had an important role in most pre-modern cultures. The subject occurs repeatedly in the myths and theology of both Hinduism and Buddhism for instance – and both of these, over the centuries, developed their own dream-compendia, interpretative manuals and a range of ideas on the subject. In Hinduism the function of dreams is discussed in one of its most ancient Vedic scriptures, the *Chandogya Upanishad*. Here, dreaming is posited as one of four states of consciousness (wakefulness, dream-sleep, deep sleep, and beyond) but is also categorised as an example of illusion, in common with hallucinations. However, on the more popular level in India, dreams and their interpretation have long been involved with the familiar, everyday practices of predictive astrology.

The Buddhist view on dreams, as expressed in early canonical texts and commentaries, regards them as largely created by the mind, but also allows for supernatural intervention. Like the Greeks, they distinguished between the dreams caused by the 'provocations' of anxiety, indigestion and external disturbances and those of more consequence. The usual cause of dreams, in the Buddhist view, is akin to that of modern research, namely, that during sleep the mind is free to 'replay' stored thoughts and experiences – and dreams of this sort are not regarded as particularly important. But Buddhist doctrines also assume that a remembrance of experience from previous existences may occur in dreams, and even that the influence of future events may be felt. These and similar 'prophetic' dreams of external origin are considered to be important, although much rarer. It is also accepted that telepathic communications can occur in dreams, and that some communities may have collective dreams, but that these too are infrequent phenomena.

The dream in Buddhist fables, as in Greek literature, tends to be heavily symbolic – usually marking a distinct stage in the main characters spiritual development. In fact the story of Gautama Buddha's life itself is traditionally marked as beginning at pre-conception when his mother dreamt that a six-tusked elephant pierced her side (usually interpreted as indicating an immaculate conception). Five of the Buddha's own dreams are recorded in the scriptures, but these texts have become highly elaborated. The Buddha also used the image of the dream in his well-known *Vajra (Diamond) Sutra* – 'All conditioned *dharmas* are like a dream, like an illusion, like a bubble, like a shadow, like a dewdrop, like a lightening flash. You should contemplate them thus'. Unlike Hinduism, Buddhism has actually produced little mythology of its own, but dreams feature prominently in the folklore narratives of the South-East Asian lands within its sphere. Notwithstanding the reservations of scholarly Buddhism towards dreams and their interpretation, these regions have their own popular traditions of divination and prognostication, which in some cases is involved with healing.[50] The commonalities of the three great monotheistic religions,

---

[50] In Tantric Buddhism (the kind that is practiced in Tibet), dreams are generally regarded as an illusion, but this illusion is considered an experience similar to the Bardo, or 'intermediate' state, experienced by the mind immediately after death. Despite this qualification, Tibetan monks habitually use dream-interpretation in therapeutic situations

Judaism, Christianity and Islam, are reflected in their attitudes towards dreaming. They all subscribe to the notion of prophetic revelation in dreams, but are more suspicious of dream interpretation as a general method. This is practiced, particularly at a popular level, but tends to be looked down on – and while recognising the possibility of supernatural influence, all three traditions are cautious in their approach. The Old Testament of the Bible refers to many divinely-inspired dreams, mostly in the book of Genesis – the Christian New Testament far fewer, just eight in fact. But both Judaism and Islam are ambiguous in their approach, recognising the possibility of the evil origins of bad dreams, as well as inspirational dreams (there is a Jewish rabbinic proverb which holds that a dream is a sixtieth of prophesy; a Muslim one that it is a forty-fifth).

For Muslims, since the passing of the prophet Muhammad, dream-revelations offered the only possibility of insights into those truths that are unavailable in waking reality – however, the official line is that only beneficial dreams, i.e. those originating from Allah, are of any value. These can be morally directive, predictive, and in special cases, may warn of potential danger. There are many references to dreams in both the *Qu'ran* and the *Hadith* (Islamic Holy traditions), the primary sources of spiritual guidance for all Muslims. The orthodox view of dreams also accepts that they can convey communications from important religious figures of the past, but these are heavily qualified. There is a traditional, accepted role for the interpreter of dreams, the *mu'abbir*, who is trusted to differentiate between 'good' and 'evil' dreams according to a conventional series of rules. But on a more popular level, as in so many other cultures, collections of the 'meanings' of dream-events have long been available in the Islamic world – notably, the many (still available) versions of the *Dictionary of Dreams*, supposedly compiled by the early Islamic scholar Ibn Seerin (635-728). Characteristically, dreams and their interpretation have a higher status in the mystical, Sufi branches of Islam.

*

Varied as the explanations of dreams may have been in pre-modern cultures, this brief survey reveals certain consistent themes. It is clear that people have always been intrigued by the content of their dreams; that they ascribed divine or mystical qualities to them; that they were regularly scrutinised for significant meanings; that dreams and their interpretations were frequently collected into compendia; and that they appear in fables and other works of fiction in most cultures. Naturally, dream narratives will always have been coloured by cultural expectations. In a world that was permeated by animistic spirits, or one in which the influence of the gods was felt as a real presence, these beliefs would undoubtedly have formed the background to the dream-experience. The introduction of writing, and later of widespread literacy, not only transformed society, but would have influenced the forms of dreaming – in fact the very act of recording and interpreting dreams within a particular tradition was bound to have created a format for further dream narratives to follow. The modern era, which saw the introduction of such new technologies as the telephone, cinema, radio and television probably also had a significant effect, possibly making our dreams more 'cinematic'. And the advent of global electronic inter-connectedness, combined with the rapid take-up of social media, has not only profoundly changed the way we think and view the world, but is bound to have influenced the ways that we frame our dreams these days. Our narratives, cultural and personal (including our dream narratives) are necessarily and intricately involved with our experience of the world.

6. Persuasive Narratives

'Leadership appears to be the art of getting others to want to do something you are convinced should be done'
VANCE PACKARD

'Our social instincts include the intense desire to belong. The approval of others is rewarding, disapproval is aversive. These social emotions shape our behaviour according to received social values'
HANS HASS

Advertising and Deception

There is no distinct line of demarcation between the straightforward dissemination of information and the use of persuasion as to the value of that information. Neither is there a clear distinction between persuasion, induction and outright deception – all of these activities lie on a sliding scale, with the simple conveyancing of information at one end and criminal deceit at the other. But humans are not unique in this regard. The whole spectrum of informing, persuading and deceiving is ubiquitous in nature, where it is an established part of the evolutionary survival tool-kit. Sexual displays, camouflage, aggressive postures etc. all convey information – and are sometimes deceptive.

Our primate cousins the chimpanzees are notorious persuaders and deceivers and have been credited with high levels of 'Machiavellian intelligence'[51], and since we are so closely related it is perhaps not so surprising that we humans exercise these skills from time to time – in fact it could be said that they are found, to a greater or smaller degree, in *most* human transactions. That is to say that the exchange of ideas, opinions, commodities etc. are rarely made without some, at least minimal, attempt to influence the recipient. If this sounds like a depressingly cynical view of human interactions then consider how difficult it seems to be for any of us to be impartial or objective when passing on information – how easily enthusiasm slips into exaggeration, how natural it is to want to impress others with our knowledge, and how misgivings so easily become disparagement. We are all persuaders by nature; opinion is the coinage of the social economy.

We are also advertisers. As social animals we are conscious and attentive of the image of ourselves that we present to others. The ways that we dress, how we furnish our homes, the sort of car we own, all of these things proclaim to whosoever may be interested (or not) the kind of person we are – or rather, would like to appear to be. And beneath these openly declared identifying markers there are those rather deeper indications of personality that we convey by the subliminal advertising methods of body-language, posture etc. All this means that when in contact with our fellow humans we are engaged in a fairly continuous exchange involving intentions and assertions of identity. The principle motivating factor behind this sustained effort of self-presentation is, of course, to do with status. Although generally unacknowledged, we humans, in common with other social primates, have an inordinate preoccupation with our personal

---

[51] The Dutch primatologist and popular author Frans de Waal has written extensively about this. In particular see *Chimpanzee Politics: Power and Sex among Apes*, 1982

standing in the social milieus that we inhabit. For us, the need for peer acceptance and approval is as unremitting a drive as those more obvious instincts of hunger and sex, and it accounts for more of our time and energy than most of us would care to admit – or even realise.

Understandably, the business of commercial advertising takes advantage of all of these basic human instincts. In our fortunate society, which produces a surplus of goods, and where one brand of toothpaste, beer or motor-car is essentially as good as any other, much hangs on the persuasive power of the copywriter when promoting their products. The obvious approach for the ad-man/huckster, is via the line of least resistance – by appealing to the buyers sense of snobbery, or greed, or libido or exploiting some other aspect of their unconscious hopes and fears. Because of this, advertising rarely attempts simply to convey information. It may be mildly entertaining or otherwise fill a space in our lives, but its primary function is obviously to sell a product – so it is at the very least persuasive, is invariably selective in what it conveys, and is sometimes positively misleading. It has been characterised as 'the organised creation of dissatisfaction'.[52] However, it is also quite clear that there is a general, careless acceptance of the role of advertising in our societies. There is a mild scepticism about its real value – most of us feel that it is probably a waste of money and that it is frequently dishonest, and certainly few believe that the celebrities who endorse products actually use them in real life. In other words, there seems to be something of a partial suspension of disbelief in our attitudes to advertising and its claims are generally taken with a pinch of salt. Despite this, advertising clearly continues to work, otherwise its persuasive activities would not continue to be so widely used – and in our industrialised consumer societies it has become one of the principle shapers of opinion. It is not easy to see how this state of affairs can change, indeed it may

[52] See *Our Inner Ape*, 2005 by Frans de Waal

indeed be the case that these persuading, cajoling activities are an absolutely necessary function of our complex societies – but there are undoubtedly aspects of commercial advertising which reflect that mischievous human impulse to 'put one over'.

Power over Opinion: Propaganda and Persuasion

In more rigorously state-controlled, societies the role of influencing the minds of the masses is usually monopolised by an official propaganda machine – indicating that there always seems to be a felt need, for some at least, to corral the body-politic. The term 'propaganda' derives from the Catholic missionary foundation *Sacra Congregation de Propaganda Fide*, which was set up by Pope Gregory XV to counter Protestant influence after the Reformation (it was founded in 1622 and is still in existence). Its methods, of presenting the facts that it wanted to convey, entirely from its own perspective, is still the basis of propagandist techniques. The distinction, then as now, between straightforward 'information' and 'propaganda' tends to be blurred – since most religious or political propaganda tends to be at least *presented* as information. However, the first extensive use of propaganda in the modern sense was made by the British in the First World War, where control over public opinion was felt to be an essential part of the war-effort. This project culminated in the establishment of both a 'Ministry of Information', for home consumption, and a parallel 'Enemy Propaganda Department'. Remarkably, both were run by famous newspaper magnates; the former by Lord Beaverbrook, the latter by his rival Lord Northcliffe. Between them, they managed a virtually complete control over every available outlet of information – the press, movie leaflets and posters were all co-opted to disseminate officially approved themes.

However necessary this may have been considered at the time, it proved to be a bad precedent. The methods were admired and copied by all the totalitarian regimes that were set up following the political chaos that ensued after the Great War. The Nazis in particular modelled their propaganda machine on the British model – which Hitler blamed for the earlier German defeat and subsequent demoralisation (this formed part of the *Dolchstosslegende*, see Chapter 10). He saw the role of Nazi propaganda as bringing 'certain facts' to the attention of the masses – by which he meant his own warped interpretation of Germany's destiny. As a result, in Germany during the 1930s, it was virtually impossible to read a newspaper or book, see a movie or listen to the radio without encountering a Nazi interpretation of events – and their brutal solutions.

The Russia Communist approach was essentially similar, again involving total control of the media, but the Bolshevik government made a distinction between influencing those already sympathetic to communist ideology and 'the masses', who were to be subjected to a relentless diet of slogans and admonitions. These totalitarian experiments demonstrated that state control of the means of communication had an extraordinarily distorting effect on the body-politic, and although these regimes (Nazism, Stalinism etc.) ultimately failed they offer a disturbing picture of the extent to which intensive persuasion can be taken.

Understandably, the association of 'propaganda' as a means of social control within totalitarian regimes gave this term something of a bad name – nevertheless, its value was realised by the politicians and commentators of the succeeding democracies, particularly in the USA, and 'propaganda' was transformed into 'perception management' in both the political and commercial spheres. After World War II research into mass communication and how it could be used to influence behavioural changes was greatly increased. Politicians wanted to know how they could best shape public opinion; advertisers, as ever, simply wanted to sell products; purveyors of the 'News' wanted to reach ever more citizens – and all needed to know how to present information/persuade in the most effective ways. As a result, a whole new industry of persuasion came into being which has developed a range of manipulative skills that now penetrate into every aspect of contemporary life.

Spinning a Yarn: Cons and Hoaxes

In purely evolutionary terms cheating may often be cheaper than telling the truth, and for this reason it is a strategy that is widely adopted in nature. According to Frans de Waal, bluffing, conning and other deceptive forms of behaviour are fairly common among chimpanzees, but interestingly, (since they are our nearest relatives) they also exhibit 'proto-moral' attitudes of fairness and empathy.[53] In human society cheating and conning ones fellows is regarded as distinctly immoral, but it is nevertheless widespread – and the possibilities to do so are greatly extended by our use of language. Our higher intelligence enables us to manipulate and outwit others in more complex ways and, in purely evolutionary terms, this instinct clearly has survival value for us, just as it does in ape societies. In the human sphere, whether it is done for material gain, sexual advantage, or simply 'putting one over' for its own sake, fooling others in this way usually involves telling a story – and in the case of dedicated con-artists and hoaxers these can be extremely elaborate.

This behaviour reflects one of the most important aspects of language, namely, to influence the actions and minds of others – whether it benefits them or not. As the author Matt Ridley has put it 'deceiving people, detecting deceit, understanding people's motives, manipulating people – these are what the intellect is

---

[53] See *Our Inner Ape*, 2005 by Frans de Waal

used for'.[54] In fact the literature on 'Cons and Hoaxes' is itself fairly extensive, which is indicative of an enduring popular fascination with the subject. Although we hate being conned or fooled ourselves, it would appear that we enjoy reading about it happening to others (*schadenfreude* is a base emotion, but a common one).

There are clear overlaps between conning, hoaxing and pathological lying, and there may be an element of what the American psychologist Dr. Paul Ekman has described as 'duping delight' in each of these (Ekman describes this as a degree of satisfaction deriving from a sense of superiority at having tricked another).[55] But there is also the common element here, in passing off a false narrative as a truthful one – a further, if rather negative, indication of the importance of the story in human social exchanges. We are suckers for a good story and the greater the extent to which we are drawn into a tale the more we are likely to give it credence. Stories, then, have a social *instrumentality*, which may be used for good or malign reasons. The ability to spin a yarn has clear social/evolutionary advantages – in acquiring material benefits, attracting a mate, gaining respect from one's peers etc. – but there is a down-side to this aptitude (quite apart from the ignominy of being caught out), and that is of the story taking over. It is well-known that habitual liars can come to believe their own made-up stories, and that many others go on to become habitual swindlers, using their story-telling abilities to further their criminal activities. There often seems to be an element of compulsion in this.

Most of us, of course, do not go down this path – as a species we are trusting by nature most of the time, and feel that this is the best way to be. And it is; it has been shown that 'trusters' have better lives overall. But our narrative-dependency does make

---

[54] According to Ridley this tendency is probably genetically hard-wired, see *The Red Queen*, Penguin Books, 1993

[55] Paul Ekman in his book *Telling Lies* (1992)

us susceptible to being taken in by convincing but fraudulent accounts. The more elaborate and emotionally charged the tale, the more likely we are to believe in it, particularly if it offers material inducements. We have always to be wary of announcements that we have just won a huge Lottery prize (which we can't actually remember entering); cautious about African princes who want to transfer massive funds into our bank accounts (for some dubious but entirely plausible scheme); and suspicious of those who would sell us the Eiffel Tower at an absolutely knock-down price (although this has been done – many times!).

Hypnosis and the act of believing

'Hypnosis does not cause the brain to malfunction.
It avails of psychological possibilities that are normally latent'
DAVID HEALY

Most hypnotic stage-shows include demonstrations in which individuals, or groups of volunteers, are led to experience strong hallucinations. When a hypnotist makes a bunch of people shiver because they believe that they are at the North Pole, or reduces them to a state of terror because they feel that they are being confronted by a ferocious lion, it may be very distressing for them, but it is usually the highlight of the show for the audience. These positive illusions are intriguing enough phenomena, but even more striking are those associated with negative hallucination. In these, typically, the hypnotised subjects are rendered completely unable to see objects which are perfectly visible to everyone else. This induced selective blindness can be worked into a hypnotist's routine by having the participants witness an 'Invisible Man' (they see his clothes, but not the man wearing them), or by his holding a child aloft (the hypnotised subjects then see a 'flying' child, but again, not the hypnotist himself).

No wonder stage-hypnotism retains its appeal. What could be more remarkable, if somewhat unsettling than having one's own, or witnessing others, basic sense-perceptions so completely subverted in this way? And yet these extraordinary effects are part of the standard repertoire of stage-hypnotism, and have been repeated countless times. There is no questioning the authenticity of most of these shows. Moreover, it would appear that the skills necessary to perform these surprising entertainments are relatively easily acquired.

Now, putting ethical considerations aside (and there are undeniably many troubling aspects of stage-hypnotism), how are we to account for this strange phenomena? What is behind this complete, and apparently uncritical, acceptance of ideas prompted by the words of a complete stranger? It all seems so peculiar; what, one wonders, are the mind-mechanisms involved, and how do they fit with the present scientific understanding of how the brain works? From all accounts, the illusions and hallucinations experienced during stage-hypnosis, or any other form of trance are usually as vivid and real as those of ordinary perception and genuine experience. How is it that the bidding of a hypnotist's inductory patter can seed ideas that so effectively compromise a subject's entire visual, auditory and other sensory apparatus? All of us, after all, are totally reliant on our senses, and most of the time they are thoroughly reliable.

There are many fascinating aspects of trance and hypnotic effects – not least, the difficulties that the medical and mind-science establishment has experienced in coming to terms with the subject. In fact, the whole field remains controversial, and there is still no generally-accepted theory that accounts for hypnotic phenomena in their entirety. Taking a broader, cross-cultural view, it seems that the many and various manifestations of trance behaviour are strongly culturally stylised; in most pre-modern cultures trance has a more established and secure social role. However, in the 'developed' world, despite all the evidence of its power to influence minds, hypnosis still tends to be treated in a non-serious, perfunctory way by conventional psychologists. It is clear that a high proportion of people seem naturally receptive to the trance-state, and that it is relatively easy to induce by an experienced professional, but the precise neurological mechanisms involved in hypnotic induction and suggestion are still unresolved (although cerebral asymmetry is believed to play a part).

In essence, the process of induction appears to work by circumventing the mechanism that, in our normal lives, enables us to distinguish between our imagination (and its fantasies) and the real world. This involves a de-coupling, and then a hi-jacking, of the 'internal storyline' which each of us carries as part of our psychic identity. It seems extraordinary that such a highly evolved faculty can be so easily short-circuited in this way, but of course something similar happens when we dream. Here too, the imaginative, story-telling part of our mind is let off the leash, so to speak. The absence of a reality-check allows it to roll out the most involved fantasies – which, as we experience them, seem entirely credible. The hypnotic state, then, is a bit like a waking dream. In its most extreme form, in the condition known as *rapport*, the hypnotised subject becomes completely oblivious of all external influences and entirely fixated on the hypnotist's words. Subjects in this state are reported to have been completely insensible to clamorous background noises, even of gunshots, but immediately responsive to their 'controllers' barely audible commands.

Another intriguing aspect of this topic is that, contrary to commonly-held beliefs, hypnotic susceptibility does not correlate with intelligence or 'strength of character'. It is not at all the case that 'weak-minded' individuals are more open to suggestion – indeed, there is some evidence that hypnotically sensitive subjects tend to have more flexible (and more efficient) brains than the average. It is also well known that the conviction that one can resist hypnosis is no indication at all of the actual degree of susceptibility to hypnotic suggestion. By contrast, the setting of a hypnotic event, that is to say the surroundings and the associated expectations, seem to be very important. In particular, any collective situation can be extremely potent. In a crowd situation, especially one experiencing a heightened emotional state, all manner of illusions and visual hallucinations can be induced by an experienced hypnotist, and adopted *en masse*. In these circumstances suggestion appears to derive extra power through the collective contagion of ideas and emotions – a technique that has of course long been exploited by rabble-rousers and would-be demagogues. As with all forms of hypnotic induction, the primary act of any individual attempting to gain control in this way is to establish psychological dominance.

But the most important aspect of hypnotic proceedings of any kind is the story. In its basic form, hypnosis relies on a persuasive *narrative*, accompanied by compelling images, which then displace one's own story-line, and one's own hold on reality – 'You are four years old again in the classroom and someone has upset you ...', 'When you wake up you will have completely forgotten your own name, address and identity ...', 'You are a chicken that thinks it is a dog ....' etc. In their strongest form the hallucinations induced by such suggestions can traduce all the senses – vision, hearing, smell, taste and touch – which is surely the most compelling evidence of the extent to which our realities are constructed around a perceived narrative. So, far from being an anomaly or a pathological symptom, this curious sensitivity to, and acceptance of, persuasive presentations not only accounts for the abiding human appetite for stories of every kind, but actually provides an important insight into the complex mechanisms of human identity and socialisation. Ultimately, of course, it is language and our habitual narrative interpretation of events that provides the keys to all of this.

Placebo: The healing narrative

The Placebo Effect, in common with hypnotic suggestion (with which it has obvious points of resemblance) is another phenomenon that the modern Western medical tradition is uneasy with, despite a great deal of evidence as to its efficacy. The reasons are obvious. Placebos, by definition, have no objective value for the conditions that they are prescribed for. In the form of medicines they are inert, non-reactive substances; as procedures they are shams. They should not work, but a great many tests have shown that they do – and because of this they present the medical profession with serious and complex ethical dilemmas. Since at best the placebo effect is based on encouraging the *belief* in a particular treatment, and more frequently on the outright *deception* of the patient, it is unlikely ever to gain acceptance as a respectable medical tool. But although as a treatment it continues to be regarded as ethically dubious by the medical profession, many doctors will admit privately to having resorted to the use of sham injections or fake pills; in reality, the effect pervades most forms of therapeutic treatment.

Tests have repeatedly shown placebos to be found to be effective in a wide range of medical conditions. In relatively minor presentations, such as post-operative wound pain, headaches, coughs and anxiety, it can be expected that approximately a third of patients will respond well to placebos. In the literature there are equally impressive results in many other more serious areas including placebo treatment for arthritis, ulcers and hypertension. They are studies that have shown that they have even been an effective treatment in such intractable conditions as Parkinson's disease.

The placebo effect has long presented very real problems when testing novel treatments – it is notoriously difficult, for instance, to eliminate placebo responses from controlled trials of new drugs. These difficulties have been confirmed in investigations which indicate that pain relief from placebos tends to follow the same pattern as genuine analgesics, i.e. peaking an hour after being administered, then gradually tapering off. To further confuse matters, inert placebo drugs have been known to cause side-effects (including dermatitis, conjunctivitis and fluid retention). All of this is obviously highly vexatious to those who want to test new medicines, and for practitioners seeking reliable, entirely pharmacological treatments of disease. The only way to overcome this problem is to adopt the 'double-blind' method, in which neither the participants nor the experimenters know who is receiving a particular treatment. But what in fact is going on here?

There appear to be two interconnected factors that determine placebo effectiveness, namely the *setting* and the *narrative*. The long and short of it is that to be effective placebos must *convince* – and at the most basic level, simply being in a healing situation is conducive to this. Patients who feel that they are being listened to and taken seriously are much more likely to respond well to the drugs that are administered, whether genuine or placebo. And a good bedside manner, from a therapist who is attentive, optimistic and encouraging, can in itself transmit a positive placebo effect (this might seem like plain common-sense, but strong evidence that a 'warm, caring and friendly approach' might be clinically helpful was presented in the March 2001 edition of the *Lancet* as something of a revelation).[56]

However, while it is clear that a person's beliefs and hopes about a given treatment can affect outcomes, it is also the case that they may be strongly influenced by a narrative, even when

---

[56] *The Lancet*, 10th March 2001, Vol. 357, Issue 9258

this is delusive. It is well known, for instance, that morphine will be far more effective if the patient is *told* what they are getting. Similarly, a particular treatment is likely to be more effective if the patient is informed that it has worked well for others. Placebos that have noticeable side-effects (by harmlessly producing dryness in the mouth for instance) are more likely to produce good outcomes. In fact there is a sort of hierarchy of placebo effectiveness. An injection will be more effective than a pill, a nasty tasting pill more effective than a sweet tasting one, and large, unpleasantly-coloured pills better than smaller, bland ones. It seems also to be the case that the more that is paid for a placebo the better the results. Most effective of all are dummy surgical operations involving full anaesthetic. There are obvious ethical problems in using such a potentially risky and completely unnecessary procedures, but when this was tried in the 1950s to treat angina it lead to huge improvements in the patients well-being. The criterion for placebo effectiveness then seems to be the degree of patient confidence and expectation.

On occasions the testing of placebos has been inadvertent – and the results all the more striking for that fact. In one classic example a number of patients suffering pain after wisdom tooth extraction got noticeable pain relief from the application of an ultrasound device – even though it later transpired that the machine had been out of action for several days and that neither the patients nor the therapists had noticed. Anyone who has undergone wisdom tooth extraction would be forgiven for being sceptical about the value of placebo pain-relief in these circumstances, but those conducting an extended study in precisely this area found that saline injections were as potent a painkiller as a 6-8mg. dose of morphine, *if the patient was told* that they were getting a powerful local anaesthetic. In similar tests, involving the treatment of acute asthma, doctors were able to produce a measurable dilation of the airways simply by telling patients that they were inhaling an active bronchodilator – even when they weren't.

In contrast with these 'placebo-plus-storyline' experiments are those studies where a genuinely powerful analgesic was administered to patients without their knowledge, via a computer-controlled infusion pump. Predictably, in light of the accounts above, when a patient has *not* been told that they are receiving painkillers (even at a very high dose), and without sympathetic attention, their effect is very much reduced. The important role of narrative in treatment then would appear to be strongly correlated with the ability to form expectations. This is confirmed by observations that those suffering from Alzheimer's disease, who have sadly lost this capacity, no longer respond to placebos of any kind. It is known that Alzheimer's results from damage to the prefrontal cortex, the area of the brain that is concerned with hopes, plans and expectations. Interestingly, the prefrontal cortex is also the centre of social/self-regulation. At the deepest level then, it would appear that our expectations work in tandem with our social awareness and the conditioning we have received from our respective social story-lines. We are highly social animals and many of our responses when we are unwell, as at all other times, are in accordance with social expectations. It is noteworthy in this regard that if the setting is convincing enough it is fairly easy to get a conventional 'intoxicated' response from fake alcoholic beverages.

In view of all this it is perhaps not surprising that people should respond particularly well to suggestion if they are in a somewhat subordinate social position. There have been a whole slew of placebo experiments on students for instance – many of which seem to have involved the use of stimulants and sedatives, fake and otherwise. In one such test American college students were given either a glass of warm milk or strong black coffee before going to bed; the cover-story was 'to test once and for all whether coffee kept one awake at night'. Predictably, the milk drinkers slept well and the coffee drinkers had disturbed, restless nights. They were later informed that the coffee was decaffeinated, and that the milk had been laced with pure, tasteless caffeine – the results were the exact opposite of what they should have been. In Cincinnati in 1971 a group of medical students were given harmless placebo pills, but some were told that they were amphetamine stimulants, others that they were depressants or tranquilisers – in general the students duly responded with the expected, suggested effects (unfortunately, a few of those taking part were quite severely affected by the inert substances). In Glasgow, in the late 1960s, staff at the Department of Psychological Medicine were involved in blind tests involving placebos and stimulants, with very mixed results – some got high on the inert placebos, but others had no reaction at all to powerful stimulants. Tests of this sort, no matter how they are constructed, invariably show positive placebo bias.

Many of the strongest reactions to placebos, however, come from self- rather than external suggestion – in particular the various recorded cases of *addiction* to placebos. It is known that placebos can be used to treat addictions of various kinds – they can be very useful in helping smokers to quit the habit for instance. But there are plenty of case-histories that involved patients becoming highly dependent on completely inert pills that they believed to be pharmacologically active. In these cases, as with the effects of placebo analgesics mentioned earlier, the pattern of use exactly mirrors the formal expectations of genuine drug dependence. Placebo 'addicts' experience a compulsion to take the placebo pills and, if allowed, will settle into a pattern of dependency. In this situation there will be strong desire to increase the frequency and quantity of use, and any sudden deprivation of the 'drug' is likely to induce all the classic symptoms of withdrawal. It seems probable here that the patients involved are following the behavioural patterns of genuine substance addiction, which of course are very well known, not least through portrayals of addictive behaviour in the popular media. And notwithstanding the seriously addictive power of narcotics it is clear that 'junkie' behaviour patterns themselves are highly ritualised (and highly mythologized) – in other words, that it too has aspects of a 'learned' behaviour.

This would seem to indicate that the refractory problems associated with addiction are always bound up with these established *concepts* of drug use and, as is the case with placebos, it is virtually impossible to separate the expected from actual pharmacological effects. This was born out by studies of heroin use in New York in the late 1970s, after the Vietnam War, when the drug was in very short supply. It was found that the average bag of street heroin was less than 4% pure, which effectively meant that much of the available product was adulterated to such an extent that habitual users had unknowingly been on a slow-reduction regime. The amounts of heroin in their scores were so low in fact that they could have produced little genuine effect and in actuality were barely addictive – but this did not of course change things. The setting and the narrative of the established drug sub-culture were maintained, and the scene, with its own language and ritualised behaviour of buying, selling and using (and the recruitment of new would-be addicts), all carried on as before.

Because the implications of the placebo effect have such a bearing on every aspect of medical treatment there has been a great deal of research into the subject in recent years. But it remains something of a bugbear. The effect itself is undeniable – test after test has shown that placebos work, whether in the form of pills, creams, injections, inhalants or sham surgery. There is little doubt that suggestion can be relied on to produce an expected result. The challenge for the medical profession is how to harness the obvious healing potential of the effect without compromising their own learned values (and their own well-established narrative) – and this is far from straightforward.

Nocebo: The harming narrative

The Placebo Effect has its shadow aspect; the benefits of a placebo, however real at the time, may evaporate if a patient is later informed that he or she has been given a fake treatment. And just as 'tender loving care' is guaranteed to assist recovery, a neglectful and indifferent attitude can set it back. But there are more emphatically harmful results from such 'negative placebos'. In the 1970s a US patient was diagnosed with terminal liver cancer and told that he had just a few months to live. Although the man died in the predicted time, an autopsy revealed that the diagnosis had, unfortunately, been mistaken and it was not his condition that had killed him but his own expectation of death. Thankfully this negative prediction effect does not work on everyone, indeed it can prompt the opposite result with patients being determined to 'live life to the full' after a serious prognosis – and sometimes living very much longer than expected as a result. In general though, negative medical suggestions, however 'realistic', can have a bad effect – and this also applies to the perceived cheerlessness of a 'therapeutic' setting. Some people have such a dread of the hospital experience and such poor expectations of the outcome of treatment that it can seriously interfere with their prospects of a good recovery. There is some recognition of the importance of this effect, and there are now far greater attempts to create a more positive, uplifting atmosphere within hospitals, but this principle is a long way from gaining universal acceptance.

Cultural dislocation is another area in which serious medical effects can appear without apparent rational causes. One of the most extreme examples of this in recent history was the outbreak of a series of apparently inexplicable, premature deaths among Laotian immigrants to the U.S. All those affected belonged to the Hmong ethnic group, who had fought on the American side in the Vietnam war, had been bailed out, and were allowed to stay in the U.S. at the end of that disastrous conflict. But these were all people from hill-tribes, who found it very difficult to adjust to their new, completely alien setting – and soon, many of the younger men, in their early thirties, began to die in their sleep. The numbers of deaths, which had no apparent physical cause, mounted, and within a fairly short time there were over a hundred reported cases. The deaths were ascribed to SUNDS (sudden unexpected death syndrome), but this was just a terminological let-out, the real cause remained a mystery.

It turned out that the Hmong were the victims of their own beliefs – that, in short, this was a transplanted 'culture-bound' syndrome. The Hmong experienced a great deal of stress as a result of their sudden removal from their familiar cultural setting, and their alienation was compounded by not having recourse to their traditional shamanic healers. As a result of their inability to fulfil necessary religious obligations, including those to protective ancestral spirits, they felt vulnerable to powerful malevolent forces. The actual cause of death (in terms of western medicine) was diagnosed as 'heart arrhythmia during sleep paralysis'. This is an uncommon, but not unknown condition, which presents as a temporary paralysis on half-waking, and can be accompanied by an overwhelming sense of dread. For the SUNDS victims though, this was experienced as an encounter with *Tsog Tsuam*, a familiar but vengeful evil spirit. In the U.S.A. the Hmong were culturally isolated, spiritually exposed and defenceless against *Tsog Tsuam*'s depredations, with fatal results.

Studies of so-called 'culture-bound' syndromes indicate the extent to which illnesses of all kinds are tied to a cultural setting – the impression they convey is that, in reality, all illness is culture-bound to some extent. However, it will always be likely that less familiar cultures will present more 'exotic' medical conditions – such as *Tsog Tsuam*. And even a modern, materially-advanced country like Japan has cultural values that are so different from those of the West that it can produce medical conditions that are entirely unfamiliar in the West. *Taijin Kyofusho*, for instance, is a form of extreme social phobia that appears to be almost exclusively Japanese. Sufferers from this syndrome experience truly crippling anxieties of embarrassment, based on a pathological fear that their shortcomings might cause embarrassment *to others*. This condition, which involves an exaggerated concern about one's appearance, is not uncommon in Japan, where the individual psyche is more subordinate to the group, but it is not found elsewhere (particularly not in Western societies). Typically, a *Taijin Kyofusho* sufferer produces the very range of symptoms that seem calculated to confirm their irrational fears – blushing, sweating, inappropriate facial expressions, flatulence etc. – an especially Japanese sort of nightmare, with a script that is not found elsewhere, and whose treatment consists in a reassuring 'talking cure' (which is effectively a gradual, confidence-building rehabilitation).

Multiple personalities and Alien abductions

Emotional distress finds different expression in different cultures, since meaning, even in such negative expressions as mental disorder, is strongly influenced by culture. Within a given cultural context the forms that anxiety, fear and embarrassment can take may be debilitating, but will at least appear *appropriate* to their setting. *Dissociative Identity Disorder* (otherwise known as Multiple Personality Disorder) is a case in point. This syndrome, which involves the patient adopting other, or indeed a whole range of personalities, is taken very seriously in the U.S.A where it is listed in the official, defining register of mental disorders, the 'D.S.M.' (The Diagnostic and Statistical Manual of Mental Disorders) – but curiously, this condition doesn't actually occur to any extent outside the U.S. In *Dissociative Identity Disorder* an individual is 'taken over' by a distinctive other persona (or several), that appear to have their own developed view of the world and their own agendas. The condition has featured in popular dramatisations – notably in the 1957 movie *The Three Faces of Eve*, and in the 1976 TV mini-series 'Sybil'. In Joanne Woodward's 1950's movie the eponymous character developed shadow-selves that had entirely different values and led entirely different lives. The real-life person on whom this drama was based purportedly had 22 personalities living in her body; 'Sybil' was believed to have developed just 16. As can be imagined, the split-off personalities created by this condition tend to make life very complicated for all those involved, both in real life and in its dramatised versions. However, without demeaning or questioning the veracity of D.I.D., it seems rather more than coincidental that it appears in the records with much greater frequency *after* the original media exposure. And it is easy to see why this 'split-personality' psychosis should have appeared in America. Essentially, it would seem to reflect a somewhat disordered version of the 'American Dream', part of which has always offered the possibilities of the recreation or reinvention of the self.

Another 'syndrome' that originated in the U.S. (and which also has roots in its media), is the alien abduction phenomena. Currently, according to internet search engines, there are upward of four and a half *million* websites dealing with this subject – a degree of cult status that has made it a very successful export. At the time of writing alien abductions are still predominantly an American phenomena, but the numbers of reports in various other parts of the world are increasing. Now, unless you really believe that malevolent aliens are regularly drawing innocent citizens up into their spacecraft to 'examine' (i.e. sexually molest) them, implant devices in their bodies (for uncertain, but presumably inimical purposes), transport and subject them to all manner of other bizarre experiences – then this is an extraordinarily attractive collective fantasy. But it does have quite deep literary roots.

The notion of alien *visitation* was, of course, presented in the earliest Science Fiction stories (in H.G. Well's *War of the Worlds* for instance, and other classics of the genre). The idea that intelligent alien beings might be taking a closer, more intimate, interest in humans was developed rather later. But, according to the sceptical author Robert Sheaffer, most of the major elements of contemporary UFO abductions were in place by the 1930s, and actually can all be found in the comic-strip adventure, *Buck Rogers in the 25th Century*. Wherever its precise origins, the broad narrative of visitation by intelligent aliens is apparently now believed by a third of U.S. citizens, and a surprising 3% claim to have direct experience of alien abduction in some form or other.

Over time, however, the abduction narrative has deepened and broadened. The aliens themselves have evolved into distinct types with their own defining characteristics; they now include the 'Greys', the sinister 'Reptilians', and the more (apparently) benevolent 'Nordics'. The original accounts of encounters have also been elaborated upon, to include the rationale of an alien desire to breed with humans in order to create hybrids, their desire to pass on 'truths' about governmental conspiracies and cover-ups, and other highly involved narratives. Moreover, despite a complete lack of any physical evidence that might support the claims of these alien encounters, it is now possible to join one of the many Abduction Support Groups, and even to buy insurance cover against the event (although the procedure of claiming in the event of it taking place does seem rather hazy). For many the fantasy has become a reality. Interestingly, sceptical investigators of this phenomenon, having conducted a number of interviews with 'abductees', have often found them to be ordinary, reasonable types – not at all the hysterical, fantasy-prone individuals that one might expect.

Death Spells

Of all the evidence of the power of a persuasive narrative though, none is quite as striking as those incidents involving the so-called 'Voodoo' or 'Kurdaitcha' death phenomena; a fatally effective death-spell. In his classic essay on this subject, Walter B. Cannon presented a number of anecdotal accounts of events of this kind, all involving a ritual curse, with no other apparent physical cause for the deaths.[57] Naturally, these phenomena only appeared in societies that recognised the potentiality of such drastic actions – usually as punishment for some perceived violation of their social or spiritual code.

The accounts that Cannon refers to are drawn from a whole range of different tribal societies, from Africa, South America, Australia and the Pacific Islands, but the proceedings, while marked by cultural differences, have certain outlying similarities. Essentially, a curse of this seriousness amount to a total social exclusion. For whatever reason, the subject has invoked the collective anger of the group to which he belongs, and the inevitable outcome of the curse will be recognised and expected by all. This may even have resulted from an innocent breaking of a taboo, such as unknowingly eating a forbidden animal or fruit. But whatever the cause, the effects are usually dramatic and fairly rapid. In most accounts the individual that had been cursed suffered intense emotional disturbance, often resulting in such physical symptoms as shaking, vomiting and

---

[57] *Voodoo Death*, Walter B. Cannon, American Anthropologist, 1944

the loss of colour; the subjects also appear to be possessed of a pessimistic fatalism. In Australia the subject of a 'boning' typically crawls away to die – other reports describe the subjects as pining away, and succumbing 'within a day or two'. In various recorded instances, even when there were attempts at medical intervention, these generally proved useless. In some of the more remote areas of Northern Australia the practice of *Kurdaitcha*, or 'pointing the bone', is still well enough known that hospital staff there are trained to deal with it.

Cannon himself, and other later commentators, have speculated on the physiological aspects of these deaths. There seems to be little doubt that most incidents were genuine; in those instances where an autopsy was performed no evidence of poisoning or any other suspicious activity was found. In terms of Western medicine the symptoms appeared to resemble those of shock, and were attributed to fear-induced anxiety (but of a most extreme kind). It seems clear that, as with classical shock, there was an abnormal metabolism, involving a degree of failure of the circulatory system, accompanied by a weak, rapid pulse, cyanotic skin and a compromised sympathetic-adrenal system. It is worth noting that even in advanced societies the normal symptoms of shock can include acute mental changes, including anxiety, foreboding and confusion.

There is a particularly revealing aspect of the 'voodoo death' syndrome that provides one the strongest of all indication of the human susceptibility to narrative suggestion. In those rare cases where a medicine-man/witch-doctor figure had been persuaded to rescind a curse the results were often as surprising as the effects of the bewitchment itself. In these circumstances a subject's recovery can be astonishingly rapid and complete. Health and strength may be regained within hours, and in some cases recovery is almost instantaneous. This procedure may have its complications – typically, the lifting of a curse will involve an elaborate ceremony, and this itself is a measure of the potency of these narratives. They are not easily reversed.

7. Compelling Tales
and collective delusions

'*Because of the unusual character of the story there is much eagerness to pass it on*'
IBN KHALDUN

Modern mythology

Every culture has its stories. They are, as noted throughout this book, one of the primary ways that we humans are able to make sense of our world. And we are by nature imaginative creatures, hence the perennial appetite for unusual or sensational accounts – and the occasional acceptance of entirely unfeasible explanations of events. Moreover, we tend to identify with such narratives, however plausible or unlikely they may be – but there are good evolutionary reasons for this. The faculty that allows our imagination to come into play at the instigation of narratives of all kinds is bound up both with our capacity to project possible future scenarios and with our need for social interactions. A narrative shared is a narrative that binds us to others. However, in practice, our imaginative, interpretive skills do not always work to our best advantage, since it is pretty evident that we can become thoroughly enthralled by highly dubious accounts of events. There is another factor at work here though, namely the universal human need for a certain level of emotional stimulation. For most people a lack of stimulation leads to the dreaded state of boredom, which is existentially uncomfortable. This means that sensational stories are a welcome diversion from the tedium of everyday life (along with various other purposeless diversions like gambling, alcohol, drugs etc.). The human instincts of curiosity, but also of credulity, come to the fore when presented with a captivating narrative – with the result that the distinction between fact and fiction can easily be blurred.

The present-day appetite for sensational news stories, rumours of all kinds, conspiracy theories, modern legends – together with an endless supply of thrillers and horror stories – are now well provided for these days on the TV, internet and popular media generally. But actually there is nothing new in this. Humans have long enjoyed sensational/mythical tales – of the lives of the Gods, of the adventures of heroes and tricksters; of the devastations of floods and lost continents; of past Golden Ages and of impending apocalyptic disasters. The massive cultural phase-changes caused by the introduction of the printed word, and more recently of social media, do not seem to have substantially altered our fondness for such engaging stories. On the contrary – there is a receptive audience across the entire, extended range of media outlets for mysterious and unusual reports of every kind. The modern list is endless, but includes elusive creatures (Abominable Snowman, Bigfoot etc.); inexplicable disappearances of personalities, ships etc. (Bermuda Triangle); alien appearances and 'abductions'; hostile conspiracies of course, and 'end-of-the-world' prophesies, in endless variation. Interestingly, the lack of general or official approval (or interest) in most of these accounts seems to provide an almost essential element to their appeal; 'Fake News' has been around for a very long time.

Many of these above notions, in common with crazes and contagious ideas generally, are much affected by fashion. They tend to have a high point of interest, but are then likely to fade in favour of newer, more novel wonders. However, some narratives, both in the past and present, are remarkably persistent, almost becoming fixtures in the collective psyche. Many of these are objectively harmless (like believing in fairies), but some of the more outlandish have had detrimental consequences for their over-identifying followers – in much the same way that delusion can tip into psychosis.

The problem is that humans, some more than others, tend to accept constructed narratives that seem to provide answers to a whole range of situations, particularly those that correlate with deeply-held fears and anxieties. Very occasionally these narratives can take a particularly sinister turn. The UFO craze, for instance, was relatively benign in most of its manifestations[58], but at least two notorious cults (the *Heaven's Gate* group and the *Order of the Solar Temple*) believed that their redemption would come from outer space, and both of their narratives became positively homicidal, leading to murders and mass-suicides. If nothing else the moral of these and similarly macabre developments should be that the motivating power of a shared narrative should never be underestimated.

---

[58] Wikipedia lists around twenty UFO-linked religions – most of which claim that they are in communication with extra-terrestrial beings. The most common attitude towards these super-intelligent aliens is that they have the earth's best wishes at heart. The planet is in crisis and they have come to teach its inhabitants a way to avert the impending catastrophe. Another common scenario is that the aliens intend to 'rescue' the more spiritually sensitive humans and remove them to a more desirable location

There are actually many historical precedents for this last sort of doom-laden, suicidal outlook (see below), just as there are parallels for visions of inexplicable events in the skies; the portrayal of scary, imagined monsters living on the periphery of civilised life and naturally, any number of end-of-world and salvation narratives. But how is it that people persist in believing weird things, against all evidence to the contrary?[59]

Adopting a new narrative: The catharsis of Conversion

The psychological process of 'conversion' (religious, political or whatever) involves the individual in a sort of rebirth, with an abandoning of their previous personality and the adoption of a new one. It does not usually result from a rational analysis of the new creed but is generally an intuitive response. The new sense of personal identity that is formed will be thoroughly identified with the aims and ideals of the adopted value system, and the convert usually becomes convinced that this new narrative will provide all the answers that they had been looking for. There are features that are common to most of these experiences that occur regardless of which set of ideas are abandoned and which taken up. In reality, virtually *any* system of thought or group identity can be the subject of conversion – to or from.

Conversion is frequently described, and experienced, as a sudden state, but it is generally preceded by a period of mental conflict that may be accompanied by feelings of inadequacy and apathy. Naturally, there is a sense of dissatisfaction with the familiar older patterns and explanations or new patterns would not have any appeal – so the acceptance of a new outlook and new explanations is basically remedial. The experience can alleviate previous feelings of rejection and sense of purposelessness – by

---

[59] For a thorough examination of this phenomena see Michael Shermer's *Why People believe Weird Things*, 1997

contrast, life after conversion has new meaning and purpose. Furthermore, identification with fresh ideas and a new group usually brings the companionship of similarly-minded others. Above all, the irrevocable commitment to a new formulated belief can produce a previously unrealised sense of certainty and through this a sense of security. The process can be an emotionally transformative experience – and this explains why converts are notoriously more enthusiastic than existing believers.

The fundamental change of attitude and outlook that are awakened may also lead the convert to exaggerate the value of new beliefs. Indeed, the feeling of belonging to the chosen, select group may promote a sense of narcissistic gratification – which may in turn breed intolerant attitudes towards non-believers. The new conceptual scheme can then become the basis of a fanatical outlook, particularly if the group's demands are themselves equally severe – as is the case in the current wave of radical Islamic 'Jihadism'. In such cases irrevocable commitment to a cause makes reversal extremely difficult – and, unfortunately, can provide a justification for every imaginable excess.

Cognitive Dissonance

The theory of 'Cognitive Dissonance' is concerned with the state of tension that arises when an individual attempts to hold two sets of ideas or attitudes that are mutually inconsistent. Because this state is psychologically disagreeable people are inclined to react to it by reducing the perceived dissonance. This can be achieved in various ways – by changing one's attitude to one or both cognitions to make them seem more compatible, for instance, or by taking on new ideas/attitudes that bridge the gap between the perceived incompatibles; in other words, by rationalising or justifying the anomaly. The classic Aesop's fable of *The Fox and the Grapes* is illustrative – having failed to reach the grapes, rather than admitting defeat, the fox rationalises that, in any case, they are sour and not worth having.

The originator of the theory of Cognitive Dissonance, Leon Festinger, argued that this effect usually appears when a perception of events conflicts with previously-held beliefs, and surmised that the pressure to reduce cognitive discomfort would increase in proportion to the perceived disparity.[60]

The failure of prophesies made by various leaders of religious cults throughout history presents a case-study of the hypothesis. If, as has occurred many times, a specific prophesied event fails to materialise (coming of the Messiah, end of the world etc.), this non-event has to be explained and drawn into a some more general framework of understanding. Disillusion may occur at such times of course, but it is more often the case that disconfirmation results in a greater, rather than diminished, enthusiasm. Generally speaking, reasons tend to be found to continue with a sect's mission.

In the 1950s Festinger's group was presented with an opportunity to test their theories by infiltrating a local (Chicago) Doomsday cult run by a Mrs. Marian Keech. This charismatic lady had attracted a small band of followers who fervently believed the messages that she claimed to have received from the distant planet Clarion – which were that the world would be destroyed on the following December 21st, but that she and her group would be saved by a fleet of flying saucers. The time came, but the prophesied events failed to materialise; creating an unnerving sense of disappointment among her followers. However, Mrs. Keech was soon privileged to receive another message from Clarion – the disaster threatening the planet earth had been averted, due to the selfless, unflagging devotion

---

[60] Leon Festinger, *A Theory of Cognitive Dissonance*, Stanford University Press, 1957; Festinger et al, *When Prophecy Fails*, University of Minnesota Press, 1956

of the group. Most interestingly to Festinger *et al*, they were not simply relieved by the explanation for the events failure to materialise (many had given up their jobs, possessions, houses etc.), but their devotion to the cult was now redoubled. From being a somewhat inward-looking, quietistic group they went on to become enthusiastic, proselytising devotees – anxious to convince others that they had saved the world, and to convert them to the cause.

This behaviour, involving the rationalisation of disappointed beliefs and an escalation of commitment is characteristic of both individuals and groups when faced with such crises. Historically, it is the usual outcome in cases of failed prophecy.

Flying Saucers and Science Fiction

At the time of writing an internet search for 'UFOs' generates around a million and a half entries; if this is qualified by the term 'hard evidence' the number of sites is greatly reduced; if 'scepticism' is added the list is diminished to a mere 50,000 (many of which provide neither hard evidence nor scepticism). But this casual survey presumably provides some indication of the extent of continuing interest in this subject at present. The emerging picture is of an abiding fascination, bordering on obsession among a hard-core of believers, and a more widespread half-belief. It is now over seventy years since 'flying saucers' were first observed, and despite a paucity of any real evidence for alien spacecraft (the hard-nosed would say that there is none at all), despite this, there is still a huge body of interest and belief in the existence of UFOs, and a virtual cottage-industry of speculation, based on their existence.

As is the case with many collective phenomena, events were precipitated by a trigger. The saga began back in June, 1947 when a businessman, flying his private plane over the Cascade Mountains in Washington, noticed a group of mysterious objects, apparently flying in formation at high speed. When he landed he reported what he had seen to a local newspaper: 'They flew as if they were linked together, swerving in and out of the mountains with flipping, erratic movements'; 'Like a saucer would if you skipped it across the water.' The story was so intriguing that it was immediately wired to other newspapers across the U.S. – and it rapidly took on a life of its own.

Despite the fact that the original report did not refer to the UFOs as saucer-*shaped* this profile became their defining image. The craze soon spread from America to the rest of the world, and people began to see flying saucers all over the place; newspapers were absolutely inundated with reported sightings. This initial phase of the flying saucer craze, when it began to grip the popular imagination, took place in the late 1940s - early 1950s. During this period it was also taken up by Sci-Fi magazines who published many accounts which carelessly blurred the distinctions between fact, fantasy, rumour and low-grade journalism.[61] It was in these publications that the connection was established between flying saucers and beings from outer space. These imaginative, usually over-heated, stories went on to provide much of the later stock repertoire of saucer mythology – their extra-terrestrial origin, their super-intelligent alien crews, their highly advanced technology etc. There was less agreement about the visitors' intentions towards the human race; these were sometimes portrayed as benign, though they were often depicted in a more menacing light.

There are obvious comparisons to be made between the broad, almost subliminal influence of these writings and that of the fantasies promulgated by medieval and post-medieval authors. Each provided a framework that could explain and give meaning to all manner of unusual phenomena – and, as

---

[61] Titles include – *Astounding Science Fiction*; *Amazing Stories*; *Super Science*; *Imagination*; *Weird Science*; *Startling Stories* and *Galaxy*

with religious miracles, faith and imagination have tended to be mutually confirming.

UFO mythology is extraordinarily persistent though. Even the briefest catalogue of UFO incidents over the past half-century would be far too long to list here, but the following account from 1966 is typical. On this occasion the UFO, which was accompanied by four sister ships, landed in a swamp near Ann Arbor, Michigan. The landing was witnessed by more than fifty people, including twelve policemen and all later agreed on what they had seen. The craft was shaped like a football (American, of course); it was about the length of a car, had a greyish-yellow colour and seemed to have a coral-like pitted surface. It had a blue light at one end and a white light on the other. The spectators on this occasion were curious rather than afraid – one man sat in his car blinking a coded message with at it with his headlights, another dashed off and brought his fiddle to the scene. Others ran to within 500 yards of the craft, when, 'with a sound like a ricocheting bullet' it suddenly took off. The UFO then apparently joined its sister craft in the sky, and together they sped off. Six police cars chased the formation as far as they could, but the group soon vanished. Detailed statements about the incident tallied closely. The U.S. Air Force was reliably tight-lipped about the affair; the newly formed Flying Saucer Society chalked the incident up as yet another piece of confirmation.

There were hundreds of stories like this during the early, heady days of UFO-spotting in the U.S. They leave those of a moderately sceptical disposition nonplussed – can the testimonies of random groups of solid citizens be dismissed as utter fantasy? Are the incidents related and/or ascribable to some perfectly explicable phenomenon (or are we really being monitored by an alien intelligence?). The problem is that anecdotal evidence of this kind, however sincere, is notoriously unreliable. Past experience tends to indicate that the involvement of a larger group, rather than the statements of individual witnesses, does not necessarily provide greater veracity for their claims.

There are various well-established psychological responses that have contributed to collective illusions of the flying-saucer kind. To begin with, the UFO *credenda* has been sustained over the years by communal reinforcement – this is the process by which suppositions and theories harden into strong beliefs simply by repeated assertion. Then there is confirmation bias – the tendency to take note of data that confirm one's ideas and beliefs, and ignore evidence to the contrary. If we once again add a fair measure of self-deception and wishful thinking to the list, the stage is set for a UFO event.

Unfortunately, this field, which has always been characterised by an inclination towards untrammelled speculation, has also been the subject of hoaxes, frauds and forgeries. In fact there have been so many of the latter that it is always difficult to exclude the possibility of deception in any particular incident – so *duping delight*, that never-to-be-underestimated impulse to 'put one over', must also be taken into account in UFO incidents (the ongoing saga of 'Crop Circles' in British wheat-fields must also be a prime suspect). Naturally, conspiracy theories also play their part in the ufologist world-view; most dedicated UFO believers subscribe to some version or other of these – if only to the notion that the lack of official acknowledgement of alien appearances simply indicate that *they*, the authorities, do not want us to know what is *really* going on.

Signs in the Sky

'The most striking indication of the greatly increased suggestibility of crowds are afforded by well-authenticated instances of collective hallucination, instances which, so long as we fail to take into account the abnormal suggestibility of the members of crowds, seem utterly mysterious, incredible, and super-normal.'
WILLIAM McDOUGALL

The whole UFO phenomenon, synchronous as it was with the beginnings of the Space Age, seems so quintessentially modern that it is easy to forget that humans have been 'seeing things' in the skies for a *very* long time. Even so, it is hard to fathom what was going on in the many accounts of weird happenings in the skies of post-medieval Europe. There are literally hundreds from this period, which can only really be described as apocalyptic apparitions – many of which are recounted in great detail by apparently reliable witnesses. These were not transitory mirages – most were prolonged, and, typically appeared above huge crowds of fascinated, and frequently terrified, onlookers. Some manifested as spectral battles, and there was often a martial theme to these aerial spectacles, but others, whilst equally dramatic, were far less obvious in their meaning. Whatever form they took and whatever significance was placed upon them, these sightings were generally as ominous as they were mysterious.

In 1554, the citizens of Nuremberg were awed by the spectacle of vast hordes of charging cavalry. In 1598, at Cockermouth in Cumbria, a furious battle took place between ghostly regiments of soldiers. There are reports of another ghostly army, visited on Berkshire in 1628, this time accompanied by the sound of heavy artillery and the steady beating of a drum – an event that, at the time, was taken to presage the Day of Judgement and 'caused many to fall on their knees'. In fact, if we can believe contemporary accounts, there were similar occurrences in Britain, and all over the European continent, from around the middle of the 16th century to the early 17th.

Polish chronicles speak of an immense funereal procession of hooded black figures, treading a menacing path across the sky (1581). The inhabitants of Wittenberg were similarly awe-struck by the appearance of a huge bloody sword and cannon mounted on wheels (1547). Flaming swords also appeared over Devon, where they were interpreted as a sinister portent of impending calamity. The small town of Eisleben was the setting for an enormous crucifix, which was accompanied by a rod and two fiery pillars (1561). The heavens above Normandy and Picardy were, on several occasions, the spectacular stage for 'angels brandishing dangerous weapons'. Tales of the appearance of monstrous animals (dragons, bears, lions or serpents) fighting in the sky were widespread, as were accounts of triple suns, inverted rainbows etc. There were many such narratives of strange and prodigious sightings around this time – and practically all induced a sense of foreboding.

What really was going on here? Phantom armies; incomprehensible but portentous signs; wild, aggressive animals; mystery, threat and fear – this is surely the stuff of nightmares. To the modern mind the accounts of these events raise a whole range of questions – not least, their reliability. Were these descriptions the product of a few inflamed imaginations? Were they grossly exaggerated for some underlying religious or political motive? Is it really conceivable, even in a far more credulous age, that hundreds of people, in widely separate localities, could have had such similar experiences, and agree in the details of their elaborate fantasies? And could they really have occurred with the frequency that the records indicate? Are, in fact, mass-hallucinations of this kind possible at all?

To begin with the last point, it would seem that, surprisingly, the answer has to be in the affirmative. So many of the contemporary accounts indicate that this was the case, and there are enough comparable examples from more recent times to believe that many, possibly the majority, of these events were experienced as real by those involved. That said, there remain many aspects of these strange occurrences that warrant further investigation – and which have a strong bearing on the subject of collective delusion in general. The setting is always a prime consideration in these matters – including, of course, broader concerns of cultural conditioning and expectations. Europe, in this post-medieval period, was undergoing massive social change and political upheaval. At the time of these 'Signs in the Sky' incidents there was widespread political and religious instability. These were tense, edgy days. Now, there is well-established psychological effect that a degree of dissociation may occur as a reaction to emotionally charged situations. Dissociation, particularly in conditions of anxiety and heightened emotional anticipation, tends to make the subjects involved more vulnerable to suggestion. Moreover, this response is enhanced in any collective milieu. In such circumstances the power of suggestion, particularly if it is from an authoritative source, can be very compelling. These are, in fact, precisely the conditions in which collective hallucinations may occur.

There is another factor. Hallucinations do not usually come out of thin air; they appear in response to suggestion or persuasive imagery, around which they are able, so to speak, to nucleate. In other words, suggestion and vivid imagery can give form and content to a prevailing mood or underlying anxieties. The principle source of the imagery that fired unsettled imaginations at this particular time came from the multitude of tracts, pamphlets and popular anthologies of prodigies that were then in circulation. There were older traditions of omens and portents in the sky, from biblical and even classical sources, so they had a cultural familiarity. But since the advent of printing, images of the sort of sky-signs that might be expected became more widely available – moreover, they were presented in graphic and sensational forms. This popular literature became very influential, often fuelling and providing the graphic imagery for apocalyptic notions of an impending cosmic battle between good and evil. The old certainties of medieval life were disappearing; many felt that they were living in the Last Days – and printed imagery showed them what to expect.

In post-medieval Europe, ideas that had once been the province of the learned few, together with fantastic tales that had once been passed person-to-person, were now widely available, and were being presented in explicit detail, carrying all the authority, and persuasiveness, of printed words and images. The impact must have been enormous. One can then imagine that the appearance of unusual cloud patterns provided a sort of screen on which groups of agitated people could project their collective fears and fantasies. In collective phenomena of this kind, however unusual, there is generally a high degree of agreement on the details of the experience. Always allowing for the possibility that there may be an element of telepathic rapport in mass-hallucinatory imagery, there is in any case always likely to be a consensus on what is seen, simply as a result of common preconceptions and expectations. This certainly appears to have been the case in post-medieval Europe. The visions were fantastic and ominous – and were generally agreed upon. They offered both a confirmation of the fears and tedium of ordinary life at the time and, paradoxically, a distraction from them.

Monstrous Races

Earlier I touched on the extraordinary developments in 'alien abduction' fantasies, in which notions of 'The Aliens' had evolved into a whole range of distinct beings ('Greys', 'Reptilians', 'Nordics') each with their own defining characteristics, all part of an elaborate explanatory narrative of their supposed motives and intentions. There are parallels here too, with certain older notions of strange, possibly malevolent, alien beings of remote origins. I am referring to the roster of imagined races that lived beyond the civilised European world – and haunted the medieval imagination. These were a formidable crew. They included the headless, club-wielding *Blemmyai*, who bore their grimacing faces on their chests; the grotesque *Cynocephali* or Dog-heads; the *Panotii* who had ears so large that they could sleep in them; and the *Sciopods* who were possessed of only one leg, but were nevertheless able to move very fast – and who, when not hopping around, used their massive feet as parasols. All of these creatures, and various others, regularly featured in medieval accounts of remote regions and on early maps of the world. They were very much part of the world-view of those times.

Many of these inventions originated in thoroughly unreliable Classical sources – principally from Pliny the Elders vast, encyclopaedic *Natural History* (which itself was partly derived from Herodotus' *Histories*). According to Herodotus the *Blemmyai* and the *Cynocephali* dwelt in Libya; Pliny had the *Panotii* living on islands off Scythia (a rather unlikely location since the Scythians occupied Central Asia). At any rate, these strange creatures were from strange lands beyond civilisation. And they were bundled up with marginally more reliable accounts of actual, if unfamiliar, humans – including those with dark skins and others of very small stature. Indeed, the entire topic reeks of xenophobia.

For the medieval European, the physical peculiarity of these alien beings was inevitably bound up with their alleged *moral* deficiencies. They lived beyond the blessed regions of Christendom, so were bound to be morally suspect (Augustine of Hippo, in his famous *City of God* seriously discusses whether or not the dog-headed *Cynocephali* were descended from Adam). These perceptions were woven into the medieval outlook, and fitted well with accepted, Biblical, versions of history – particularly with the gloomy stories of the Fall of Man, and of Lucifer's expulsion from heaven – and of course with the familiar, lurid accounts of hell and its demons. Taken together, these accounts all contributed to the unconscious ideology that sustained the peculiarly circumscribed medieval universe.

The perceptions of remote monstrous races, as with those of hell and its dreadful inhabitants, endured well into the early modern period. The early, printed version of human history, the *Nuremberg Chronicles*, has several chapters on 'monstrous races' and they also feature in Marco Polo's and Sir John Mandeville's accounts of their respective *Travels* – both of which were unreliable and plagiaristic, but very influential. Sometimes it would seem that humans have a primal need for bogeymen on which to project their fears and loathing.

Doomsday Narratives

The most salient feature of End-of-the-World accounts (in all their variety) is the sheer number of them and the extraordinary cross-cultural range of their appeal. They, and the cults that so often accompany them, are to be found in 'primitive' societies, in the ancient and the Medieval worlds, and throughout the modern period. Apart from the element of desperation in all of these scenarios the only feature they have in common is that they are acted out by human beings. They are indeed a strange phenomenon, and have a strong bearing on the general theme of this book. As pointed out in the Introduction, we humans count ourselves as the most intelligent species on the planet – and we are intelligent, rational beings most of the time – but are also capable of acting really stupidly. No other animals have such extravagant hopes and fears – and certainly no other species would commit mass-suicide in response to a suggested narrative. But of course no other creatures have our sense of self-awareness, or of our own mortality. It is this factor that is clearly at the bottom of such irrational collective movements. But there is another element that comes into play in the sort of movements described below, namely the human capacity to respond dramatically to suggestion.

The early 20th century American psychologist William McDougall was fascinated by this effect and looked for an explanation of the phenomena in terms of human evolutionary development. McDougall hypothesised that the curious effectiveness of hypnotic suggestion was strongly linked to the instinct of submission found among gregarious social animals where 'some members of a herd or flock submit tamely and quietly to the dominance of the leadership, the self-assertion of others'. He observed that these unspoken transactions are in fact part of the background of ordinary human life, where we frequently, and automatically, carry out suggestions made by others. Further, that in more heightened circumstances, the power of suggestion can by-pass rational, critical thought processes and lead on to entirely irrational forms of behaviour, creating a tunnel-vision condition of mind that disregards all other instincts – even, in the most extreme cases, that of survival itself.

Almost invariably, Doomsday narratives emanate from a cult or cult-like organisation, usually run by a charismatic leader (or leadership group), who generally exert high levels of control over their followers. Such organisations are usually hierarchically structured, with the leader or leaders possessing all the special knowledge, with the followers in a subordinate position. Such cults are characterised by the leader's coercive control, and the members' total immersion in the group's aims (and the narratives that flow from these).

In 1997 the founder of a Californian-based group known as *Heaven's Gate* convinced 38 of his followers to commit mass-suicide in readiness for transit to outer space. The group, following their leader's evolving narratives, had come to believe that they themselves were aliens, and that redemption (their rescue from this doomed planet) would be effected by a spaceship that was already on its way, accompanying an expected comet (named Hale-Bopp). The comet was real and was keenly anticipated in astronomical circles; the rest was sheer fantasy. But the group-members were very serious about their expected departure and dedicated themselves in earnest to training for the event – engaging in special exercises and living in a darkened house to simulate the rigours of their coming intergalactic journey. As the comet came close to earth, in order to facilitate their transcendence to 'a level of existence above the human', they all committed suicide. Their bodies were found some time later, all dressed in identical black shirts, sweat pants, and trainers, wearing armbands that read 'Heaven's Gate Away Team'.

The Heaven's Gate affair occurred some twenty years after the terrible mass-suicide of the *People's Temple* movement in Guyana, which was among the most lethal in the entire, melancholy history of such events. And it was just three years after the series of murders and suicides associated with another death-cult, that of *The Order of the Solar Temple*. It is clear that doom-laden cults like these tend to attract those with depression and feelings of low self-esteem, and that these emotions can, in turn, reinforce collective delusions of guilt or doom. In such cases a group's narrative, whether handed down from a charismatic leader or arrived at collectively, provides a unifying point of reference.

There are some historical examples in which this sort of collective suicidal tendency was institutionalised. The Donatists, a schismatic Christian group of the 4th and 5th century, came to make a positive virtue of self-immolation. This extreme attitude came out of the sect's frustration in their long rivalry with and persecution by, the Roman Church in North Africa. The Catholics were a majority, but only just – and since nothing was ever forgotten or forgiven by either side in their endless doctrinal conflicts, tensions based on the righteousness of their cause seems to have mounted to intolerable levels for the Donatists. The Donatists were Puritans and regarded the Catholic Church as entirely corrupt. In their reasoning, since nothing is purer than the spirit, it was a small step to contemplate its liberation from the 'contamination' of the body. The common ways they achieved this was by jumping off cliffs or by deliberate drowning – the more highly dedicated chose to burn themselves at the stake. Groups of zealots from within the Donatist community, the Circumcellions, became notorious for random, provocative attacks on Catholics, hoping to incite retaliation that would martyr them and ensure their place in heaven. There are obvious comparisons with the recent rash of suicidal atrocities committed by self-styled 'jihadis'.

This narrative, that the soul itself was free of sin and that only the body was sinful, was the basic assumption of another schismatic Christian group of more recent history – the Russian 'Brothers and Sisters of the Red Death', who seemed first to have appeared in the 17th century. They were bitterly opposed to the Orthodox Church, and if forced under duress to attend their services murmured prayers abusing the faith and the Archimandrate – who was in their eyes the Anti-Christ. In this cult every sectary was under obligation to recruit new members, and having managed to convert twelve new members was permitted to commit suicide – by which actions their admission to heaven was assured. Despite the inherent self-eliminating nature of the sect it managed to persist up to the turn of the 20th century, a date that they had collectively decided as marking the End of Times. On November 13th, in the town of Kargopol near St. Petersburg, over eight hundred believers arranged to burn their houses and themselves in an extraordinary act of collective suicide. The central authorities got wind of this scheme however, and managed to intervene in many incidents, nevertheless over a hundred were successful and they and their families perished.

There is, as I have indicated, a hidden history of such extreme events. It has to be said that they are always unusual, but from the regularity with which they appear across a whole range of human societies, throughout history, it is clear that they represent a distinct band in the broad spectrum of human behaviour. As incomprehensible as they appear to those of us living normal, regular lives the actors in these terrible events are basically no different from ourselves – other than being in a particular time and place – and responding to a different script.

8. The Sacred Word

'To be in possession of absolute truth is to have a net of familiarity spread over the whole of eternity. There are no surprises and no unknowns. All questions have been answered, all eventualities foreseen'
ERIC HOFFER

Holy Writ

For many, throughout history, sacred writings constitute the most important of all collections of stories. These provide the basis of most religious beliefs, which in turn form the basis of the moral and legal structures of most cultures. However, one way or another, they can prove to be extremely troublesome to the faiths and societies that they have originally inspired. Inconsistencies within an original text can, of course, lead to disputations, as can different interpretations of particular passages. But with the passage of time various other difficulties may arise. Problems can occur when the language in which the scripture was originally recorded has ceased to be the ordinary speech of the people – which is the case in many religious traditions. Whenever this has happened, the ancient tongue (Hebrew, Sanskrit, Latin etc.) has tended to become the prerogative of a learned, exclusive class of officials (priests, or priests by any other name) who then enjoy a privileged access to the Holy Writ. Historically, this sort of monopoly on the sacred has always been prone to abuse, and easily leads to a situation where these 'protectors' of the Holy Writ become aloof or remote from ordinary believers. The Sacred Word may even come to be regarded as *too* sacred for the ears of such common folk, even when read in a language that they do not understand, leading to such peculiarities as the 'silent' recitation of the scriptures that was practised in a certain period of early Christianity.

Then there is the question of authenticity. Any religion whose claim to legitimacy rests on its possession of an inspired text will be convinced that their scripture (or their particular version of it) is, beyond doubt, the genuine article. As a result the very letter of the scripture, the order that it is presented in, and in extreme cases its punctuation and even its pronunciation, can become sacrosanct. But the complete identification of a religious establishment with a particular version of a text can, in the end, make it vulnerable. In the event of religious dissent the scriptures themselves may easily become the centre of controversy. Would-be reformers frequently focus their attention on a perceived textual corruption of the Holy Writ (which, of course, they wish to rectify with their own rescinded text), in the face of opposition from more conservative elements (who are equally adamant that the text should not be violated by changes of any kind). As with all matters religious, views are likely be intense on both sides of any such argument and fanaticism easily intrudes onto the scene. For True Believers, be they reformers or conservatives, their own version of the sacred literature is always *bona fide*, others are either corrupt or impostors (it is almost invariably the case that both Orthodox and Heretical beliefs have their respective supporting texts). Practically all of the world's holy texts have been subject to this sort of disputation at one time or another and a great deal of strife has ensued and much blood spilled by the partisans of conflicting versions of the sacred word, in whatever form it has taken. The Russian exercise in textual reform offers an extreme example...

The Holy Text revised

In the middle of the 17th century the Patriarch of the Russian Orthodox Church attempted a long-overdue reform of the Slavonic Bible which, by this time, had become riddled with all manner of errors and interpolations. Accordingly, he acquired the most reliable of the Greek and Slavonic texts that were then available and appointed a panel of leading theologians to sort out the mess. Some years later, when they had completed their labours, the Patriarch presented the reformed text to an Orthodox Russian Church Council where it soon received official approval. But when the reformed version was introduced to the population at large it was first greeted with disbelief, then by a sense of outrage that grew to a general and outright opposition. All over Russia the masses, incited by their priests, rose in revolt. There was particular revulsion against the reviser's new (and correct) spelling of the name of Jesus. Believers were desolated by the changes: 'Woe, woe! What have you done with the Son of God?' Monks refused to accept the reformed Bible and closed their monastery gates against those sent to deliver it. Troops were brought in, and sieges and battles with the Tsar's soldiers ensued, lasting for years in some cases. Many of the leading figures in the resistance to the new Bible were permanently exiled.

The struggles between those who continued to defy the revised version and the Tsarist authorities, who insisted on its acceptance, dragged on into the following century, by which time the resistors had formed a sect that became known as the 'Old Believers'.[62] This group, who came to be numbered in millions, were to remain fanatically devoted to the old, corrupt text. They continued to be persecuted by the Tsarist government for the following two centuries, during which time huge numbers of them were driven to exile in the remoter areas of Siberia. Many prominent figures were sympathetic to their cause, including the writer Tolstoy.

Incredibly, the 'Old Believer' movement still exists – having survived Tsarist persecution, the Russian Revolution and Stalin's Terror – and still clings to its archaic, error-ridden version of the Bible (although it splintered into dozens of sub-groups, each with its own interpretations of the older Orthodox tradition). In the 1970s the Moscow Patriarchate revoked the anathemas that were imposed on the 'Old Believers' sect in the 17th century, but despite this official forgiveness very few of them ever returned to the Orthodox fold. It all goes to show that if words and their interpretation are important, *sacred* texts are *vitally* important.

The Pope who improved the Bible

The problems of a 'corrupted' biblical text were not confined to the Eastern Church. At the end of the 16th century the Latin Church Council had experienced similar difficulties with its Bible, different of course from the Eastern version, but which was also full of errors and interpolations (faulty copying during the medieval period was largely to blame in both cases). To rectify the situation a new edition of the Catholic Bible was commissioned. As with the Slavonic Bible, a panel of distinguished scholars was appointed to carefully sift through

---

[62] In the 18th century the 'Old Believers' were re-labelled as 'Old Ritualists' by Catherine the Great, but they continued to refer to themselves simply as 'Orthodox Christians'

the text and edit out the many false readings. After years of patient work, their version was presented to the Pope of the time. Unfortunately, he was less than impressed.

Sixtus V was one of the more energetic Popes in the long history of that institution. He achieved more in the way of buildings and reforms in his five years in office than had been seen in the previous fifty, and was known as 'the consecrated whirlwind'. But he was autocratic, to say the least, and highly impetuous. His response to the painstaking revision of the Medieval Latin Bible was characteristically dismissive; he threw it out and declared that he would do the job himself. To the amazement of all he issued a Papal Bull stating that only he, as Pope, was qualified to establish an authentic Bible for the Catholic Church – and that he intended to produce a full, complete and final version.

Sixtus threw himself into the task, working night and day, with the aid of just one secretary (who he drove to the point of insanity). His methods of retranslation were as idiosyncratic as the man himself; nevertheless, in a mere eighteen months the Vatican's printers were able to produce the first folio copies of the reformed text. It was an unmitigated disaster. The printers had been forced along at the same frenetic pace as Sixtus, and as a result the new, official Bible for the Catholic Church was thoroughly infested with misprints and other errors – and well overdue. The Pope spent a further six months attempting to patch up the text by writing corrections on small pieces of paper and pasting them over the worst of the printers errors. Even these corrections were incomplete on the day set for official publication, but the Pope insisted that copies be delivered to all the Cardinals of the Sacred College, and to the Vatican's many Ambassadors.

The new version of the Holy Bible created a scandal. Quite apart from the printer errors Sixtus had introduced a mass of defects all of his own. He had arbitrarily retranslated many passages and omitted others at whim. He also changed the established system of chapter and verse in line with a scheme of his own devising (an innovation that he saw as rendering all previous Bibles obsolete). But this sloppy, ill-considered, unscholarly version of the Holy Bible was, under the terms of the Papal Bull, intended to become the 'true, lawful, authentic and unquestionable edition'. No one, on pain of excommunication (or worse), would be allowed to deviate from this final and authentic text – ever! This, as many at the time recognised, was a potentially catastrophic situation.

The Pope was well pleased with his work, but the rest of the Church was almost prostrate with embarrassment. The Protestants, having heard the rumours of this fiasco, were having a field day at their rival's expense – and then, just four months after the new Bible had been shown to his incredulous Cardinals, Sixtus V unexpectedly died. The relief within the Church on the passing of this headstrong Pope was palpable, but they were still burdened by the legacy of his deeply flawed *Sixtine* Bible. They had either to admit that a Pope could be seriously fallible on a matter of supreme importance to the Church, or find some other solution to the problem of his deeply flawed, but still 'sacred' text. It was an extraordinary predicament.

Since the dignity and authority of the institution of the Pontiff itself was so obviously at stake it was decided at the highest levels that there really was little choice but to engage in a cover-up – but since Sixtus had so enthusiastically proclaimed the imminent publication of his New Bible they were left with very little time in which to retrieve the situation. With a distinct sense of urgency a group of scholars was formed to re-revise the Sixtine Bible under conditions of strict secrecy. Remarkably, their work was completed and ready for printing within a year. It wasn't perfect, but it was a huge improvement on Sixtus's version.

It was agreed by those closely involved that the new work should be published as a 'second edition' of the Sixtine Bible, with a preface explaining that the first edition contained many errors owing to the printers unseemly haste in producing it - thus entirely shifting the blame from Sixtus himself. But there remained the problem of those copies of the first edition that had already been distributed. This too was a tricky matter. It was obvious to all that the copies of the original Sixtine Bible would have an enormous rarity value, but it was equally clear that as long as they remained in existence they could fall into the hands of irresponsible heretics, Protestants and the like, who could then point to their distorted text as evidence of Papal corruption. The Sixtine Bibles *had* to be reclaimed.

Fortunately, the Church had the appropriate agencies to deal with their recovery. Discrete instructions went out both to the Holy Office (the Inquisition) and to the head of the Jesuit Order to retrieve as many copies as they could. It was made clear that the very honour of the Papacy was at stake. A sum of money was made available to purchase the volumes where possible; more drastic means were to be employed when this failed. As a result many private homes were entered and printing houses raided. However, in the event, these attempts at procurement did not meet with complete success. Many of the Sixtine Bibles had already travelled to lands beyond the Vatican's jurisdiction, and many owners were extremely reluctant to part with the unique edition that they had so recently acquired, which was, after all, a distorted version of the Holy Bible, made by Christ's representative on earth. The surviving copies remain to this day as one of the greatest of all bibliophile treasures – and an embarrassing reminder of one of the more bizarre episodes in the history of the Catholic Church.

Accretion and Proliferation

The furore accompanying the revised Slavonic Bible, and the problems created by the Sixtine Bible were, in fact, both consequent on the invention of printing, or more specifically, on the need for a reliable printed 'authorised version' and the necessity of dealing with past errors and accretions. In the previous centuries, when every copy had to be made by an individual scribe, errors were bound to occur and regional variations were ever likely to creep in. The advent of the printing process offered the Church a solution to this age-old problem, but brought an even greater need for accuracy in the official text since it could now be produced in unprecedented quantities. The possibility that mass-printing techniques offered for the close control of orthodox texts had been apparent since their introduction in 10th century China, where, as much later in Europe, unauthorised editions of scriptures were soon banned.

The printing press was not, however, the only change affecting the Church at this time. The Renaissance had already seriously dented the clerical monopoly of learning, and the Protestants, with their Reformation, were intent on a complete severance from Rome. They were also dedicated to translating the Bible into vernacular languages, a process that was to lead them to make their own interpretations of the original Greek and Hebrew scriptures – a move that was, of course, bitterly opposed by the Catholic Church.[63] Thus, as in so many religious conflicts, the era of rivalry between Catholic and Protestant, and their contending claims to legitimacy, focused on their respective versions of the holy texts.[64]

There was a long history to this. In common with all established religious bodies the Christian Church had always reserved to itself the right of interpretation of its scriptures.

---

[63] Not least of the Catholic objections to the Protestant Bible was the exclusion of seven Apocryphal books in their entirety (1 and 2 Maccabees, Judith, Tobit, Baruch, Sirach, and Wisdom). These are not accepted by Jews either. The Orthodox Church, by contrast, includes a few more Apocryphal books in their version of canonised scripture

[64] As well as excluding certain Old Testament books, the Protestant versions changed the *order* of presentation

The sacred writings were its property, so to speak, but there is a very real sense in which they were also its creation (although this fact was scarcely acknowledged). Most religious texts tend to become sacred, that is to say assembled into canonical form, at a much later period than their origin. The Christian canon, for example, was not put together until the 2nd century AD, at which time material that did not fit with the new Church's emerging dogma was rigorously excluded. Only writings that confirmed this rising, conventional view were allowed. Many other documents were ignored and some did not survive at all. In the first Christian century various oral teachings of Christ's message vied with written traditions, and there were many other Gospels in circulation than those finally settled on as 'canonical'. All of this non-canonical material was discarded by the new class of priests, sometimes with little justification – the choice of just four Gospels, for instance, appears to have been made on the basis of numerological principles.

The historical development of the Christian Church was thus bound up with the business of the selection, translation and 'explanation' of the various sources of their founder's words. As most of the first Christians were Jews the very earliest of such interpretations were made within the messianic Jewish tradition, but as Christianity spread to the larger, Greek-speaking, gentile world the message had to be adapted accordingly. Thus began the process by which the Church assumed the right of selecting (though not without considerable controversy), and later of interpreting, the scriptures. There was a certain circularity in all of this: the Holy Writ, every word of which was later deemed to be a sacred and complete record of the Saviour's life and message, and on which the entire authority of the Church rested, was actually shaped by the contingencies facing those trying to organise the new religion. It was natural, as the authority of the Church grew, and as it fought off rival claimants to the Christian message, that its chosen canon should become more authoritative, at least in its own eyes. There were others who thought differently, but they were increasingly regarded as heretical nuisances.

This process of textual evolution was not exclusive to Christianity; a similar progression can be found in most of the religious traditions that rely on sacred writings (including Judaism, Islam, Buddhism, Confucianism, Taoism etc.). There is a remarkable consistency in the overall sequence of events.

Sometime after the passing of the 'founder' (and possibly of his companions), a definitive version of religious doctrine is enunciated. This is usually supported by a religious canon, which has generally been selectively assembled from available textual material – and by the suppression of contrary interpretations. After a time this sacred canon becomes sacrosanct. Any challenge to its verity is then interpreted as a challenge to the religion as a whole. However, even the holiest of texts are not immune to the forces of change, as we have seen. And there are, of course, many variations of this broad pattern within the different religious traditions.

Once Christian doctrine was in place, and its canon established, the Church came to treat the whole collection of its sacred book as equally inspired, and the alteration of absolutely any part of it as an act of sacrilege. The intense controversies that had been generated in the 2nd century, over which books should be included and which left out of the New Testament, were themselves written out of Church history. In religions, as in most other matters, the winners write the texts – and usually compel their acceptance of their version. It is worth recalling that Willian Tyndale (c. 1494-1536), who first dared to translate the Bible into English, was strangled, and then burned, at the stake for his 'heresy'. A sacred text can easily become the symbol and instrument of religious authority.

A similar process of 'sacralisation' had, in fact, already taken place with the older part of the holy book, the Hebrew Bible, from which the Old Testament was derived. By the 1st century the Hebrew Bible had a history of revision all of its own. Although the Jewish scriptures were collected between 600 and 100 BCE, they were later edited to conform to contemporary beliefs and political necessities. This means that as a guide to Israelite history (which in part they purport to be) they are entirely unreliable, since it is virtually impossible to disentangle the earlier writing from later accretions and 'interpretations'. This leads onto that other great difficulty with sacred texts, in a sense the opposite problem to that of maintaining a single definitive text – namely, the tendency towards proliferation.

The Jewish Holy Books themselves are a case in point. The *Torah* (Law) was originally an authoritative set of rules of conduct, handed down by the priests in the name of God. It was a collection that bore on all moral, ceremonial and religious duties for believing Jews. This, when it was written down, became the Pentateuch, the first five books of the Old Testament. But over time the moral code was refined and extended to include the *Halakha* (Rules), which also began as oral law, but were also written down, and which eventually came to be regarded as coeval with the *Torah*. The *Halakha* is actually part of the *Mishna*, an encyclopaedic collection of legendary and historical material of every kind. The *Mishna* forms part of the text of the *Talmud*, which also contains a commentary, the *Gemara*. In addition, this canon was amplified and explained in the *Midrash*, which consists of a vast number of comments on the Old Testament. But the interpretations of scripture did not stop there. Dispossessed of their land, these sacred books became the principle focus of Jewish religious life. So, over the centuries Jewish scholars produced commentaries upon commentaries upon commentaries. With its texts, commentaries, super-commentaries and other references, the *Talmud* came to comprise thirty-eight volumes, amounting to ten million words – and, of course, nothing was ever discarded of this enormous fabric of exposition.

In the Jewish Holy Books, then, we see an extraordinary mix of religious laws, moral precepts, history, myth and legend, followed by layer upon layer of commentaries and interpretations, each, in its turn, adding to the stock of devotional literature (and each tending to add to the essential prescription for a devout life). Naturally, the exhaustive process of re-examination and reinterpretation of religious texts became ever more inward looking and restrictive. In this tradition, in which mystical speculation was frowned on, those who sought a 'deeper', spiritual, understanding of the available texts were driven to analysing the very letters of the Hebrew alphabet: these were the Kabbalists. Amongst other activities the Kabbalists ascribed numerical values to individual letters in an attempt to uncover their inherent, divine power. Using occult procedures, letters that had been converted into numbers were used in various permutations as keys to 'unlock' obscure biblical passages, supposedly revealing their hidden meaning. In reality this all too often led to exotic speculative fantasies.[65]

The multiplication of texts in the Jewish tradition, bewildering as it is, pales by comparison however with the Buddhist canon of authoritative works. As in other religious traditions the Buddhist scriptures were originally transmitted orally, and only at a later stage were they written down. Predictably, different schools wrote different things. Buddhists, though, were more relaxed about their master's inspired sayings, and never felt the need to define their doctrinal position too closely – an approach that resulted in a positive luxuriance of sects, and of sacred writings. The *Pali* Canon alone, which is restricted to a single sect, amounts to 45 huge volumes in the Thai edition, quite apart from its voluminous commentaries; the Chinese

---

[65] There has been a long history of contradiction in the Jewish world between the rationalising and mystical streams of thought. Kabbalists themselves see their tradition as at the core of Jewish belief, for the more Orthodox it is an extraneous, foreign import

scriptures comprise 100 volumes of 1,000 closely printed pages each, and the Tibetans have 325 volumes of their own. Each of these compilations are accompanied by their own extensive commentaries. Needless to say, the proliferation of Buddhist scriptures provided endless scope for doctrinal disputes between the various sects, which, even in this peace-loving religion, has led to extended, sometimes violent, clashes.[66]

It is interesting too, that the original Chinese translators of the Buddhist texts slanted their interpretation by representing Buddhist concepts using terms of their native Taoism, in a deliberate attempt to make the new religion more acceptable to Chinese scholars. They were successful in this, but as a result basic Buddhist doctrines were subtly changed. For their part the Chinese Taoists were to claim that Buddhism in fact derived from a diluted version of the doctrines of their founder, Lao-Tzu, which had been transmitted to the foreign barbarians – they later produced accounts of his travels to the West elaborating on this theme.

Confucianism in China emerged from a mass of myths and legends about the founder, whose origins are in fact thoroughly obscure.[67] The *Analects* are now regarded as the most reliable source of his teachings. These present a collection of the Master's conversations and sayings, ostensibly put together by his disciples - a collection that dates from the 5th - 3rd centuries BCE. As Confucius' reputation increased over the following centuries, so did the commentaries on his works. Some 500 years after its origin, during the Han dynasty, Confucianism

---

[66] There are a proliferation of lineages in Buddhism. The largest are *Theravada* and *Mahayana* (which has the offshoot of Tibetan Buddhism); these are primarily defined by geographical location. *Hinayana* is a derogatory term for Southern (i.e. *Theravada*) beliefs and practices, used by *Mahayana* Buddhists. *Theravada* Buddhists only recognise the *Pali* Canon

[67] It is believed that he may have been a minor court official in the ancient state of Lu

became established as an official cult, and subsequently went on to become the orthodox state ideology. By this time, however, it had become suffused with many other influences, and the *Analects* themselves had come to be regarded as mere commentaries on a later series, known as *The Confucian Classics*. The *Classics*, which had begun as a relatively small corpus of texts, had been greatly expanded, with the addition of more and more books, glossaries, interpretations and commentaries. Ultimately, this collection came to constitute a huge body of work, which was comprised of the *Thirteen Classics*, the *Four Books*, the *Sub-Classics* (6), the *Spring and Autumn Annals and Commentaries* (4), and the *Ritual Classics* (3). But, of course, it did not end there.

There were many further translations, interpretations and 'cleansings' of these texts by later philosophers during China's long eventful history, and by the time of the Sung dynasty (960-1276) there were some 1776 works of classical scholarship relating to these works which, taken together, came to have a status as sacred scriptures comparable to that of the Bible in the Christian world. As a revered text this vast canon was seen as providing the moral foundation of Chinese society – although from time to time it was subjected to revision, usually to comply with current orthodoxies. And for centuries it had a role in the notorious 'Public Examinations' for the Civil Service.

If the Jewish, Buddhist and Confucian scriptures are extensive, what can be said of the Hindu texts – immense, prodigious, almost beyond reckoning...

The *Vedas*, of which there are four (the *Rigveda*, the *Yajurveda*, the *Samaveda* and the *Atharvaveda*) constitute a huge body of revealed work; each *Veda* has four principle sub-classifications, concerned respectively with mantras and benedictions (*Samhitas*); rituals, ceremonies and sacrifices (*Aranyakas*); commentaries on these (*Brahmanas*); and texts concerning matters of meditation, philosophy and spiritual knowledge (*Upanishads*).

The *Vedas* are regarded as *apauruseya* – that is, of Divine origin[68]; and there are other, vast canons that are *smriti*[69] – which include a range of *Shastras* (precepts) and *Itihansas* (epics), such as the *Ramayana*, *Mahabharata, Harivamsa Puranas, Agamas* and *Darshanas*.

And these are just the bare bones. Here is not the place to attempt to list the totality of Hindu holy texts, but believe me it is truly vast – enter 'List of Hindu scriptures' into your favourite search engine and you will see what I mean...

By comparison with the holy books of most other religions the Islamic *Qur'an* is relatively short and, so far as can be judged, is a reasonably authentic version of its founder's utterances. The authorised version of the *Qur'an* was compiled just eighteen years after Mohammad's death by his successor the Caliph Othman (in 650 AD). It is recorded however, that Othman, having established a canonical version of available fragments, *had all others destroyed* (though not without upsetting many pious believers). Nevertheless, this version, despite its curiously muddled construction, managed to gain general acceptance. Effectively, it became the centre-piece of the new state-religion of Islam. For the most part the *Qur'an* is assembled according to the length of its chapters or *Surahs*, with the longest at the beginning – since the earlier *Surahs* tend to be the shortest, this effectively means that it is laid out in an approximate reverse chronological order. Over the centuries minor variations in detail managed to creep in (fourteen readings are recognised), but Othman's compilation remains *the* Holy Scripture for all Muslims: it is regarded as inviolable and, importantly, its original Arabic text is sacrosanct – meaning that it is held to be untranslatable into any other language. This had the effect

---

[68] *Apaurusheva* is a basic concept of the Vedanta and Mimamsa schools

[69] There is a distinction between Smriti and Shruti; the former refers to written texts that have an attributed author, the latter to more ancient authorless texts, including the central canon of Hinduism

that wherever Islam was adopted the Arabic language followed as an authoritative tongue. In addition, by the 9th century, after a period of intense theological speculation, the *Qur'an* came to be regarded as the uncreated 'word of God' – as eternal as God himself. This doctrine has meant that the sort of objective scholarly analysis that has been applied to the Christian and Jewish canons, is virtually impossible in an Islamic context. To Muslim believers the *Qur'an* is entirely beyond this sort of examination or critical comment.

However, although the *Qur'an* held its position as Islam's Holy Book, as Islamic culture expanded and became more sophisticated the need arose for authoritative guidance on many of the aspects of ordinary life that it did not address. In response to this demand scholars began to collect the sayings of the Prophet Mohammad and contemporary accounts of his (exemplary) life. These collections of Holy Traditions (*Hadith*), originally transmitted orally, were themselves written down and in the course of time became sacred texts, whose importance was only just below the *Qur'an* itself. This collection of sayings then became the principle source of reference in matters concerning Islamic law, religious dogma and ritual. In time a great body of law was built up that was largely derived from these traditions. The pious collections of *Hadith*, and the writing of commentaries on their every aspect, went on for centuries until eventually there was a prodigious mass of sayings and stories attributed to Mohammad, well over 600,000 – far more, in fact, than one man, even an inspired prophet, could have spoken or enacted in a single lifetime.

It became increasingly clear, and a matter of concern to many pious jurists, that a great deal of extraneous material had been introduced into these collections. Much of it was indeed suspected of being outright forgery, often reflecting the interests of a particular group at a particular moment in time. It seemed that every emerging Islamic dynasty and every

Muslim sect tended to justify its actions and claims to authority by reference to some *Hadith* or other. In fact, by the second Islamic century these collections held so many inconsistencies and contradictions that the authenticity of many of them was increasingly questioned. Serious attempts were then made to identify and eliminate false traditions – but the effort to achieve veracity and consistency vied with a pious respect for the existing *Hadith*. The attempt to differentiate 'reliable' from 'unreliable' sayings was not undertaken in any objective, rational way, but rather by examining the 'chain of transmission', and however suspect a particular saying might appear there was always someone ready to defend it. Eventually, the problem of ensuring whether a given passage was, or was not, uttered by the Prophet some two centuries or more after his death became quite hopeless.

In the end, the aura of the sacred tended to overcome doubts and scruples. The inconsistencies between *Hadith* were ignored, and even those that contained the most obvious anachronisms came to be considered reliable. They remained decisive in all matters to do with the law (although Sunni and Shia Muslims made different interpretations according to their different legal systems).[70] And as the language of the *Hadith* became less intelligible to later generations of believers many volumes of commentaries and 'explanations' were produced. In time these commentaries themselves came to attain an almost canonical standing – by which time the authenticity and relevance of the *Hadith* in general was no longer questioned.

It is worth pointing out however, that even where there is a high degree of agreement on a religious text, as there is in Islam with the *Qur'an*, this has never guaranteed unity – despite the

---

[70] In Sunni Islam the *Hadith* came to include the words and practices of the Prophet's companions as well as Muhammad himself. Shiah Islam included the Prophet's family, particularly his daughter Fatimah, and her descendants, the Twelve Imams

fact that the notion of a transcendent unity is an article of faith in this religion. In fact, serious religious disputes followed closely on the death of the founder and have persisted to this day, in Islam – as in all other major religions.

*

Most religions are founded on sacred writings, and the books or scrolls themselves are usually treated with great respect. The customs associated with them are remarkably similar across the different religions - they are invariably beautifully bound and often wrapped in fine cloth; they are not allowed to be covered by other books; they should be held only by clean hands and not allowed to touch the floor; prayers are often recited before their use, and often the texts themselves become objects of veneration.

Despite this, most Holy Scriptures have at some time or other been the subject of serious rancour – usually over conflicting interpretations of some aspect of their contents. As we have seen, they are all too likely to accumulate errors, and to be edited, altered or even forged in accordance with doctrinal adjustments – and naturally, religions and sects that are centred around a particular text invariably pour scorn on those of all others.

Many scriptures have been lost to history (those of Mazdaism, Mithraism and the Ajivika movement for instance), and the texts of these losers, however sacred they had been to their adherents, and whatever insights they may have provided for humanity at large, are as forgotten as the religions themselves.

The reason for this is clear - a religious text may be perceived as timeless and transcendent, but humans, their societies and institutions are not. However inspired a particular set of revelations might be, and however profound the insights they might provide into the great questions of man's place in the order of things, situations are bound to arise that were inconceivable at the time of their inception. The 'eternal' quality of the 'Sacred Word' has always been subject to the forces of change – and to man's restless, interfering, territorial nature.

Textus Receptus: Textual Authority and Literalism

Religious Fundamentalists of every persuasion tend to adopt a literalist interpretation of their holy texts. For fundamentalist Christians the Bible was inspired by the Holy Spirit and is absolutely inerrant; likewise, Jewish Haredi fundamentalists believe that their *Torah* is utterly flawless in every detail. Similarly, for hard-line Muslims every word in every *Surah* of the *Qur'an* has to be literally true since it was dictated to Muhammad directly by God. All of these fundamentalist movements claim to be true inheritors of their respective, ancient texts, but in reality all are deeply reactionary, essentially anti-modern, and of relatively recent origin. All literalist fundamentalists are strongly defensive of their scriptures and concerned to avoid any admission whatsoever that they might contain the slightest error. For them, 'God's word' is timeless and eternal, and criticism (sometimes even of punctuation marks!) is anathema.

The reality, however, is that all of their texts, and indeed all other religious canons, were selected, compiled and edited by human agency – often in a highly uncoordinated way.

The Christian New Testament is a case in point. The 'Timeless and Eternal' accounts of the life and message of Jesus found in the Gospels were actually compiled one hundred and twenty years after his crucifixion – by which time there were around *seventy* other works on the subject in circulation. These 'Apocryphal' versions included such titles as *The sayings of Jesus*, the *Acts of Apostles*, the *Martyrdom of Apostles* and the *Apostolic Epistles*. The reason for the proliferation of these writings, and many other oral traditions concerning the life of Jesus was, ironically, the shortage of genuine accounts of the life of Christ – for over a century his followers had relied on Jewish sacred texts for their religious inspiration. But by the 2nd century a convincing, officially-approved, text was clearly needed, both to revive the failing hopes of the (mainly Jewish) Christians who were still expecting the prophesied 'end of the world', and to satisfy the demands for an authoritative script by the hordes of gentile converts to the Jesus-cult that were coming in from the pagan world.

To this end, during the middle to late 2nd century, the early Church devised a 'test of doctrine' to apply to the confusing mass of available material in order to establish a definitive canon – which then became the New Testament. There was, naturally enough, a great deal of controversy around this process, arguments that were compounded by the proliferation of 'heretical' beliefs that had grown up around the Jesus fables since his death. In the event, even though they were accepted by the incipient Church, the four canonical Gospels themselves were, and remain, riddled with contradictions. It was all a bit rushed, and this meant that, objectively, the notion of a complete and consistent account of the life and beliefs of Jesus from apostolic times is entirely untenable – instead, the approved and 'holy' version amounts to a highly selective collection of unreliable, legend-like stories of these events. The 2nd century Greek philosopher Celsus complained about this at the time, observing that the Christians were forever correcting and altering their Gospels. The reality, then and now, is that there is virtually no Biblical text (of either the Old or New Testaments) that is contemporary with the events it describes.

Other major religious texts show similar levels of inconsistency and illogicality – not that this ever deters True Believers, because they have completely identified their own *persona* with these stories. Because we seem to be prejudiced in favour of the *written* word ('if it's written down it must be true'), there are particular psychological difficulties in accepting revisions of established texts. Humans are capable of forming and abiding by the most convoluted sets of beliefs, rigidified in their texts, which then tend to become entrenched, vigorously defended systems of thought. One of the obvious dangers of this cast of mind is that such an overwhelming belief in one's own moral ascendency all too easily provides justifications that can sideline any moral or ethical scruples whatsoever, particularly in regard to those who choose not to agree with these 'obvious' truths.

Pious forgery (*Pia Fraus*)

As indicated above, a consummate belief in one's own moral ascendency can lead to the use of dubious methods in support of committed beliefs. This can begin, as it did in Christianity, with the selective construction of a canonical version of basic texts (from the 50 or so *Apocryphal* Gospels) – which went on to become the accepted, incontrovertible version of the life and message of Jesus. But *Pia Fraus* in the Christian tradition went much further than this. The relative paucity of accounts of the life of Christ in the officially sanctioned New Testament were felt as a disadvantage by many of the early Church Fathers in their arguments with unbelievers – so they used forged documents, extensively, to support their claims for the new religion.

The rationalisation in constructing these fakes, to convert the unbelievers or strengthen the conviction of the faithful, was that they supported a 'higher' truth. Accordingly, in the 4th century a 'Gospel', purported to be written in Jesus Christ's own hand appeared; as did examples of his personal correspondence; a letter written by his mother the Virgin Mary; and a 'Confession of Faith' supposedly made by Pontius Pilate (there are distinct parallels here with the later production-line manufacture of Holy Relics).

This last forgery was part of a pattern of false documents that referenced older, Roman authorities to bolster their authenticity. The *Decree of Marcus Aurelius*, for instance, was presented as a letter from the Roman Emperor to his Senate, calling for a halt to the persecution of Christians – in fact it was a clumsy forgery that was actually fabricated by the Church Father Tertullian. In reality, Marcus Aurelius was a follower of the classical philosophy of Stoicism and was contemptuous of the Christian cult. A supposed correspondence between the Roman philosopher Seneca and St. Paul also appeared around this time – but again, was completely spurious. For many of early Christian theologians the scant reference to Jesus by the contemporary historian Josephus in his famed *Antiquities of the Jews* was an acute embarrassment. So his meagre historical accounts of Jesus and the Crucifixion were augmented by interpolations – by both the Church Fathers Origen and Eusebius – to claim the author as a witness for the recognition of Jesus as the Christ.

In fact he 4th century Bishop Eusebius was known as a prolific forger (he was responsible for the so-called *Letters of Emperor Antoninus*, supposedly in defence of Christians) but is also notorious for rigorously defending his counterfeiting activities. He wrote that – "It will be sometimes necessary to use falsehood as a remedy for the benefit of those who require such a treatment".

The long-running dispute between the Eastern and Western halves of Christendom (between Rome and Byzantium) was also responsible for a huge number of forged documents – in fact for centuries Rome was known to the Greeks as the 'Home of Forgeries'. Whenever the latter brought up a matter of contention between themselves and the Romans they almost invariably managed to produce a document verifying their claim.

The Donation of Constantine was the most famous of these – supposedly from the first Christian Emperor, it constituted a massive transfer of legitimacy, conferring on the Pope and all his successors, ecclesiastical primacy over all other bishops (including the Eastern Patriarchs), together with their palaces and regalia. Quite a donation! This is now known to be an 8th century forgery, probably written by the then Pope-to-be, Paul I. *The False Decretals* were another great collection of papers, again conferring rights and privileges on the papacy – this time purporting to be from a number of early Pontiffs. In actuality they were 9th century forgeries. *The Clementines*, a strange 4th century forgery of some twenty books, supposedly written by the 1st century Pope Clement I, makes the first claim for St. Peter as the first Bishop of Rome; and so it went on. Naturally, many of these forgeries had profound religio-political consequences...

And it goes without saying that the forgery of important documents, religious or otherwise, for whatever motives, is not limited to Christianity. The dubious accumulation of the 'sayings of the Prophet Muhammad' in the Islamic tradition has been noted; together with the fact that scriptural invention and counterfeiting was clearly rife in the Buddhist sphere (the Lotus Sutras and other Mahayana Sutras are now officially accepted as not having been spoken by Buddha). Forgery seems also to have been endemic in Chinese religious culture. In the early 18th century a group of Chinese scholars exposed many ancient Chinese texts as forgeries. In particular they cast doubt on more than 90 Shangshu scriptures, revered classics of Chinese literature, most of which have since been confirmed as late forgeries. One of these scholars, Yau Ji-hung, was scathing in his accusations of those who, for centuries, had failed to distinguish between the genuine and spurious versions of these works – "Can they be called Scholars at all?" he asked.

'**Scriptures:** *The sacred books of our Holy Religion,*
as distinguished from the false and profane writings on
which all other faiths are based'

AMBROSE BIERCE
(The Devil's Dictionary)

9. Heresy!

*'There are twenty sorts of Infidels, but the Heretics are
more Infidel than any.'*
From 'The Sea of Precious Virtues',
an Islamic Medieval 'Mirror for Princes'

*'All autonomous agencies and authorities, sooner or later, turn into
self-perpetuating strongholds of conventional thought and practice'*
HUXTABLES LAW

Holding the Centre

All belief is systematised, and all belief systems require a
narrative. This means that those who dare question this
narrative, the accepted, established truths in whatever arena,
are challenging not only authority, but the entire body-politic
of believers – and this why heresy is worse than unbelief. It
is, after all, one thing for those who have never been properly
exposed to the faith to question it (there is always hope that
these 'infidels' may be persuaded), but it is quite another to be
aware of the proper system of belief and to gratuitously reject it,
or to place a different interpretation on the accepted norms...
So runs the logic of the 'defenders of the faith' in the religious,

scientific, medical and political spheres, or actually, in any other organised system of beliefs and practices.

Historically, holy texts have long provided authority and legitimacy for hierarchical forms of government – with the general rule that the more authoritative the text, the more hierarchical the governance (and the least resistant to change). Ruling establishments of all kinds, throughout history, have naturally tended to portray their own political and religious order as proper and inevitable. So when new ideas appear that challenge established views they are bound to be interpreted as an affront to the entire existing order. When that order rests on a particular cosmological viewpoint contradiction may be almost intolerable. Perhaps the most famous example is the Catholic Church's resistance to the idea that was to shake the entire medieval world-view, namely the Copernican notion of a Sun-centred universe...

Copernicus denied, Galileo refuted

On the Revolution of the Celestial Spheres, by the obscure Canon Koppernogk, was finally printed in 1543, just before his death. His work was intended as a simplification of the Ptolemaic system of astronomy that had placed the Earth at its centre – and which had held sway since the 2nd century A.D. But its conclusions had far-reaching, not to say revolutionary, consequences. Copernicus was probably wise to have delayed publishing his Sun-centred theories, anticipating the furore that his publication would create (to cover himself he had indicated that his conjectures were simply a hypothetical exercise). In the event, they excited interest and controversy among his fellow astrologers, but remained of academic interest until their broader implications became more widely known (in fact the first edition of his book never sold out). But eventually the Church smelled heresy; the Inquisition was notified, and the book was placed on the *Index Liborum Prohibitorum*, the Vatican's Index of prohibited books.[71]

Galileo Galilei was the first notable scientist to openly acknowledge the truth of Copernicus' theories. This was seen as a provocation. In 1633 the Inquisition called him to their court and after a trial whose conclusion was pre-ordained, compelled him to recant his observations (which had effectively proved Copernicus' hypothesis that the Earth moved around the Sun). Famously, he is said to have left the court muttering 'all the same, it moves'. In reality though, the idea had already taken hold by this time. Even during the trial, the Vatican was divided on the verdict, but there were a majority of reactionary Churchmen who were completely resistant to these new developments in astronomy.[72] According to the prominent Jesuit theologian Father Melchior Inchoter, 'The opinion of the Earth's motion is, of all heresies, the most pernicious, the most scandalous'. The Cardinal Francesco Barberini (who happened to be the then Pope's nephew) was of a similar opinion. As one of the members of the Inquisition that investigated Galileo he denounced the Copernican theory with the following, ludicrous assertion: '*Animals, which move, have limbs and muscles; the Earth has no limbs or muscles, therefore it does not move. It is angels who make Saturn, Jupiter, the Sun etc., turn round. If the Earth revolves it must have an angel in the centre to set it in motion; but only devils live there; it would therefore be a devil who would impart motion*

---

[71] This listing was intended to 'protect the faith and morals of the faithful', and it had serious implications for the selling and distribution of books. The inclusion of such important figures as Johannes Kepler, Immanuel Kant and Descartes was a reflection of the extreme reactionary nature of some within the Church at this time. Interestingly, the works of Machiavelli were placed in the most severe category of the Index

[72] Ironically, the new Copernican scheme for the Solar System, with its central, fixed Sun and planets in circular orbits around it, was initially far less precise than Ptolemy's long-established model in predicting the future position of the planets. It did need refining

to the Earth. The planets, the Sun, the fixed stars, all belong to one species – namely that of stars. It seems, therefore, to be a grievous wrong to place the Earth, which is a sink of impunity, among these heavenly bodies, which are pure and divine things.'

Galileo's trial, and subsequent conviction, led to his being placed under house-arrest for the rest of his life; when he died he was refused burial in his family grave. All of his published works were placed on the Index of forbidden books – where they remained until 1822! Some 359 years later, in 1992, the Vatican finally admitted their mistake, that Galileo was right, and forgave him.

It might be asked why the notion of a Sun-centred planetary system should have been considered such a serious religious heresy in the first place (particularly since the matter is scarcely mentioned in the Scriptures). Actually, this had more to do with the medieval Churches adoption of a cosmology, which was derived from a combination of pre-Christian Aristotelian and Ptolemaic views (pagan both!). However, the Catholic Church had come to regard itself as the sole authority in these matters – it would follow that to doubt any aspect of their dogmatic assertions was regarded as heretical. It was all to do with maintaining the *status quo*, and their hold on Power.

'Error has no Rights'

By the time of Galileo the Church had a long and sorry history of dealing with heresy; well over a thousand years, in fact. Even before the Emperor Constantine effectively converted the Roman Empire to Christianity (in the 4th century), the Church was plagued by troublesome groups who questioned its religious authority, but when it became an official arm of the Roman state, the notions of orthodoxy and heresy became far more pressing; the religion of the meek and oppressed had become an instrument of state policy. In fact, Constantine's reign marked the end of governmental persecution of Christians and the beginnings of the persecution of heretics and other non-believers – religious views became not simply a matter of theological speculation, but a question of loyalty to the state.[73] However, the processes involved in transforming religious faith into a viable organisation inevitably led to compromise and distortion. As part of the incorporation of the Church into Imperial government, Bishops became official appointments for instance, and a formal hierarchical Orthodoxy sprang into existence However, since there were serious disagreements within the Church on basic matters of belief, there was a distinct urgency in sorting these out; a party-line, as it were, had to be established. In 380 A.D the *Theodosian Edict* was issued as the definitive doctrinal statement of orthodoxy. This was intended to clarify matters, declaring that only those who professed the Nicene Creed could be considered genuine Christians – '*All others we pronounce to be mad and foolish, and shall bear the ignominious name of heretics*'. After this, not to agree with the Creed was heretical – although in reality it was a hopelessly botched-up compromise that soon gave rise to further dissent. In short, the outcome of the combination of religious power with civil authority gave rise to a history of bitter divisions, schism, defection and persecution from the very beginning.

There had in fact been little uniformity of belief among early Christians. Outstanding matters such as the divinity of Jesus (was he god or mortal or what?), the realities of the Second coming (precisely when and in what form), along many other basic disputed doctrines, had to be resolved by a Church that claimed to know all the answers.. This was not an easy problem since Christianity had gone in several different directions before Constantine made it a state religion; it had taken

---

[73] As an indication of these new rules, when the Church became the official religion of the Roman Empire any marriage between a Christian and a Jew became a capital offence

many forms, with many distinct narratives. Notwithstanding, following the Theodosian Edict, there were attempts to destroy all 'heretical' books – however, all too often the condemnation and persecution of heresies led to a wider dissemination of their beliefs. It was also the case that many of these matters of belief had become bound up with ethnic and tribal differences.

Although most of the early heresies were, at least ostensibly, concerned with doctrinal disputes, later dissenting movements were more to do with the rejection of wealth and property, and a renewal of the Church's mission. Naturally, these new challenges to the Church's authority had to be dealt with severely. In one of the more shameful episodes in the Church's long history of the persecution of unauthorised belief, the Franciscans, as advocates of poverty, came to be regarded as heretical. Their vows of selflessness, of living a simple lifestyle and working with the poor, were declared a 'perversion of scripture' by Pope John XXII, and in 1337 the first Spiritual Franciscans were burned at the stake for holding the opinion that Jesus and his disciples had stood for absolute poverty. There were many more in the following years.

But the pressures for reform were ultimately irresistible. In the end, the Protestant Reformation saw the end of the Catholic monopoly of faith, and the Renaissance the end of the clerical monopoly of learning and education. A wave of rational thought, powered in part by the importation of ideas from the infidel, Islamic world, proved an unstoppable force. The 19th century American agnostic Robert Ingersoll put it succinctly: 'Religion is like a palm tree; it grows at the top. The dead leaves are all orthodox while the new ones are all heretics'. And this rule does not only apply to religious thought. In the end, every form of knowledge needs heretical thinking to progress – uncritical acceptance of any set of ideas inevitably leads to stagnation.

Heresy and Science

The prosecution of Galileo for his view that the Earth moves around the Sun, which was entirely based on rational observation and mathematics, was part of a rear-guard action against the new threat to religious dogma represented by the progress of scientific thought. Actually, this was not a new thing. The hostility of religious authorities towards natural philosophy goes back at least to the pre-Socratic philosopher Anaxagoras, who taught that the Sun was simply a red-hot metal and that the Moon was made of stone.[74] For his pains, Anaxagoras was charged with impiety by the authorities, who felt that his attitude towards the Gods was intolerably irreligious. Being unwilling to suffer martyrdom for his beliefs (unlike Socrates), he managed to escape from Athens and return to his native Ionia.

Over the centuries Science was at the forefront of this sort of free-thinking, truth-seeking speculation – and it was to have its own panoply of Heroes and Martyrs - until, in the modern era it has become the dominant world-view. But science itself has not proved immune from turning into a 'self-perpetuating stronghold of conventional thought and practice'. And like the Church it has often needed its own heretical thinkers to shake complacent modes of thought – and to introduce new, more appropriate narratives.

This is essentially because, paradoxically, one of the greatest obstacles to new knowledge is old knowledge. The Aristotelian/Ptolemaic cosmological system worked for a millennium and a half, it was an extremely powerful description of the Universe, but essentially wrong – and its very existence impeded more accurate theories. Coming up to date (and though it is hard to

---

[74] Anaxagoras also theorised on the nature of stars, eclipses, meteors and rainbows in scientific terms. He was the first to propose that the Moon's light was simply reflected sunlight

conceive), it is quite possible that such scientific articles of faith as the Big Bang and Quantum theory may be superseded – in the way that Newton's theory of Gravitation was replaced by Einstein's theory of Relativity.

The most famous account of the essentially discontinuous process of scientific discovery was spelled out by the American philosopher Thomas Kuhn in his *The Structure of Scientific Revolutions* (1962). Kuhn saw the development of science as consisting of 'normal' and revolutionary phases. The normal phase, with its ruling 'paradigm', means that, for much of the time, science tends to discover what it expects to discover. But over time anomalies may accumulate, the standard explanations in the field are no longer considered adequate, and discontent arises. Crises of belief in accepted views lead to their being seriously questioned, with a greater openness to alternative explanations. Eventually, a 'paradigm shift' comes about, with the adoption of a new framework for the particular branch of science involved. Just as with the religious *status quo*, until a new norm is established this can be a painful, unsettling time for all concerned. As I said in the Introduction, anomalies are uncomfortable – it is intolerable to live in conditions that do not make sense.

Heroic Heresy

High on the list of 'Martyrs to Science' must be the wildly free-thinking Dominican friar Giordano Bruno. Bruno took the new Copernican idea of a Sun-centred solar system much further – he had the nerve to imagine that the stars might be distant suns, with their own planets, and that they might even have their own life forms! As if these pronouncements weren't enough, he proclaimed that the universe was actually infinite – containing goodness knows how many other worlds. These notions, to a Church that already felt under siege from the cosmological ideas put out by Copernicus, Kepler and Galileo, were insufferable. In addition, and perhaps even more unacceptable, was his dismissal of many of the basic doctrines of Catholicism (such as the Trinity, Eternal damnation, the Virgin birth etc.). Bruno was captured by the Inquisition, tried for heresy in 1593, and finally sent to the stake in 1600. In a final act of Inquisitorial vindictiveness he was suspended upside-down as he was burnt.

But for many scholars Giordano Bruno was not the ideal scientific martyr. Free-thinking heretic he certainly was, but the Church was offended as much by his occult beliefs as by his scientific theories. He was committed to Hermeticism, a set of beliefs that accompanied the great flow of more genuine classical knowledge that triggered the Renaissance. The Hermetic corpus included Magic, Astrology and Alchemy and had its own, entirely un-Christian, philosophy. Moreover, according to contemporary accounts, Bruno's arrogant, combative personality did little to protect him from the Inquisition. As an Iconoclast, albeit with less-than-perfect personality, Bruno was the almost perfect subject for heretical persecution, but he was not quite the ideal subject as a martyr to science – although his death is still celebrated annually in Rome, on the 17th of February, for just that.

The Deep Time narrative

The 18th century Scottish gentleman-farmer James Hutton makes a distinct contrast with Giordano Bruno's flamboyant personality, but his theories, heretical enough in their time, came to exert a far more profound influence on the course of science – for Hutton discovered 'Deep Time'. An enquiring mind, his geological investigations led him to conclude that the Earth was not 6,000 years old (as was generally believed in the 18th century), but hundreds of millions of years old. And he worked this out by literally examining the ground beneath his feet. When, after years of patient, independent research, Hutton presented his *Theory of the Earth* to the Royal Society of Edinburgh in 1785, his ideas were greeted with derision by most of the audience and dismissed out of hand.

In essence though, James Hutton was the founder of the science of Geology. He realised that the surface of the Earth was slowly being re-cycled, that the temperature emanating from deep within the Earth caused the crust to expand and form mountains, and that this same process caused rock strata to fold and deform. From observations on his farm he also became aware of the continuous operation of erosion and the relentless deposit of eroded material (sedimentation). He realised that the continuous working of these forces, over aeons of time, created every aspect of the Earth's landscape. Hutton was the first person to see all this, but his insights, although entirely accurate, were so in advance of contemporary thinking that it was a generation before they were taken seriously. His insights indicated a paradigm shift that almost amounted to blasphemy – altogether too big a step for even the most educated scholars at the time.

Lyell: Consolidating the Vision

Hutton's work was never properly recognised in his own lifetime – except by a fellow Scot, John Playfair, who promoted his ideas in a book *Illustrations of the Huttonian Theory of the Earth* in 1802. To an extent, this work helped to popularise Hutton's theories. Importantly, it was noticed, and inspired two other scientific thinkers who went on to absolutely change practically everyone's perception of the world; these were Charles Lyell and Charles Darwin.

Lyell was born in 1797, the year that Hutton died. He built on the pioneering work of Hutton and Playfair and comprehensively applied it to the whole range of geological phenomena. His *Principles of Geology*, which appeared in three huge volumes between 1830-33, was enormously influential. If Hutton founded the science of Geology, Lyell defined its curriculum; Stratigraphy, Volcanism, Earthquakes, Palaeontology, Glaciology – there was little that he did not touch on. It was a comprehensive, evidential account of the physical realities of the world we inhabit. Perhaps though, his confirmation of Hutton's notions of the immense time span involved in geological processes had the most enduring influence on intellectual sentiments.

Charles Darwin took a copy of the *Principles* with him on his epic voyage aboard the HMS Beagle. With its promulgation of 'deep time', together with its disdain of the views of religious orthodoxy, it was undoubtedly one of the greatest influences on his own, transforming theories of evolution.

'The most Important Book of the Century'

Revelatory as it was, Lyell's book did not cause any serious controversy. By contrast, Darwin's *Origin of Species* (1859) most certainly did. In fact, the *Principles of Geology* enjoyed a certain unexpected degree of popularity. But the *Origins* created a perfect storm of hatred and ridicule, admiration and controversy. When he returned from his voyages Darwin had befriended Charles Lyell, and the older man went on to make significant contributions to Darwin's thinking on Evolution. Lyell also helped with the simultaneous publication of papers by Darwin and Wallace on natural selection; the initial introduction of this idea. Darwin was apprehensive about publishing his great work, anticipating the furore that it might generate – and in the event his reservations proved correct, the publication did meet with enormous religious opposition. Even in the 21st century, among a minority of fundamentalist believers, there is still a great deal of hostility to this essentially commonsensical theory.[75] But it proved to be a foundational text; evolution by natural section became the very foundation of biology.

Darwin was supported in his early struggles with leading Churchmen by Thomas Henry Huxley ('Darwin's Bulldog'), who was an enthusiastic convert to his ideas on evolution. On his first reading of the *Origins* Huxley is said to have declared 'How extremely stupid of me not to have thought of that!' But that is often the way with new paradigms – unthinkable heresy gradually becomes obvious, taken-for-granted factuality.

The Semmelweis tragedy

It seems extraordinary these days, when the principle of bacteriological infection is universally accepted, that even as late as the last quarter of the 19th century the idea was not well understood and not generally accepted. Hospitals were dreadful places before the introduction of antiseptic procedures and their mortality rates were appallingly high. Patients undergoing a surgical operation of any kind were likely to be infected by the so-called 'Hospital Disease', and if they were, were lucky to survive. Some hospitals had worse reputations than others, but in some the death rate for operations was 50%. Although hospitals were understandably feared, many women still chose to have their children delivered there; unfortunately there was a terrible risk of infectious disease. Naturally the deaths by Puerperal, or Childbirth fever were of great concern to obstetricians, but the causes were a complete mystery.

In the middle of the last century Ignaz Semmelweis, a young Hungarian obstetrician working in a hospital in Vienna, noticed that one of his wards had three times as many cases of Puerperal fever than another. The only difference between the two wards

---

[75] T.H. Huxley once described science as 'organised common-sense'

was that the women in the 'bad' ward were delivered by medical students, while those in the 'good' ward by midwives. Initially Semmelweis attributed this disparity to the greater experience of the midwives. But a fatal incident in the hospital led him to reconsider. A colleague cut himself whilst performing a *post-mortem* on women who had died of Puerperal fever, his wound became terribly septic and within a few days he had died. It occurred to Semmelweis that there might be similar linkage between the high death rates in the 'bad' maternity ward and his students, many of who came to the ward directly from the dissecting tables, where they had been cutting up bodies to learn anatomy. Was it possible that they were transferring the 'putrefaction', by way of their hands, from these corpses to the living mothers?

At the time there was no knowledge of microscopic bacteriological pathogens, so there was no explanation for such a transfer. But Semmelweis decided to interfere with this possible line of transmission and insisted that his students wash their hands in a solution of lime chlorate before they entered the labour wards. The results of this simple exercise were dramatic. Almost immediately the mortality rate in the 'bad' ward dropped from being far higher to being well below that of the 'good' ward. Semmelweis had invented the principle of antisepsis. This important discovery did not, however, get the recognition it deserved. In fact it was scarcely recognised at all. Although the death rates in his wards continued to be far lower than those of any other hospitals his success inspired professional jealously and opposition rather than emulation. Semmelweis had never been on particularly good terms with his superiors. He had pronounced liberal views, and it was known that in 1848 he had taken part in revolutionary activities. He was seen by his superiors as a difficult personality (he had a somewhat emotional and volatile personality), and his latest obsession simply fuelled the deteriorating relationship between them. Eventually he was dismissed from the clinic in Vienna and returned to Hungary. He continued to practice obstetrics however, and continued to develop his antiseptic techniques. In the hospital in which he worked childbirth mortality was reduced to less than 1%, an incredibly low figure for the time.

Over the next ten years Semmelweis accumulated a mass of evidence supporting his methods. He published the results and sent copies to medical institutions throughout Europe. But the book was completely ignored, despite the fact that Puerperal fever continued to rage. The statistics were horrifying indeed. In the Viennese hospital from which he was sacked (and which had abandoned his antiseptic methods) 35 women out of 101 died in the labour wards during the autumn of 1860. We can only surmise the effect that this must have had upon Semmelweis when he got to hear about it.

Why was his message ignored? From a historical perspective it seems almost incredible that such clear evidence for the prevention of mortality, at such a small cost and involving only the most elementary precautions, should not have been immediately and widely adopted. Instead, these ideas met with a determined resistance from the medical profession.

The continued resistance to these ideas was utterly irrational, but in the end it was Semmelweis himself that snapped. He became prone to bouts of serious depression, and at other times would fly off into rages against his co-workers. His mental condition steadily deteriorated. In the summer of 1865 he was taken by his colleagues for a coach ride, in the course of which they visited a local mental sanatorium. Once there his friends slipped away and Semmelweis was forcibly restrained, confined by a straitjacket and placed in a darkened cell. A medical examination undertaken soon after his admittance revealed that he had an injury to his right hand that appeared gangrenous. It had been accidentally self-inflicted during his last obstetric operation. He died two weeks later of a puerperal-type infection. An autopsy revealed some organic brain damage. Semmelweis had been insane – but was nevertheless a martyr of rational thought.

In one of the most poignant coincidences in medical history Joseph Lister performed the first ever surgical operation using antiseptic dressings on the day before Semmelweis died. Despite the success of his experiments Lister was also ridiculed – but the tide of opinion was changing. The theory of the bacteriological transmission of disease, and of the necessity of antiseptic methods was slowly but steadily accepted by the medical profession. Lister's pioneering achievements eventually brought him great honours (he was knighted and made a Baron), but Semmelweis who had anticipated his ideas by at least fifteen years has been almost completely forgotten.

Disregarded Genius

There is a sad parallel between the tragic case of Semmelweis and that of Ludwig Boltzmann, the pioneer of Thermodynamics. Boltzmann, who was born in 1844, was the first physicist to connect the properties of matter on the macro scale to the behaviour of individual particles. In a sense he was the first truly modern physicist. He understood the basic mechanics of nature from the bottom up, as it were, and had worked out the implications of his concepts in great mathematical detail. But his contemporaries lacked his vision, and were fearful of his portrayal of matter as made up of nothing more than the purposeless jostling of atoms. This denial of an underlying Creative Purpose was just too heretical (rather paralleling the resistance to Darwin). Boltzmann, like Semmelweis, suffered deeply from the non-acceptance of his ideas, which he knew to be of profound importance to science. After years of rejection he was driven to such a state of despair that he eventually lost his reason and killed himself. His ideas and his calculations were perfectly sound and, when they were finally accepted, formed one of the pillars of modern physics.

The best one can say of this unfortunate affair is that Boltzmann was spurned because he was just too far ahead of his time, and the same was true of his near contemporary Gregor Mendel, an Austrian monk, whose experiments with peas were to lay the foundation of modern genetics. Mendel was completely ignored by established biologists during his lifetime. Like Boltzmann his ideas were perceptive, his methods thorough and his conclusions correct. After years of patient experimentation he published his results and sent them to the appropriate academic centres. Unfortunately they attracted no attention whatsoever, and just sat on the shelves gathering dust. His attempts to communicate his ideas to established biologists met with indifference. He was, after all, an outsider.

Mendel later became the Abbot of his monastery; a move that left him no time to pursue his interest in plant heredity and his scientific career was effectively ended. It was not until sixteen years after his death, when his papers were rediscovered, almost by accident, that the importance of his ideas was appreciated. This shy Austrian monk, whose genius was completely overlooked in his own lifetime, did at least give his name to a branch of science. His explanation of heredity, Mendelian genetics, has now long been the universally accepted version.

The Continental Drift heresy

The examples above of disregarded genius and those of Lister and Pasteur in their earlier careers, all belong to the 19th century. One might expect that by the 20th century, when science had assumed an even greater role in human affairs and when scientific ideas were examined and argued over to a far greater extent than they had in the past, that any sound scientific thesis would be sure to be thoroughly assessed on its merits, however controversial it might initially appear. Unfortunately this was not the case. Where original thought conflicts with long-held views it is always likely to meet institutional resistance, however strong the supporting evidence. To adjust to an entirely new outlook, a new paradigm, can be a painful process, virtually a self-denial.

This can be the only explanation for the incredibly long drawn-out resistance to the principle of plate-tectonics, which were first espoused by Alfred Wegener before the First World War, but not fully accepted by the Geological establishment until the late sixties. The observation that the outlines of the continents seemed to roughly fit together was made soon after the appearance of reliable maps, in the mid-16th century (Abraham Ortillas, the famous early Netherlands cartographer, remarked on the apparent parallelism between the opposite shores of the Atlantic, as did the Englishman Francis Bacon). Many amateurs over the following centuries went to work with scissors and sticking tape making a passable fit of the landmasses, but the subject never attracted the interest of serious geologists. Wegener, a German meteorologist, was intrigued by the effect, but unlike previous dabblers he approached the matter in a more consistent and scientific way. He first laid out his thesis of 'Continental Drift', in 1912, proposing that the continents as they exist today are the remnants of an original, far greater landmass, a veritable super-continent, which he termed Pangaea, meaning 'all lands'. They gradually moved to their present position, and are still moving. He published his findings in a book, *The Origin of Continents and Oceans* in 1915, but he was looked upon as a mere crank, and his ideas ignored by the Geological establishment.

Wegener continued to develop his theory however, and continued to accumulate hard evidence to support it. He concentrated on the remarkable similarity between the rocks, the geological structures and most importantly the fossils on opposite sides of the Atlantic. It was a long haul however. Wegener was accused of 'auto-intoxication' – i.e. of being an obsessive crank. He was refused admittance to any German university and had to move to Austria. In the 1920s and '30s his proposals began to generate a certain amount of interest and debate, but much of this was hostile. Until that time the continents were generally assumed to have always occupied their present position. Wegener did manage to garner some support for his theory, but it was evident, both to those who were inclined to accept his ideas and those who ridiculed them that, if they had any basis whatsoever, all geological textbooks would have to be rewritten.

The principle obstacle to the notion of Continental Drift was the lack of a convincing mechanism that could be held to account for it. This was, in fact, the weakest aspect of Wegener's theory. But the fact that his suggestions of a tidal mechanism were shown to be inadequate to produce such vast effects tended to mask the possibilities of some other, so far unconsidered, explanation. Sceptics seized on this weakness in the theory, but in the late 1950s studies of the Earths magnetism and evidence of seafloor spreading inclined the argument strongly in favour of Wegener's hypothesis. A search for a mechanism then began in earnest, and a plausible 'convection' hypothesis appeared. It was finally established that the continents are indeed moved by convection currents from within the upper mantle. Like the currents generated in a heated saucepan they stem from the Earth's efforts to dissipate its internal heat.

The theory of continental drift was marked by official recognition by the publication of *Tectonic Plate Theory* in the science journal Nature in 1963. But well into the '70s there were a number of distinguished Earth scientists, particularly in the U.S., who remained unconvinced. Nevertheless, Wegener's notion that the present distribution of landmasses derives from the disintegration of an original supercontinent has become the orthodox geological version. Current thinking envisages a cycle of dispersion and consolidation of about 500 million years (we are presently about 200 million years along the dispersion part of this cycle). Wegener's term for the original supercontinent, Pangaea, has been retained, but apart from this, recognition of his major role in the furthering of this idea, which is now so basic to Geology, has been niggardly to say the least. In fact he has never really been accorded the credit he deserved. Part of the reason for this was that the acceptance of the idea of Continental Drift was so gradual (it took more than half a century), and that Wegener himself had died before it received general support (he died in 1930 on an expedition in Greenland).

It was also the case that Wegener, as a meteorologist, tended to be seen as an interloper. That his theory was sound, that he built up a mass of solid evidence to support it, that it unified many aspects of Geology was, for many, of less account than his perceived image as a crank or, worse still, guilty of scientific trespass.

*

In summary, we have always needed those whose who questioned accepted norms – no matter how unconformable their ideas may seem (and no matter how cranky their personalities). And this rule is as relevant now, in the enlightened modern era, as it ever was. The notorious maverick physicist Fritz Zwicky was recognised as brilliant, but on a personal level insufferable. His hypothesis on the nature of supernovae, neutron stars and cosmic rays seemed quite crazy when he presented it, but turned out to be completely correct. The Australian researchers Barry Marshall and Robin Warren challenged orthodox belief when they showed that duodenal ulcers were caused by a bacterium, *Heliobacter pylori* – eventually, after a great deal of resistance to the idea, it too was found to be completely correct, and quietly absorbed into orthodox belief. There are many more examples. One is reminded somehow of Sir John Harington's famous quote… 'Treason doth never prosper: What's the reason? Why, if it prospers none dare call it treason'.

10. Cover Stories
Rationalisations and Justifications

'The talent for self-justification is surely the finest flower of human evolution, the greatest achievement of the human brain. When it comes to justifying actions, every human being acquires the intelligence of an Einstein, the imagination of a Shakespeare, and the subtlety of a Jesuit'
MICHAEL FOLEY

Being in the right

As I've indicated earlier, there is a basic human need to operate within some sort of framework of values. This is necessary for our existence because it sustains our sense of purpose – nothing is more psychologically harmful to a group than the impairment of its underlying ethos. These assemblages of beliefs and associated values provide the most basic of *social* functions and are bound to be identified with in a highly personal way. In sociological terms they are 'internalised'. They enable us to know who we are and what we make of the world – but this means that mind and consciousness are as much a social product as a personal one. The desire to feel that one is 'in the right' is very much part of this. There is a strong tendency to concur with generally held opinions, to go along with conventional interpretations of events, and to adopt similar views and forms of behaviour as one's peers. Collective commitment confirms conventional beliefs and allays doubts in most matters – but of course these common habits of thought can lead to all kinds of unreasonable behaviour.

People are not so much motivated to *be* right as to *believe* that they are *in* the right, particularly in a group context. This means that consensual explanation is always a greater factor in our outlook and beliefs than more obvious, objective truths. In addition, humans are equipped with an almost infinite capacity to rationalise their beliefs and actions. These strong rationalising tendencies lay behind our capacity to form and defend the strangest beliefs on the most flimsy evidence; this is the principle way in which our socialising instincts can lead us to irrationality. For any of us it can be an uncomfortable experience to be presented with evidence that contradicts a firmly held belief. The normal initial response is to find the easiest way to relieve this discomfort, even if this involves some absurd exculpatory delusion. Indeed, once an idea or set of ideas is subscribed to by a group it can actually be strengthened rather than abolished by reasonable challenges or disconfirmation. People not only try to reduce the difficulties caused by anomalies and inconsistencies, they habitually avoid information and situations that conflict with their views.

It is perfectly natural to defend basic beliefs, indeed if these are seriously disturbed the consequences, for an individual or an entire culture, may be catastrophic. Explanations, rationalisation and justifications are the ways in which a positive self-image, of the self and the group, is preserved (although, as we have seen, these responses are also found in many forms of psychotic delusion). Naturally, these habits of self-justification can easily lead us into all kinds of irrational or immoral behaviour – on the other hand, which of us has not at some time or other smoothed over awkward contradictions in something that we have believed in, or fooled ourselves that apparent incongruities are in fact reasonable and consistent? As the quote above indicates, humans are expert at this. The reality is that most forms of objectively unreasonable behaviour seem reasonable and rational from the 'inside'. We have seen in Chapter 3 that one of the main tasks of our left-brains is to constantly devise defensive explanations for our actions and beliefs. This means that despite being essentially moral creatures we can quite easily persuade ourselves, or be persuaded by a group consensus, into objectively unprincipled activities. Indeed, much of the most socially destructive forms of behaviour are carried out by people who feel they have some kind of permission for what they do – unfortunately there seems to be virtually no limit to the extent that humans are able to justify their beliefs and actions.

We are also inclined to stick to our stories. Having committed to acceptable explanations (of events, principles, beliefs etc.), we are generally very reluctant to abandon them, either on a personal or on a cultural level – although, as we have seen, people may occasionally switch entire sets of beliefs in favour of another in the psychological somersaults of conversion. The fact that the precise details of the before and after narratives of conversion may show considerable variance, but that the emotional processes involved have distinctive common features, provides some of the best evidence of the pressing human requirement for a sustaining narrative. Humans abhor a narrative void.

*

Explanations, rationalisations and justifications, then, are all around us, so they are not difficult to find, but here are just a few classic (and rather extreme) examples, some of which have played an important role in world history:

The *Requerimiento*

The Spanish colonisation of the New World (which was asserted to be a civilising process), was a based on a legally justified declaration of sovereignty, the *Requerimiento*. This was essentially a demand to the local populations that they should submit, instantly and unconditionally, to Spanish rule – on pain of death or enslavement. It was drawn up, shortly before the colonial adventures in the Americas and provided a religious justification for their conquests on the basis of any reluctance to accept the authority of the Spanish Crown, as granted by the Pope. Each *Conquistador* carried a copy of it with him during their invasions of New World territories. The *Requerimiento* was usually read out at a distance, and in a language that the local inhabitants obviously couldn't understand. It included the stipulation that in the event of 'disobedience', 'You shall be blamed for all deaths and losses, not the King, nor I, nor my soldiers'. Having read out this declaration to uncomprehending native populations the invading Spanish forces proceeded about their brutal business. In effect it was an entirely hypocritical licence for mass-murder, torture, enslavement and forced conversion – a classic example of the self-justification, referred to above, of those who have forfeited their basic human capacity for empathy.

'Yahweh loves you'

The early Israelites were originally one of many ethnic groupings in the Near East, and one of the smaller. In the course of realising their distinctive identity they adopted Yahweh, originally a minor member of the Canaanite pantheon, as their particular patron God. This was not unusual; every tribe raised their own client God to occupy the highest position. During the glory period of the Jewish monarchy (with the Kings David and Solomon) a Temple, dedicated to Yahweh, was built in Jerusalem. The Jewish world-view at this time was polytheistic, in common with other neighbouring nations, but there was a gradual transformation, in the course of which Yahweh, whilst retaining his position as the patron God of the Israelites, came to be perceived as the sole God.

However, despite the presumed affection of Yahweh for his people, the Israelites fell into a political decline that culminated in defeat and humiliation. This created a theological dilemma. If their God was all-powerful and held them in particular esteem why had he allowed them to suffer such indignities? Their priests came up with an ingenious theological solution. Yahweh was indeed omnipotent, it was He that shaped the destiny of nations – and he used such powerful empires as those of Assyria and Babylonia as instruments to punish the Israelites for their repeated failure to respond to his overwhelming devotion to them alone. In this way the disasters that befell the Jews were able to be interpreted as divine punishment, but *also* as proof positive of their God's power, and righteousness – and naturally, recovery from disaster could equally be constructed as divine reward. In either eventuality they were confirmed as an elect. The many adversities that befell the tribe of Israel (and their occasional successes) were all taken as evidence of Yahweh's power and devotion to their cause. This belief in their unique Covenant with the one 'true' God meant that the Israelites, as the 'chosen people', were set on a course that was naturally inclined towards exclusivism. In time they ceased to proselytise, and their religious aims tended increasingly to be concentrated inwards, on deepening the spiritual life of the community.

'For you are a people holy to Yahweh your God; Yahweh your God chose you to be a people for his possession, out of all the nations on the face of the Earth. It was not because you were greater in number than any other people that Yahweh set his love upon you, for you were the smallest of all nations; it was because Yahweh loves you.' (Deuteronomy 7, 6-8)

The success of the Russian October Revolution of 1917 saw the adoption of Marxism as an official ideology by the newly formed Bolshevik state – with the result that the aspirations of the newly-formed Soviet Union and those of International Socialism became thoroughly entangled. This in turn led to the incongruous situation in which advocates of the Marxist brand of revolutionary socialism, wherever in the world they happened to be, adopted a form of transferred nationalism and, by stages, the promoters of a renascent Russian Imperialism. As a result many well-intentioned left-wingers, who were perfectly sincere in their beliefs, became apologists for one of the most despotic regimes that the world had ever seen. Marxism under the Soviet regime gave rise to a reign of terror that was responsible for executions, forced labour and mass deportations on an unprecedented scale – but it continued to enjoy the greatest support from left-wingers outside Russia precisely during those years that it was most savagely repressive (the early to mid-1930s).

During this period the external supporters of Russian socialism were led into ridiculous justifications for its excesses. When, for instance, the age of liability for capital punishment was lowered to 14 years under Stalin this was hailed by the leader of the French Communist Party as an indication of the new health and vigour of Russian youth under socialism. Many similar pernicious idiocies were spouted by liberal-minded Western intellectuals during the 1930s. The accounts brought home by sympathetic visitors to the Soviet Union were overwhelmingly favourable, but in reality they were systematically deceived as to the realities of the situation there by the Soviet authorities, who were adept at exploiting the visitors' optimistic preconceptions. After the English socialists and social reformers Sidney and Beatrice Webb visited the USSR they had nothing but praise for OGPU, the dreaded Soviet secret police – as did that other famous visitor George Bernard Shaw. Their notorious (though at the time well-received) study of the Soviet Union was originally titled *A New Civilisation?* – but in the second and later editions the question mark was removed. Not even the faintest whisper of doubt could be allowed.

For many left-wing sympathisers there were no negative aspects of the regime that could not be denied, explained or justified – famine used as a weapon, forced labour, deportations, colonisation of the border-lands, the Purge Trials etc. etc. And in the face of overwhelming evidence to the contrary, committed Marxists kept up these rebuttals for decades.

Certain because impossible

The second century thinker Tertullian, whose apologetics were a major contribution to the ideological foundations of the Latin Church, defended the 'impossible' aspects of Jesus' crucifixion and resurrection with the phrase *Certum est, quia impossible* ('It is certain because it is impossible'). In doing so he contrived to turn sceptical doubts about these events into 'proofs' that they really did occur (as in 'water to wine'). This was achieved by the somewhat convoluted logic that, since the early Christians believed these improbable occurrences (and they were not stupid), these accounts must be true, even though they might appear impossible. Following this train of thought Tertullian urged that, in matters of faith, believers should disbelieve the evidence of their own eyes, ears and reasoning in favour of the supernatural assertions of the established creed. Because of his theological contributions to the incipient Latin Church, Tertullian was later recognised as a 'Church Father'. Details of his biography are scarce, but it is believed that he may have had an earlier career as a practising lawyer – which figures.

Nobel's expectations

It is a curious fact that Alfred Nobel, the chemist and arms manufacturer, who left the bulk of his considerable wealth to found the Nobel Prizes, was a life-long believer in pacifism. But he was obviously conflicted in his wish to reconcile these beliefs with the enormous profits he made through selling weaponry. During his lifetime Nobel filed literally hundreds of patents in the field of arms and explosives and founded over 90 factories to produce them. He became known as the 'King of Dynamite', but he entertained delusions regarding his conflicting interests. In a letter to Bertha von Suttner, an eminent novelist and pacifist of the time, he wrote 'My factories are perhaps more likely to make an end to war than your Peace Congresses. On the day when two Army Corps can annihilate each other in a second, all civilised nations will probably shudder back from a war and dismiss their troops.' Made a decade or so before the First World War, to which his innovations and armament factories made a massive contribution, this proved to be an extremely unlikely rationalisation.

The *Dolchstosslegende*

The German defeat in the First World War came as an enormous shock to their Military, and to many civilians, both of whom had been led to believe that their armies were on the point of a victory. In fact the German forces were completely overstretched by late 1918 – largely as a result of the effectiveness of the Allies' Naval blockade they were out of reserves and were being overwhelmed by the Allied forces, which included fresh contingents of American troops. Failure was inevitable, but entirely unexpected by the German Nation at large. In the event, the leading Generals left it to politicians to start peace negotiations with the victorious Allies. The ensuing blame-laying saw the Generals claiming success in their last big push, and the politicians on all sides blaming each other. No-one wanted to accept responsibility for the defeat. Out of this quarrelling there arose the notion of the *Dolchstosslegende* – the idea, originating with the defeated Generals themselves, that the Army had been 'stabbed in the back' by cowardly politicians just as they were on the point of victory.

This was a completely false representation of the facts, but it suited the military and deflected the blame for the debacle away from them. In reality, with the failure of the Spring Offensive and their serious under-reporting of German losses, the Generals did have much to answer for. But the Stab-in-the-Back proposition gained considerable traction, particularly among influential right-wing circles, who actively disseminated it throughout German society. The Republican politicians who were obliged to sign the Armistice were endlessly portrayed as traitors. In the difficult ensuing years, after the inequities of the Versailles Treaty, the theme was developed by those who could not accept the idea of defeat – Germany had been betrayed by treacherous Jewish-Bolsheviks who had conspired towards this outcome for their own sinister reasons. For most right-wing nationalists there was no other explanation, and through their efforts the legend became widely believed – and added to the weight of Hitler's savage fantasies in his *Mein Kampf*. There is little doubt that the *Dolchstosslegende* was a factor in the destabilisation of the Weimar Republic, and it was installed as a constant feature of Nazi propaganda. General Ludendorff, who helped conceive the myth, became a prominent right-wing leader – and the *Dolchstosslegende* a cornerstone belief of the regime that went on to commit some of the most appalling crimes in the history of mankind.

The Omphalos Hypothesis

Fossils had long been objects of curiosity, but in the course of the 18th and 19th centuries the notion that these were the remains of life-forms from the distant past began to be taken seriously. A problem arose however, in that the new geological theories with which they were associated seemed to contradict traditional, Biblical versions of the age of the Earth, with its six-day Creation. Explanations were clearly required – and they came in various forms.

The 'modernists' among believing Christians tended to accept the new precepts that the Earth was in fact far more ancient than had been realised, and might even be millions of years old. For them it was a simple matter of interpreting the 'days' of the *Genesis* story as epochs, and that was seen as solving immediate concerns. Predictably, the Biblical literalists were not as lenient – many clung to the notion that fossil remains were leftovers from the Flood. Some of them also put forward the idea that there had been a 'pre-Adamite' phase of Creation (which, it was proposed, could have occurred between the first and second verses of *Genesis*). Other fundamentalist believers postulated that there had been not one, or two, but a whole series of Creations, each coming to its own catastrophic end; fossils were remnants of these earlier stages. In fact hundreds of books were published in the mid-19th century presenting theories that attempted to reconcile the new discoveries of geology with the Biblical version of the Creation. Among this explanatory tide there was one that stood out from all the others – *Omphalos: An Attempt to Untie the Geological Knot* by Philip Henry Gosse, a naturalist and dedicated Christian. In this work Gosse proposed a 'Prochronic' solution to the existence of fossils, whereby God deliberately created the world complete with fossils, and other indications of evolution over time, to test the faith of believers. In this way the Creation could have occurred in the six-day period described in *Genesis*, and within the then conventional time-scale of the 5,860 years of the world's existence.[76]

This extraordinary hypothesis, that the world and everything in it could have been created in an instant, all pre-aged as it were, to present a mere *appearance* of enormous antiquity can now only be seen as a quite desperate attempt to reconcile the authors conflicting beliefs in Science and Scripture. Stranger still that this rationalisation *ad absurdum* should come from an otherwise intelligent naturalist. Gosse was a prolific and popular producer of books and articles on a wide range of topics. His interests in nature had taken him to many different parts of the world, he is regarded as an early conservationist and, most curious of all, had a great respect for Charles Darwin.

The Lightning Problem

The phenomena of lightning had long presented something of a problem to the Church. The Church Father Tertullian, who could always be relied on to provide a definitive assertion, firmly identified lightning with hellfire (a notion that seemed to be supported by the 'sulphurous' smell experienced during thunderstorms), and since he was regarded as a founder of the Latin Church, this notion became incorporated into its official dogma. However, there were other ideas in circulation that associated lightning with specific demonic activity. These contending theories led to a further viewpoint that sought to combine the various streams of thought on this subject, holding

---

[76] In 1650 Archbishop James Ussher published his chronology of the origins of the world, which fixed the moment of Creation as beginning on the evening of Saturday, 22nd October, 4004 BC. His conclusions met with general agreement in the Church of England and were even inserted into the Authorised Version of the Bible, where they came to be regarded as the last word on the matter. As we saw in the previous chapter the Chronology only began to be seriously questioned by theologians towards the end of the 19th century, as a result of James Hutton's revelations of Deep Time

that thunder and lightning were indeed the result of demonic activity, but that God was using them for his own greater purpose.

By the time of the Middle Ages, and with the building of magnificent new cathedrals throughout Christendom, theological elucidation on the subject of lightning had become rather more pressing, since God, or some malignant agency (with or without His sanction), was in the habit of visiting unmistakable signs of displeasure on these monuments to His greater glory. It was all very mysterious. Those more obvious abodes of sin, taverns, bathhouses, brothels and other low dives, were seldom struck by lightning, but churches and cathedrals were – and with embarrassing frequency. What was God's intention in this? Why did he strike his own consecrated House, or even allow Satan to do so? Quite apart from the amusement that it offered to certain low types, there was always the danger that the lack of any convincing explanation of these events would encourage those unspeakable heretics who were forever prating on about the Church's greed, luxury and godlessness.

However, to the Church's continuing discomfort, these visitations were inexplicably sustained. Such records that have survived indicate that it was a relatively common event for a church to be struck by lightning. In fact many were struck repeatedly and frequently incurred such damage that their spires needed to be entirely rebuilt – indeed, some cathedrals were hit so often that their congregations became afraid to use them. However, although the need was pressing, no theological explanation of lightning strikes could be generally agreed on. The weakness in the argument of those who favoured the Daemonic, as against the Divine, nature of lightning was, of course, its origination, which was clearly from the heavenly direction – and as everyone knew only too well, Satan and his fiendish crew were ensconced in the lower regions. The theologians had their work cut out to explain this discrepancy, but they managed to come up with a doctrine of a diabolical 'power of the air', by which means certain demons were able to gain control of the airy element for the sole purpose of tormenting humanity. Surprisingly, this curious doctrine became the Church's official explanation of lightning strikes – except, of course, in those cases in which an obvious sinner had been struck. And this rather unconvincing explanation went on to be sanctioned by successive Popes throughout the entire Middle Ages.

*

With this sorry tale I will draw this collection to an end – although, of course, the list of such specious arguments could go on almost indefinitely. The historical catalogue is vast concerning such matters as the rationalisation of the suppression of women, of the institution of slavery, of racism, of the use of torture; in the justifications for wars; for the persecution of minorities – and of the intolerant defence of the *status quo* generally. Religious authorities, it has to be said, have always been among the most consistent offenders in this.

The strange thing is though, that despite the examples cited above, and an absolute multitude of other explanations, justifications and rationalisations, humans are basically moral creatures. We need a convincing narrative to overcome our doubts and scruples – and we always look for rational (or rationalising) explanations for our actions. Unfortunately, our capacity for self-deceit and self-delusion, particularly where constructed narratives are involved, has left us with a serious intellectual blind-spot. And this is *Homo Sapiens* greatest weakness – as we shall see in the following chapters.

11. 'We Shall all be Saved'
Narratives of Redemption

'And I saw a new heaven and a new earth; for the first heaven and the first earth were passed away... And I saw the holy city, new Jerusalem, coming down from God out of heaven, prepared as a bride for her husband'
REVELATIONS CHAPTER 21

Culture and catastrophe

Much of this book has been concerned with ways in which our narratives impose a framework on what we are able to understand, emphasising that we interpret the world according to deeply held cultural storylines. At times of great stress, when such accounts, and the cultures themselves, are seriously disturbed – by natural catastrophe, or by the onslaught of war, famine or disease – new explanatory narratives may have to be found. As we saw in the example of confabulating patients whose thought processes were compromised, a coherent interpretation of events will always be sought. To retain mental and cultural equilibrium in the face of such challenges, and no matter how dire or incomprehensible the situation that is presented, an appropriate narrative *has* to be constructed.

The Ghost Dance

'When the sun died, I went up to heaven and saw God and all the people who had died a long time ago'
JACK WILSON (WOVOKA)[77]

By the 19th century the incursions of European settlement into North America were having an overwhelming effect on indigenous tribal societies. From the time of the early appearance of these white-skinned settlers, and as a result of the problems brought about by their ever-changing contacts with them, there had been a melancholy history of decline among the Indian populations, particularly those of the Great Plains. Many tribes had been displaced by white land-grabbing and where they did come to an accommodation with settlers there was a constant pattern of treaty-breaking. The once plentiful buffalo herds had been severely depleted and hunting and fishing patterns were disrupted. In addition, the effects of introduced European diseases had been devastating – some tribes saw huge declines in their population. Many of the old relations between tribes had broken down, and the basic narratives of tribal life in general seemed under threat. In these new, fraught conditions old ceremonial practices were being lost, and social rituals were becoming irrelevant.

Against this background there arose a revelation of a new, revitalising movement. In 1889 a shamanistic member of the Pawnee tribe named Wovoka fell seriously ill just at the time of a solar eclipse (an event that caused consternation among the

---

[77] Wovoka was from the relatively small, peaceful Paiute tribe who, after sporadic conflicts, had surrendered to the Whites in 1862. He had been rechristened Jack White by a settler family for whom he worked.

members of his tribe). On his recovery Wokova began to tell of his experiences when he had 'died'.[78] He related that he had been transported to an idyllic world, where there was plentiful game, and had met with all the people that had died in the past. During this visit he had been commissioned to return to his tribe with a message, which he duly delivered. They were to live peacefully, love one another (including members of other tribes), not lie or steal, and should abandon all of their old warlike practices. If they followed these instructions they would be reunited with the dead, and old age, sickness and death would be abolished. He also had instructions for a new, powerful celebratory dance – the *Nanissáaanah*, or Ghost Dance.[79]

This was a communal dance of a familiar kind, with the participants holding hands to form a large circle, swaying and shuffling around to a regular, rhythmic beat. The dance and Wokova's prophetic message were correlated. If it were performed correctly the dance would revitalise the tribe, their lands would be restored, the white man's ways would be abandoned, and the spirits of the dead would return, together with the buffalo. The whites themselves would be blown away by a high wind. Both the dance and predictions were enthusiastically adopted. For the culturally depressed Pawnee, the five-day Ghost Dance gatherings, with their singing, feasting and expectations of a blessed prophesied future, proved to be an exulting collective experience. Trance was an important part of these proceedings, and it was common for participants to have their own visions of

[78] This seems to be something of a pattern. Charismatic figures often appear, with their teachings/redemptive messages, after an episode of physical or mental trauma

[79] Wovoka's prophetic ideas drew from an earlier Ghost Dance cult (1870), which was also accompanied by beliefs of the return of the Ancestors. It is also possible that it had some experience of the Indian Shaker movement, which drew much inspiration from the Protestant Shakers, who originated in England (The United Society of Believers in Christ's Second Appearing).

the happy new world to come. It was a mass expression of emotional release, of communal joy.[80]

Such was the aura surrounding this movement that word spread rapidly, and delegates from other tribes came to investigate. As a result, the cult and its teachings soon spread, becoming an extraordinary cross-tribal phenomenon. As it was taken across the western lands the dance and its rituals gathered momentum by incorporating local variants of old tribal beliefs, and its accompanying prophesies became more elaborate. The new age would be accompanied by catastrophic events. There would be earthquakes, landslides and great winds; hills would pile up on each other; the earth would roll back, cleaning itself of every last trace of the white man's interference, and the settlers would leave, returning to their own lands. The concept of Ghost Shirts was another innovation that was adopted – special clothes imbued with a magical power to stop bullets.

These developments did not go unnoticed by the white settlers, who became increasingly concerned by the rapid spread of this mysterious cult among so many different Indian tribes. Unfortunately, the dance itself came to be misinterpreted as a War-dance (which it quite definitely was not). As a result of mutual misunderstanding between the two sides, their relationship deteriorated, and a series of violent incidents ensued, culminating in the infamous, and completely unwarranted, Massacre at Wounded Knee.[81]

This tragic event effectively put an end to the Ghost Dance movement, as practitioners became fearful of further attacks. To a limited extent, among some tribespeople, the dancing carried on surreptitiously.

---

[80] The sociological term for this is 'expressive contagion', the extreme examples of which were the 'Dancing Plagues' of Medieval Europe.

[81] The tragedy of the Wounded Knee affair came about as a result of a seriously misguided attempt to disarm a group of Lakota Indians, who had no intentions to cause harm. In the fracas that ensued between 250-300 Indians were killed, half of them women and children.

Colonialism and Cargo

It is usually the case that when realities contradict our deeply held notions of what is happening, it is the realities that tend to be rejected (for as long as they possibly can be). When confronted with *extremely* unusual circumstances, efforts to explain the situation are redoubled. The bizarre 'Cargo Cults' of the South Pacific present some of the most striking example of this response. Although seemingly irrational to outside observers, the strange forms of behaviour that these cults gave rise to were essentially an attempt on the part of indigenous peoples to make sense of situations that controverted everything in their cultural experience.

The arrival of Europeans in the South Pacific islands, which only really got underway in the 19th century, made a profound impression on the inhabitants. In some places these newly appearing, white-skinned beings, were taken as the returning spirits of dead ancestors. The encounter with colonialism, and the whole range of new ideas and artefacts that it brought, gave rise to new magical-religious movements in many locations. There was a great deal of misunderstanding in this process – and bewilderment. From their point of view, it seemed that even when the islanders tried to adopt European ways of life, and attempted to follow the missionaries' religious instructions, they were still unable to get at the much-desired material goods ('cargo') that the Europeans seemed to acquire without apparent effort. Various cult-like responses arose out of the islander's confused interpretation of this situation.

A narrative spread that the 'cargo', of which the foreigners seemed to have an endless supply, had actually originated from their own ancestors and was intended for themselves – but that it was somehow being diverted and claimed by the Europeans. To counter this they built their own wharfs to entice the 'cargo' ships, and later, airstrips to attract the 'cargo' airplanes. There was also a widespread adoption amongst cultists of other aspects of exotic European behaviour: tables were built, laid with tablecloths and decorated with vases containing flowers, and the cult-followers, dressed in their best clothes, would spend hours sitting at these. Military-style drills, based on those of the colonial police and military organisations, also became very popular. To their great frustration, none of these attempts seemed to work, and the cargo still failed to come their way.

The cultural dislocation was expressed in other ways. A movement known as the 'Vailala Madness' began on the southern coast of Papua when a local native went into trance and spoke of visions of ancestors and their promises of a steamer full of cargo. This visitation gave rise to a cult, (which incorporated some missionary teachings), whose followers adopted a trance-like 'automatic' behaviour. The cultists attempted to imitate western modes of dress and manner in curiously exaggerated ways, and pieces of paper were carried around as 'Bibles'. In its essence this was a form of 'sympathetic magic'; European behaviour was emulated in an attempt to acquire European wealth (in the form of tobacco, calico, knives, axes and foodstuffs).

A similar popular movement known as 'John Frum' started in the New Hebrides. A preacher calling himself 'The King of America' and 'wearing a coat with shining buttons', was urging islanders to spend all their money, promising that their youth would be restored, that they would no longer need to work or keep pigs, and that ancient customs, looked down on by the missionaries, would be reinstated (including kava-drinking, dancing and polygamy). Like the Vailala Madness, this new movement, named after its initiator, spread rapidly, to the consternation of both missionaries and the colonial authorities.

These curious, but understandable, reactions to the impact of European incursion were thoroughly compounded by the incomprehensible struggles *between* the rival would-be colonial powers, particularly during the World Wars. At different times and places the British, Dutch, German, American and Japanese all claimed sovereignty over various of the islands – and fiercely contested their assumed rights. During WWII a succession of these alien forces landed in the South Pacific, fought incredibly fierce battles and built innumerable military structures and airstrips. In the course of all this, villages were destroyed, their inhabitants displaced and many of them were enlisted into conflicts of which they had little understanding. The impressions that these momentous events must have created in the minds of local people can scarcely be imagined.[82]

Retrospectively, the 'Cargo Cults' can appear both sad and ludicrous – it is only when we consider the extraordinary circumstances that the islanders found themselves in that their responses become intelligible. These were people in extreme cognitive discomfort, caught between two utterly different ways of life, set in their old ways, but yearning for the goods of the new. Their reactions, of denial and fantasy have to be seen as imaginative responses, part of a sustained attempt to absorb entirely new concepts and information – and as such their actions had its own internal logic. To make a convincing interpretation of events is one of the most important functions of our mind/brains – and to remain in control of one's thoughts it is always necessary to weave a consistent, comprehensible story.

---

[82] During WWII, for instance, the Solomon Islands went from a remote colonial outpost to becoming the focus of one of the most intense struggles of the war in the South Pacific. The Islanders first experienced the unannounced arrival of Japanese, who behaved as badly as most occupying powers do; then there was an invasion of vast numbers of Allied troops intent on re-capturing the islands. This was a major, bitterly-fought campaign. Each side was highly advanced technologically, but appallingly unmindful of the lives, property and culture of the inhabitants.

The Burned-over District: A plethora of narratives

'Creative discovery, religious conversion and the formation of delusional systems appear as the result of unconscious processes over which people have little voluntary control.'
ANTHONY STORR

The 'contagion' of religious enthusiasm is not, of course, limited to unsophisticated tribespeople; there are countless examples of enthusiastic religious revivalism in more technologically advanced cultures. The U.S.A. has had its fair share of these...

One of the most famous, the Great Western Revival, which started in Kentucky in 1801, went on to sweep the entire country in a wave of near-hysterical preaching and penitence. These events took place against a background of general anxieties about the enormous social changes occurring in America at that time – including rapid population growth, an economic depression, and a sort of competitive panic that was particularly associated with the rush for land.

In the new frontier regions itinerant preachers ('circuit riders'), spread their message in the more remote areas, but the Western Revival also took place in great open-air evangelical 'camp meetings', which attracted huge crowds.[83] These festival-like assemblies saw great numbers of mass conversions in an extraordinary outpouring of collective religious fervor, but also became notorious for the curious, spasmodic body movements, 'the jerks', that affected many of the participants during the proceedings.[84]

---

[83] Many of the preachers were self-taught. Camp meetings were so called because those who came usually stayed in their own tents for the duration.

[84] If reports are to be believed, there was also much leaping and dancing, even barking on all fours. A psychic release from a sense of guilt and anxiety seems to have been the underlying factor in this outbreak of collective hysteria.

The religious enthusiasm of the Western Revival spread to many other parts of the U.S.A., including north-eastwards to the outlying regions of New York State, which was itself still a frontier at this time. By the early 19th century, this territory, once the ancient homeland of the Iroquois Indian nation, had become available to settlers. The construction of a great new canal project, the Erie Canal, encouraged a whole new huge influx on its own account. Whatever their motivation, these new arrivals were to prove to be particularly receptive to the Revival – and at the forefront in the formation of a whole range of innovative religious and political movements. Because of its sustained enthusiasm for these new dispensations, this area later became known as 'The Burned-over District' (figuratively, burned by spiritual fervor).

What seems remarkable now is not simply the range of religious and social experiments founded here, but how influential they were later to become. The Mormon religion began here, as did the Seventh Day Adventists and the Jehovah's Witnesses. The American Shakers, the Millerites and the Dispensationalists all originated in this area, as did the important movements against Slavery, and for the Prohibition of Alcohol. The advocates of Spiritualism, of Celibacy and of Free Love all flourished in this part of America – and naturally, each of these had their own leading figures, their own ruling precepts… and their own narratives.

Many of the purely religious movements had their origins in British non-conformism and dissent (including Baptists, Quakers, Shakers etc.), which flourished when transplanted to the new American setting – and were soon producing their own religious innovators and motivators. One of the most colourful of the earlier leaders was Jemima Wilkinson. Jemima acquired her mission on recovering from a serious illness, and adopted the name 'Publick Universal Friend'. The 'Universal Friend' would forthwith only respond to this name, was self-described as 'neither male nor female', and habitually wore male clothes. This habit was emulated by her/his female followers, many of whom declared the 'Friend' to be a genderless Messiah (to the great annoyance of all other Christian denominations). The 'Friend' and followers were rooted in Quakerism and broadly followed their moderate doctrines – although they were later repudiated by mainstream Quakers. The Publick Universal Friend founded a religious community, and was in fact the first American-born figure to do so. However, the group generated considerable opposition, not least for their advanced social views – on women's rights, anti-slavery and the treatment of indigenous people – although disapproval tended to focus on the transgender aspects of the movement. Some modern commentators have portrayed the Publick Universal Friend as a transgender evangelist and a pioneer of androgynous acceptance, but the Friends teachings were very much of their time – including sexual abstinence and the imminence of a Day of Judgement. In the end, although influential in its heyday, the movement did not survive the death of the founder. However, other charismatic religious innovators from the Burned-over District were to leave more enduring legacies…

The Baptist preacher William Miller was one such. In common with many non-conformist Christians at the time, Miller was much preoccupied with notions of the Millennium and the timing of the Second Coming of Jesus Christ.[85] His conclusions, after years of deliberation, and based on his own numerological analysis of certain biblical passages, was that Jesus would appear on Earth, to begin his 1,000 year reign,

---

[85] Millennialist ideas, i.e. that a thousand-year Paradise will appear on Earth prior to the Final Judgement, were a consistent feature of prophesy in both Christianity and Judaism. Similarly, the Second Coming of Jesus (or Advent), which is referred to in the New Testament, has been the subject of prediction since the earliest days of Christianity.

sometime between the 21st March 1843 and the 21st March 1844. In 1838, given the imminence of this epochal event, he published his findings.[86]

Even before this time Miller's enthusiastic preaching about the Second Coming had attracted many followers; after the publication the ranks swelled to thousands. The validity of his prophecies were given credibility by the appearance of celestial 'signs and portents', which occurred just as he had predicted (actually they were a meteoric shower). In 1840 Miller was joined by another, media-savvy, salvationist cleric the Rev. Joshua Himes, who took control of the campaign and boosted it still further. So by the time of the expected Advent there was a great deal of anticipation on the part of Miller's followers. Many abandoned their homes and sold their worldly belongings, made 'ascension robes' and even wings in readiness for the ascent to Heaven.

But the allotted time came and went, and the Advent failed to occur, causing a great deal of confusion and anxiety among Miller's followers – however he soon re-set the date for October 22nd 1844, and the build-up continued, with even greater fervour. When it failed yet again the faithful experienced what came to be known as 'The Great Disappointment'. Thousands of disillusioned followers left the movement, mocked by their unbelieving neighbours. The Baptist Church disowned Miller, and there was acrimony among the leaders of the sect, leading to factionalism. But that was not at all the end of the story...

As we saw in Chapter 7, according to Leon Festinger's Cognitive Dissonance theory, the failure of prophesy creates

---

[86] In a tract entitled *Evidence from Scripture and History of the Second Coming of Christ about the Year 1843*. Williams fully accepted the Biblical narrative that, following the Resurrection, the righteous dead would join the living faithful in an ascent to Heaven; that Satan would be rendered powerless by being bound and cast into a bottomless pit, where he would remain for the 1,000 year duration; and all righteous believers would then live in eternal bliss.

an urgent need for explanations that will provide reasons to continue with the sect's mission. Many may be disillusioned of course, but those who stay can become even more zealous – and make great efforts to persuade others of any new interpretation to allay their own doubts. In the case of the Great Disappointment there were a range of responses, leading to a whole range of new dispensations. Miller himself continued to expect the Second Coming until his death in 1849, but other of his followers came to the conclusion that an 'investigative judgement' had in fact begun in 1844, unperceived by most, when Jesus had entered the Second Compartment of Heaven (in order to sort the sinners from the faithful). This group came to call themselves the Seventh Day Adventists – they maintained a belief in the imminence of the Advent and its consequences, and do so to this day.

Other ex-Millerites provided other strands of interpretation. One of these, Jonas Wendell, using his own Biblical calculations, set the Second Coming for 1868, then when that failed, for 1873. Another, Nelson H. Barbour also initially favoured 1873, then 1874, and then he and his followers decided that Jesus *had* returned, but invisibly. This notion was confirmed by Charles Taze Russell who developed it into the elaborate theology that became the Jehovah's Witnesses (though not without many further schisms, Armageddon date-setting, and failures thereof).

With hindsight, the continued prophetic failures, and the endless theological revisions that followed, make these groups and their instigators appear entirely unconvincing to rational enquiry. But their appeal was never to rationality. It derived, from the beginning, on the charisma and declared certainty of the leader's beliefs – notwithstanding the fact that many of them were deeply flawed characters. The emotional certainties offered by religious beliefs, together with the intricacies of their explications, probably offer the greatest testimony to the power of narrative.

If religious success is measured purely by the numbers of present-day adherents, then the Seventh Day Adventists are the most successful of all the religions that have their roots in the Burned-over District; they claim 25 million worldwide. The Jehovah's Witnesses are also high on the list, with around 8 million worldwide. The Church of Latter Day Saints (or Mormons), which must count as the most original of the Burned-over religious movements, are big in the field too, claiming 16 million adherents in no less than 160 countries.

The Mormons are original because their founding text connects the main-stream Judeo-Christian tradition to ancient America. Their founder, the visionary Joseph Smith, initiated the Church after being directed to a buried book of golden plates by the improbably named spirit Angel Moroni. The *Book of Mormon* was his translation of these 'ancient texts', which he published in 1830. They purport to be a history of an ancient American civilisation, written in what Smith referred to as 'reformed Egyptian'. This scripture, which was later mislaid, is both the focus of Mormon theology and of critical inquiry about the movement – for the former it is a holy text, for the latter it is a jumbled fabrication. Sceptics have pointed out that there seems to be no relation at all between the locations described in the *Book of Mormon* and known American archaeological sites, and that there are absolutely no linguistic or DNA connections between indigenous American populations and any Middle Eastern population. Despite these objections, Mormons consider the Book of Mormon to be a historically accurate document and have always defended it as such. As the author Michael Shermer has put it 'The veracity of a proposition is clearly independent of the number of people who believe it.'[87]

Regardless of the veracity or otherwise of their founding text, the Mormons went on to establish their own cultural identity in the developing U.S.A. After the death of their founder Joseph Smith in 1844, the movement followed his successor

---

[87] In *The Believing Brain*, Times Books, 2011

Brigham Young to the Great Salt Lake in what would become Utah. They managed to survive in this unpromising, arid land, attracting many further followers and building a secure modern economy. From the perspective of the subject of this book it is a supreme example of the formative power of narrative, however objectively dubious.

The Burned-over District was prominent in other movements that were to exert a profound influence on civil life in America, in particular Anti-slavery, the Prohibition of Alcohol and The Rights of Women. In the 1840s this area saw a great upsurge in Abolitionist sentiment with many wanting to form a political party whose aim was the immediate abolition of slavery. This issue, which had strong moral elements, was cross-linked with those of Temperance and gender equality. The Abolitionist movement grew ever stronger of course, particularly in the Northern States, culminating in the American Civil War, but was ultimately successful in its aims. The anti-alcohol campaign, by contrast, led to the 'Noble Experiment' of Prohibition (1920-33), which is generally judged to have been a self-defeating failure. Women's rights, even in the 21st century, is of course an on-going struggle, but the 19th Amendment, enacted in 1920, did at least secure the right to vote.

In addition to these consequential reform movements, the Burned-over District saw the founding of Spiritualism, by the Fox sisters (Newark, Western N.Y.)[88], and the formation of the extraordinary free-loving, 'Perfectionist' community (Oneida, N.Y.)[89]. The prodigious author Washington Gladden, with his

[88] The table-rapping phenomena, popularized by the young Fox sisters, is a curious example of a hoax that got a momentum all of its own, leading to the international movement of Spiritualism

[89] Perfectionism was based on the belief that Jesus had returned in AD 70, allowing the possibility of the creation of a sin-free millennial kingdom. John Humphrey Noyes, who declared himself sin-free, founded the Oneida Community in 1848. The group practiced 'complex marriage', which allowed free consensual sexual relations.

'Social Gospel', was another leading figure to have added his radical voice to the list of important Burned-over reformers.[90] There were many more.

The influence of this relatively small geographical area during this relatively short period, not only on American social attitudes, but in the greater world, has been the subject of sociological research for many years. The term 'hot-house environment', a time and place of intense intellectual/emotional activity, must surely apply here.

Japan's 'Rush-Hour of the Gods'

If there is a common factor in all of the examples mentioned above it is surely that exceptional social conditions can produce anomalous modes of thought and behaviour. When familiar narratives are shattered others, almost of necessity, arise to take their place. The ruined state of civil society in post-War Japan offers further examples...

By 1945 Japan had endured eight long years of militaristic dictatorship and war, and then the shock of defeat, including the atomic bomb attacks on Hiroshima and Nagasaki, for which the population was utterly unprepared. This left a traumatised and thoroughly demoralised country. After the war America occupied Japan and set about rehabilitating the Japanese state. There was much to do. Japan's industry and transportation infrastructure were devastated, the economy was in tatters, there were severe food shortages and the population as a whole were shell-shocked. General MacArthur, the Supreme Commander of the Allied Powers, rapidly pushed through sweeping changes. The Japanese armed forces were disbanded, the wartime nationalist government were tried for war crimes, and all the conquered territories were returned. As a further part

---

[90] Gladden wrote at least 36 books; he strongly supported Unionism of the workplace and opposed racial segregation.

of the radical programme of reconstruction a new democratic constitution was put in place – and religious freedom was established.

This last enactment was to have extraordinary consequences. Essentially, it introduced an entirely novel concept to Japan, where religion had traditionally been associated with the *status quo* – and had been repressed by the recent ultranationalist regime (or used to promote their policies). Under the Allied occupation a whole new crop of religious narratives quickly appeared. And just as the Japanese industrial economy, whose base had largely been destroyed, rapidly applied itself to new forms of peacetime manufacture, so the older belief systems were reconfigured into a whole range of New Religions (*Shinko Shukyo*); it was said that these new religions 'rose like mushrooms after a rainfall'. By 1952, at the end of the U.S. occupation, almost 600 new religious groups were registered, and hundreds of other groups had become independent of the shrines and temples to which they had originally belonged. This phenomenon became known as '*Kamigami no Rasshu Awa*', The Rush-hour of the Gods.

Although the majority of these new movements were based on the precepts of older, traditional religions (Shinto, Buddhism, Confucianism and Taoism), these new home-grown popular religions showed a great diversity of interpretation, introducing all manner of novel, sometimes foreign ideas. Many were founded by charismatic leaders, often of lower social status and, frequently, women – surprisingly, given Japan's patriarchal society.[91] It was also the case that the aims and beliefs of some of these sects were decidedly eccentric. Famously, an electric appliance dealer founded a group called *Denshin-kyo*, which was dedicated to the

---

[91] There were historical precedents for this. In the 19th century the religion that became Tenriko was founded by a female peasant farmer Nakayama Miki; similarly, the principle spiritual leaders of *Oomoto-kyo* were predominantly women.

worship of the 'Electricity God', and to the American inventor Thomas Edison. For similar reasons, the German physicist Heinrich Hertz was venerated by other, Shinto-aligned, groups. Many of these remained as minor sects however, and did not acquire large followings – but another unusual Shinto-based religion was far more successful. *Tensho Kotai Jingu-kyo*, was established in 1945 by Sayo Kitamura, a peasant woman, and became known as the 'Dancing religion'. Kitamura claimed possession by a Shinto deity, practised rhythmic singing and dancing, and taught her followers the 'Dance of the non-self'. She propounded an essentially millennialist doctrine which went on to attract huge numbers, especially, for some reason, among the Japanese-American population of Hawaii.

Several other of the new religions experienced rapid growth. The immediate post-war period was a sort of marketplace of new religious sects; it was characterised by waves of mass-meetings, and later, as they became more confident in their mission, by building programmes and an immense output of religious publications of all kinds. The aims of some, particularly the more successful, were rather general and bland[92] but there is little doubt that they all addressed the existential loss of identity suffered by many Japanese and aimed to provide a new sense of identity and mutuality.

Most of the groups' founders were seen as *ikigami*, a Japanese term for those possessing spiritual powers. This concept, which is rooted in older shamanist beliefs, was bound up with ideas of spirit possession – it reflects the fact that in Japan the difference between the divine and human realms is not as sharply distinguished as in monotheistic cultures. This allows special individuals the ability to draw down transcendent powers. The prophetess Sayo Kitamura,

---

[92] *Soka Gakkai* described itself as 'a happiness-manufacturing machine' whereas in 1992 *Shoko Ashura* published a garbled manifesto that incorporated ideas from Indian and Tibetan Buddhism, together with those from Christian millennialism and Nostradamus.

for instance, declared that when she spoke it was like turning on a 'divine radio'. As an extension of this shamanistic power it was common for the new cults to include sickness-healing in their portfolio (a traditional shaman activity), and many of their cult-leaders claimed to have personally experienced the miraculous healing of a serious illness themselves immediately prior to taking up their mission. As noted earlier, this is something of a pattern among charismatic leaders.

But there were other aspects of these new religions that were not so positive. In the heightened atmosphere of this post-war period there were, almost inevitably, a number of less savoury candidates ready to take advantage of the new openness. The 'Rush-hour' had its fair share of charlatans, fraudsters and perverts; some cult leaders were considered mentally deranged, others were clearly morally corrupt. The movements were also highly prone to internal factionalism and schism – and in some cases to scandal. In one of the most notorious incidents involving a major New Religion, the offices of *Reiyu-kai* (Spiritual-Friendship Association) were raided in 1949 for suspected tax-evasion. In the course of the raid police uncovered a huge undeclared cache of gold bars, plus cocaine. This group, one of the larger organisations, were raided again in 1953 and were found to be involved in political bribery, black-market dealing, intimidation and embezzlement. Surprisingly, *Reiyu-kai* managed to survive these setbacks to its reputation, and the upheavals of internal dissent; it now boasts well over 5 million members.

The prophetess Nagako Nagaoka was another leader that made the headlines. She, through her movement Jiu, was one of the more vocal sectarians, with very strong ideas on the restoration of the Japanese social system, and of world renewal. She led her followers by way of a series of oracles received while in trance, some of which were highly critical of authority – and legally and morally dubious. Despite this, her teachings were taken up by two notable public figures, a Go Master named Go Seigen, and a Sumo Grand Champion, Futabayama. Unfortunately for the movement, many of Nagaoka's oracular utterances went way beyond social convention, and common-sense (a matter that seemed to surprise her as much as her followers). In the end the group's increasingly erratic behaviour and pronouncements provoked the authorities into a response, leading, again, to a police raid. The ensuing fracas, and the resulting media uproar, with photos of Futubayama fighting off police officers, proved fatally damaging to the cult and it lost much of its following.

The New Religions experienced a severe thinning of the ranks in the decades following their post-war heyday. Some, like Soka Gakkai and PL Kyodan, were highly successful and went on to become somewhat regimented mass-movements, many others just faded away. This was largely the result of the changes in social conditions in Japan through the 1960s and 70s. From being a defeated, demoralised country Japan was now relatively prosperous and confident of its role in the modern world. It was also far less culturally isolated, more connected to the rest of the world and more open to external cultural influences – and its ruling narratives changed accordingly.

These changes were reflected in the general drift away from religion common to most of the developed industrialised countries – but the 1980s also saw the emergence of the *Shin-Shin-Shukyo*, or 'new, new religions'. The focus of these new groups, again reflecting international trends, was on personal development, occult phenomena and environmental concerns – essentially reactions to the dominant post-war emphasis on materialism and technology. Like the earlier new religions, these organisations tended to produce huge quantities of promotional literature – some of which promulgated highly controversial views. One of the most notorious, *Aum Shinriko*, essentially a doomsday sect, managed to combine Buddhism with extreme terror. In the late 1980s its leader, Shoko Ashura, began to kill members of the group who disagreed with him, and in 1995 the group carried out the infamous Sarin attacks on the Tokyo subway, killing twelve people and injuring thousands of others. Ashura was later executed for his crimes. In reality Aum Shinriko had far more in common with other non-Japanese doomsday organisations such as those referred to in Chapter 7, than to any genuine religion.

Another controversial sect, the peculiarly-named Happy Science (*Kofuku-no-Kagaku*) preaches the 'realisation of love, peace and happiness on Earth', but also promoted some decidedly reactionary militaristic views. In common with other of the 'new, new' groups its teachings derive from an eclectic jumble of sources. Needless to say, the more sinister elements of these new movements have attracted the most attention, but there are others with more benign agendas. The White Light Association (*Byakko Shinkokai*) has the laudable aim of 'raising consciousness for world peace'; another, True Light (*Sukyo Mahikari*), promotes a method of 'spiritual purification that cleanses the spirit, mind and body'; neither of these show great originality, but both have attracted massive followings. Another popular new religion was founded in 1978; *Agon Shu*, offers a return to an ostensibly regenerated Buddhism, although it actually combines various older forms with traditional Japanese folk beliefs. Its founder, Kiriyama, who tends to deride conventional Buddhism, is credited with having written over 50 books. *Agon* has claimed well over a million followers,[93] and has been involved in international charity-giving on a massive scale. It has not escaped controversy however, and has been accused of extracting money from its followers 'to avoid ancestor-spirit haunting'.

---

[93] This figure is itself controversial; most of the new religions, in common with sects and political movements throughout the world, tend to inflate the numbers of their adherents.

From the perspective of this book, the primary function of all of the groups described above is to provide meaning to its followers. To do this, a movement of any kind must provide its own distinct narrative, its own aims and frame of reference. What is particularly interesting about the *Shin-Shin-Shukyo* is their willingness to take advantage of the latest developments in information technology as they have appeared. All are social-media savvy; most put out audio-visual material, including videos, *manga* (comic-books), and animations to get their messages across. And many issue videos of their rituals and ceremonies – some of which are broadcast worldwide, as they happen. Verily, the Global Electronic Religious Narrative is upon us.

Failed prophesy: The Xhosa Tragedy

Prophesy is always an uncertain undertaking; when it is concerned with national renewal and redemption it may offer new hope and meaning – but it can have absolutely disastrous consequences, as in the following account, which is drawn from the discreditable history of the colonisation of Southern Africa.

The Xhosa people lived on the eastern frontier of the Cape Colony, to the southeast of Lesotho. By the 1850s it was becoming clear that they were losing the long drawn out Kaffir Wars, in which they were ranged against both British and Boer forces. They had been repeatedly beaten in this bitter conflict, and were being steadily driven from their homeland – added to which, their dire situation had been exacerbated by years of drought. This, then, was the background to the tragedy that became known as the 'Cattle Killing', a horrible drama that amounted to a collective mass self-destruction.

These pitiful events started when a well-known seer began to announce prophesies of tribal resurrection. She had spoken to the shades of old tribal heroes who were intending to come back to their old homeland in order to deliver the Xhosas from extermination by the white colonists. They promised to bring cattle and to drive the Whites into the sea. But there was a terrible condition to their expected return – they would only come back if the Xhosa nation as a whole demonstrated their faith by killing off all their cattle and destroying all stocks of grain. The mood of the tribe at this time was that of exhaustion, frustration and desperation, a condition that made them terribly vulnerable to these suggestions, which seemed to offer a complete solution to their predicament.

News of the visions spread rapidly and were widely believed. Rumours multiplied, and there were miraculous indications of imminent salvation. The ancient heroes were seen to emerge from the Indian Ocean, armed and ready for war, before sinking back into the waves; cattle were heard bellowing in subterranean caves, their horns knocking against each other in their impatience to reappear; men that had been dead for years appeared, delivering messages to their kindred, urging them to obey the prophesies. The day of resurrection was expected on the 15th August 1856, and in anticipation of this the Chiefs began ordering the killing of cattle and destruction of food stocks. It was a time of great feasting, but so many animals were killed that it was impossible to consume all, and many carcasses were left to rot.

There was enormous pressure on the few sceptics who tried to hang on to their stock. They were seen as hindering the rebirth of the nation. Most Xhosas were fully engaged in preparations for the coming event. They cleaned out their empty cattle kraals and corn pits, and enlarged and strengthened them in anticipation of the coming bounty. On the dawn of the great day the majority rose, full of hope, and were decked out with beads and paint, ready to welcome their long-lost friends and relations. But the expected millennium did not materialise. There was no sign of the promised twin Suns, no sudden darkness, no whirlwind came to sweep off the Whites and their own unbelievers, no ancestors returned and no cattle appeared – and neither did any of these things take place over the following days.

Confusion soon turned to bitterness, and then to despair. Those who had destroyed their property sat around their villages in the vain hope that their cattle kraals and corn pits would be filled – but they were disappointed. Within days people began to die of starvation. People were reduced to digging for roots and desperately gnawed at the bones that they had so recently discarded. The land was soon filled with the dead and dying. Tens of thousands of Xhosas lost their lives in this appalling episode, a lucky few eventually managed to find work on white-owned farms in the Eastern Cape or moved to the towns. The prophecies, and their failure, had achieved what years of bitter warfare had not – the power of the Xhosa tribe was utterly broken. Their lands, and their labour, now fell under White control.

12. The Terrors of Hell

*'Without the existence of stories that diverge from the true,
without the first fictions, religion could not have arisen.
Religion depends on the power of story'*
BRIAN BOYD

The Hereafter

Human thought processes are characterised by a singular amalgam of instinct, reason, imagination, and of course, hopes and fears – which is why we love stories, and why we habitually use them to secure our place in the world. These elements also form the basis of all religious belief. Since we hominids became fully conscious entities, a development that was itself associated with the acquisition of speech, we have been inclined to contemplate our own individual relation to the greater world and our exit from it. A reluctance to accept the finality of life is one of the drivers of the elaborate narratives that we construct about an imagined hereafter. However, the problem with these accounts, as with any set of narratives, is that they can get a life of their own. This is particularly the case with notions of Heavens and Hells. Just as our dreams can at different times be comforting or terrifying, so can the stories we tell ourselves. The many versions of the afterlife produced by the many distinct cultures that have appeared were always bound to some extent to reflect the conditions of life in the societies that created them. But inevitably there would always have been feedback – that is to say, that the tone and content of these narratives were bound to exert an influence of their own. In fact, they often had a profound effect on the hopes, beliefs and aspirations of the cultures that subscribed to them.

That concerns with the afterlife have been part of human consciousness for a very long time is borne out by evidence from the very earliest burial sites, which often have indications of a respectful attitude towards death and, by implication, of some associated ritual. We can't ever know for sure what the attitudes towards the hereafter of our earliest ancestors may have been, but it seems likely, from the careful placing of bodies and the grave goods that accompanied them, that they had a strong narrative relating to these matters. There are many distinctive features in such early burials, from which we may assume that there were a whole variety of such narratives. Later burial sites, dating from the time of the Neolithic (New Stone Age), often contain more elaborate ritualistic elements, which would imply the existence of more evolved and complex belief systems, possibly amounting to a well-developed mythology – although with no written accounts these will always remain mysterious.

The earliest *recorded* depictions of an afterlife come from the earliest city-based cultures, the Mesopotamian and, it has to be said, they are not at all pleasant. Sumero-Akkadian accounts of their 'Land of no return', for instance, present a picture of a rather grim, colourless place – a great subterranean city, where the dead blunder around in semi-darkness, eat clay and (for some unfathomable reason) are clothed in feathers. Hunger and thirst are the norm in this place, and rank offers no advantage. It is pretty miserable for everyone here no matter what position you occupied in life – and of course it goes on for ever and ever. This dismal concept of the afterlife was carried on by their successors, the Babylonians, who continued to view their after-existence as a deprived, lacklustre version of life on earth, although by this time it was somewhat more hierarchical in nature. No-one was happy in the Babylonian *Kurnigia*, but some of the inhabitants were worse off than others. Generally speaking, it would seem that the Sumerians had a pretty negative view of death and the dead, amounting to an abiding dread.

By contrast with this horrible prospect, the afterlife envisaged by the Ancient Egyptians was a far more congenial affair – although getting there was far from easy. The Pharaonic Egyptians were much concerned with their version of life-after-death, and a great many of their religious activities were dedicated to attaining it. Not so surprising, when the imagined 'Field of Rushes' offered a paradisiacal version of the familiar world of the living – one with permanent blue skies, fertile fields with abundant crops, rivers stocked with fish, and boats available for navigating them. This afterlife was envisaged as a physical reality, where new arrivals would be allotted a piece of land of their own to cultivate. Everything that they had left behind – in the way of possessions, family, pets, servants etc. – would gradually be restored to them. In short, there was an expectation that one would enjoy all the pleasures of life with none of its hardships and disappointments. But as indicated, the rites of passage after death were formidable. The newly deceased had to face a severe series of trials immediately after their passing-over. A light, sin-free heart was pretty essential at this stage (it would be weighed, and eaten if it was too heavy), as was the ability to come up with the correct spells, passwords and other formulae (which was the point of their instructive

Book of the Dead). It was also important to have undergone a prescribed, highly elaborate, mortuary ceremonial – which involved being properly embalmed and placed in a sarcophagus – procedures that were far beyond the means of the poorer members of society. Failure to come up to scratch in any of these requirements simply meant eternal oblivion – not an easily countenanced proposition.

Classical ideas of the Afterlife

The older Classical Greek notions of the hereafter were not dissimilar to those of Mesopotamia, i.e. rather grim. Their *Hades* was imagined as a vast cavern that existed below the surface of the earth. In common with the Babylonian underworld it was a colourless, dismal abode, inhabited only by the shades of the dead who moved around rather purposelessly, haunted by their memories of life. However, there were qualitative differences in this afterlife. Most ordinary souls finished up in the somewhat dreary setting of the *Asphodel Meadows*, but those that had lived an honest, fulfilled life (and who were still remembered for this in the land of the living), might be entitled to stay in the rather more pleasant suburbs of the *Elysian Fields*. The exceptionally wicked, though, would be cast into the deeper, darker pit of *Tartarus* (though possibly not for all eternity). Apart from these variants there was little sense of divine retribution in this afterlife – the soul survived, not really aging or changing in any way, but in a diminished, pleasureless semi-existence. However, from all accounts, these prospects did not seem to greatly concern the Greeks during their own lives; they probably pushed them to the back of their insouciant minds. As far as the dead were concerned, it was sufficient to ensure that they had a proper, decent funeral and were well-remembered.

These mythical ideas continued to be more or less believed in by the majority of Greeks for centuries, but later thinkers became increasingly concerned with the subject of the afterlife. The Pythagoreans, for instance, in the 6th century BCE, introduced a doctrine of transmigration, a notion that they shared with the Orphics[94] and which was later taken up by Plato. In this imagined scenario the immortal soul would be well rewarded after death for having lived a virtuous life in its earthly existence. In Plato's dialogue *The Phaedo* the character of Socrates refers to the geography of the underworld and ensures his listeners that the soul that had devoted itself to the good during its lifetime would be granted a more pleasant existence than one that had merely been concerned with selfish pleasures. In time ideas of this sort were developed so that the destiny of the immortal soul came to be firmly associated with the Celestial regions – and that the separation of the deserving good away from the punishable wicked became ever more firmly associated with the newly perceived Ptolemaic distinction between the heavenly world of the Sun, Moon and planets, and the terrestrial domain below. By the time of the Roman philosopher Cicero (in the 1st century BCE), the final resting place of 'blessed souls' was firmly established as the zone of the constellations (in his *Dream of Scipio*). This of course was the root of later Christian notions of Heaven (and one of the main reasons why, a millennia and a half later, the Copernican Sun-centred Universe was regarded as such an intolerable heresy).

In most respects the Classical Romans followed Classical Greek models in these matters, as in so much else.

---

[94] Orphism was a Greek mystery religion based on the songs and teachings of the legendary musician Orpheus. Although they subscribed to a complex mythology, little is known of the details of the Orphic system of beliefs, other than an emphasis on the role of punishments and rewards after the death of the body, from which followed the transmigration of the soul. They are believed to have adopted stringent ascetic practices and followed a severe moral code

Jewish and Early Christian notions of the Nether Regions

It is sometimes asserted that there is no Jewish belief or theories concerning the afterlife; this is not the case. It is true that the references are few in the Hebrew Bible (known as the Old Testament to Christians), but in fact the ancient Jews had similar views on this to those already mentioned of the Sumerians and Greeks. Their *Sheol* was much like the Babylonian *Kurnigia* and the Greek *Hades*, a netherworld located somewhere beneath the earth where the dead continue a shadowy, rather pointless, existence as *rephaim* – very much the equivalent of the Greek 'shades'. However, as in the other cultural versions of this dismal afterlife, further notions about the hereafter were gradually developed, including those of divine retribution. References to the linked, apocalyptic, themes of the 'Destruction of the Wicked' and a 'New Life for the Righteous' became more common in the later books of the Hebrew Bible. These concepts, of separate fates for the righteous and the wicked in the afterlife, really got going however in the Jewish apocryphal literature[95] of the 1st century BCE, during the turbulent period of conflict with the occupying Greco-Roman authorities. It is around this time that *Gehenna*, as a 'place of woe', makes its appearance.[96] The concept of a retributive afterlife was accompanied in these accounts by the radical new doctrine of the resurrection of the dead at the 'End of Days'. Both were the subject of great controversy in Jewish dialectic at this

---

[95] Apocryphal – meaning 'non-canonical', i.e. discarded by later theological authorities

[96] Named after *Ge-Hinnon*, the evil smelling, constantly burning, Jerusalem town rubbish-dump. The term *Gehenna* is repeatedly used by Jesus in the New Testament, but is frequently translated as 'Hell' (which is Germanic in origin)

time[97], but both were eventually accepted into mainstream Jewish theology – and by the splinter cult of messianic Jews that went on to form Christianity. In fact the latter went on to develop similar apocryphal accounts on their own account. So, by the 1st century CE, the novel idea of eternal punishment after death for earthly wickedness (despite many theological inconsistencies), had become an established part of both Jewish and Christian doctrines.[98]

The belief in the possibilities of a blissful afterlife in a celestial heaven is also found in the apocryphal literature of both traditions – in particular, the idea of the redemption of an elect became a stock feature of religious speculation at this time. There were also accounts of visionary journeys through the heavens in their respective literary works, and each made similar references to *Gehenna*. In fact the process of the separation of Christianity from Judaism was a gradual process that took place at a local level, with different communities opting for or against the new Jesus-cult, but still sharing many commonly-held beliefs. However, after the failure of the Jewish rebellion against Roman rule in 70 CE, and the subsequent destruction of their Temple, the Jewish state collapsed. During this desperate, critical period there was a polarisation of beliefs, resulting in the dissolution of many disparate Jewish groups (and their eventual absorption into a Rabbinic Judaism) – and the emergence of the Christ-sect as a distinct, separate religious entity.

---

[97] There were clear difficulties in reconciling the notion of God as a 'loving Father' with that of eternal punishment, nevertheless this theme appears in the late-Jewish apocryphal works *The Book of the Watchers*, *The Apocalypse of Weeks* and *The Book of Similitudes*

[98] Jewish and Christian theological views were probably influenced at this time by the ancient dualistic Persian religion of Zoroastrianism, which saw existence as consisting of eternal strife between the forces of Good and Evil

The origins of the Christian Hell

There is little mention of Heaven or of Hell in either the Old or New Testaments themselves, these perceptions, which came to have such an influential role in Christian theology, really derive from a handful of non-canonical (i.e. officially rejected) texts. However, there is little consistency in these narratives, other than a sense of retributive justice in the hereafter, and most are rather short on detail. But one of the more influential of these apocryphal texts, the *Apocalypse of St. Peter* prophesised a particularly grim outcome for sinners and unbelievers – and spelt out their punishments in graphic detail. In this 2nd century apocalyptical vision of the afterlife blasphemers will be hung by their tongues; those who have persecuted Christians have their lower bodies burned, while evil spirits flog them and worms devour their entrails; murderers are confined into a narrow space and are covered and eaten by worms; adulterous women are suspended by their hair over boiling filth; homosexuals are pushed off a cliff by punishing angels (endlessly); usurpers wallow in a filthy lake of foul matter and blood; sorcerers are hung on whirling wheels of fire etc. etc. There is a distinct tone of vengeful consolation in these retributive fantasies, directed as they were to a newly-formed, persecuted and vulnerable faith. But these lurid tales were to have an enormous influence. The alarming descriptions featured here, and in various other long-forgotten apocryphal texts, went on to become the template for many of the later images that came to be promulgated by the Church[99]. Interestingly, the author of *St. Peter* itself imagines the Christian righteous to be ring-side spectators

---

[99] Some of these texts are more apocryphal than others. That known as the *Gospel of Nicodemus*, for instance, is particularly dubious and is now dated to the 4th century. Nevertheless it follows earlier examples in its blood-curdling descriptions of Hell

of his horrible sado-masochistic circus, which they are clearly expected to relish; a revenge narrative indeed.

Further developments of the notion of Hell, which can only be described as a kind of literary inflation, really got under way only at a rather later stage however, with the works of the 'Church Fathers'[100] – some of whom, ironically, had actually been instrumental in excluding the apocryphal accounts from the official canon.[101] In these accounts, made during the first few centuries of the Christian era, the earlier apocalyptical visions, including the various speculations on the afterlife, were greatly embellished. This gave rise to some extraordinary flights of punitive fantasy – and because these authors had attained a high degree of religious authority their narratives acquired theological respectability. This meant that these lurid speculations prepared the way for many of the later, even crueller, descriptions of the torments of sinners in hell – which in time came to be dogmatically asserted by the Church as facts.

The aforementioned Church Fathers played a formative role in the ratcheting-up of this savage narrative. In the 2nd century Justin Martyr, Iraneus and Theophilus all mention eternal punishment and the burning of sinners in an eternal fire in

---

[100] The 'Fathers of the Church' were those influential early Christian writers who gave the religion its theological foundation – and dogmas. The Fathers were strongly influenced by Classical Greek philosophy (although they often seem to have overlooked its more rational aspects). The list of those qualifying for this title varies according to viewpoint – the Roman Catholic Church recognises a different series from that of the Eastern Church, for instance. But overall, their pronouncements contributed greatly to notions of Christian orthodoxy – and thereby of Heresy and excommunication

[101] The pressure to establish a formal canon that was recognised by all Christians was intensified by the adoption of Christianity as a state religion under the Emperor Constantine. But it was not until 367 CE that the Church Father Athanasius put forward the first complete list of the 66 books that came to make up the recognised canon – although final agreement on the canon had to wait until the 5th century. Some seventy-plus Apocryphal Gospels were rejected in the editing process

their published works. Tertullian (c. 160-230 CE, one of the greatest of the Church Fathers) refers to 'the greatness of the punishment which continues, not for a long time, but forever'. He was the first of several Fathers to endorse the *schadenfreude* notion, that one of the joys of Heaven lay in experiencing the suffering of the damned in Hell; 'How shall I admire, how laugh, how rejoice, how exult, when I behold so many groaning in the lowest abyss of darkness, liquefying in fierce flames.' Cyprian (c. 200-258 CE) also has graphic descriptions of eternal torments; 'Let him fear to die, of whom, at his going away from life an eternal flame will lay pains that never cease'; he also refers to 'the punishment of hunger and thirst eternal.' In the 3rd century, Basil also refers to 'the eternal fire that sinners will have as their companion in eternity'; Gregory of Nyssa warns of 'the fire of *Gehenna*'; Hilary declares that 'the heathen will have material bodies suitable for living in flames'; Jerome threatens 'the worm that will never die and the fire which will never be quenched'; and John Chrysostom also talks of 'a river of fire, a poisonous worm, darkness interminable and undying tortures'. There is a high degree of mutual endorsement in these tales, but the saintly Augustine (354-430 CE), the most influential of the Church Fathers (for the Catholic Church at least) bears the greatest responsibility for the official acceptance of the doctrine of eternal punishment. In his 'City of God' he writes that 'God hath not spared them, but cast them down into Hell, and delivered them unto chains of darkness, there to be kept until the condemnation of the last judgement, then to be cast into eternal fire, and there to burn for evermore.' Augustine also shared that notion of earlier authors that a balcony view of the eternal punishments inflicted on the damned sinners was an important element of eternal heavenly bliss. Not a very Christian sentiment, one might think – but this theme, along with many other sadistic fantasies, was developed to an even greater extent during the Medieval and Early-modern periods.

There are many other contributions along similar lines from other Church Fathers, and it is significant that there was a general consensus of opinion between practically all of them in favour of the doctrine of eternal punishment in the hereafter (usually involving 'eternal fire'). What is quite remarkable is the extent to which these projections are at odds with the message of compassion and selflessness supposedly extolled by Jesus himself. The Church Fathers are considered to have provided the intellectual rigour necessary for the Church to assert its authority – but their doctrines also ensured that it became a rigidly hierarchical, authoritarian and repressive institution. Ultimately, the Church came to place great emphasis on threats of damnation, and to rely on these to a far greater extent than on promises of eternal bliss. And theologians throughout the Christian centuries came to an unquestioning belief in the existence of Hell. These frightening stories became a reality in their eyes, and indeed of the majority of believers.

Consolidating the Hell Narrative

As indicated above, the groundwork on the nature of Hell that was outlined by the Church Fathers in the early Christian centuries was developed by many later theologians – who seemed to vie with each other in the ghastliness of their, often highly detailed, visions. The rationale for their sadistic fantasies were partly because it was felt 'necessary for the uncultured poor to have before their eyes a permanent vision of future torments and future joys', a sort of ecclesiastical stick and carrot – and the images of Hell certainly provided a justification for the persecution of every kind of heretic (in order to save their souls). But although it became a powerful instrument of social conditioning, this topic was clearly also a vehicle for the malignant imaginations of controlling, and sometimes obviously disturbed, individuals. The graphic nature of the horrors of Hell – in case you hadn't paid enough attention to the priest's admonishments – were of course on display on the walls of Churches and Cathedrals in all their gory detail. During the medieval period the Church was the principle commissioner of art, and naturally artists and sculptors provided what was asked for, often adding their own horrific details to the nightmare visions.[102]

The rationalising aspect of medieval Scholasticism, in which Aristotelianism became the basic idiom of their theology, meant that there was also the matter of establishing an exact, detailed description of the conditions of Hell. The precise nature of hellfire, for instance, was of particular interest to theologians, who spent a great deal of time discussing the subject - just as they would later debate the actual location and dimensions of Hell. They were also keen to emphasise (and categorise) the reciprocity of punishments for sins – allocating specific punishments for a whole range of particular transgressions.[103] The 12th century divine St. Alberic, for instance, relayed his vision of the torments that were in store for those married couples who had the temerity to sleep together on Church festivals or feast days – which involved their immersion in a vast lake of an unlikely mixture of burning pitch, resin and hot lead.

Other narratives emanating from the cloistered environment of medieval monasticism clearly reflect some of the less

---

[102] As in the original literary accounts of Hell, a tradition of competitive gruesomeness came into being, with artists trying to outdo each other in the horrific nature of their depictions. These works were commonly located on the western walls of churches, to be viewed on leaving, after the service. The majority of medieval Masters came up with their own versions of Hell, no doubt guided by the commissioning clergy

[103] This rationalising, categorising impulse also led to the inventions of the 'half-way houses' of Purgatory and Limbo, categories in the hereafter that had absolutely no basis in Canonical scripture – or even in any of the Apocryphal texts

salubrious aspects of life at that time. This long series of visions include grim descriptions of the bodies of the tormented, squeezed together in a permanently jostling, pestiferous heap in 'an enforced and sordid cohabitation, face to face, buttock to buttock with punches and kicks; as an anonymous, claustrophobic, struggling heap of corpses, covered in shit and filth.'[104] Throughout the Middle Ages there were similarly repetitious accounts of Hell – as a sewer, a brothel, a stinking swamp, a cesspit – together with whole bestiaries of tormenting demons and the fiendish tortures that they endlessly inflict on its inhabitant. The themes laid out in the early Apocrypha – the anguish of eternal fire, tormenting demons, devouring worms, filth, stench, disease and decay – were endlessly reiterated and embroidered upon, and these awful descriptions came to dominate Christian thought for centuries.

In fact, they became a stock feature of the visions of religiously-inspired individuals for well over a millennia, particularly the most revered and 'saintly' ones – from St. Gregory (the 'Father of Christian Worship'), who related his extensive accounts of the geography of Hell in the 6th century, to Bridget of Sweden, who delivered her harrowing, obscenely masochistic, descriptions in the 14th century. In the intervening centuries there were endless catalogues of the horrors of Hell issuing from the monasteries *ad nauseum*, conveying their terrifying images to the greater Christian world. As if life in the Middle Ages wasn't grim enough…

Other Hells

Christianity is of course not alone in its fearsome descriptions of the hereafter awaiting sinners. Other doctrinal systems, notably the Islamic and Buddhist, have comparable, highly evolved notions of Hell. The subject is too grisly to examine here in

---

[104] Piero Camporesi: 1990

any more detail – suffice to mention that there are nearly 500 references to *Jahannam*, the scorching place, in the *Qur'an* – and that at least one Buddhist system has eight major Hells, together with a further sixteen minor Hells. But it should also be observed that none of the threats of eternal punishment or promises of eternal bliss, in the Christian tradition or elsewhere, appears to have had the required, chastising effect in any permanent sense. One suspects that many sensitive individuals suffered severe mental anguish over these things, but that most citizens just learned to ignore the threats and promises, or at least live with them, no matter how hard they were cranked up by the religious authorities.

13. Versions of Utopia

'The world of reality has its limits;
the world of imagination is boundless'
JEAN-JAQUES ROUSSEAU

As Dostoyevsky observed "Ideas have consequences", and these may be profound – unfortunately, they may also be quite different from those imagined. All the common human errors that are likely to affect our view of the present (misinterpretation, distortion, wishful-thinking etc.) are equally likely to influence our aspirations for the future. As a result, Utopian visions are notoriously unreliable. In the end, one person's ideal may be another's purgatory, as the following accounts show...

The Social Contract

The Victorian historian Thomas Carlyle was notoriously loquacious. On one occasion, at a dinner-party, he was giving forth in his customary manner when a fellow guest, tiring of the philosopher's spate of words, interrupted him, saying "But these are ideas, Mr. Carlyle, nothing but ideas." Carlyle turned to him and said "There was once a man called Rousseau who wrote a book containing nothing but ideas. The second edition was bound in the skins of those who laughed at the first."

Carlyle was, of course, referring to Jean Jacques Rousseau's *Du Contrat Social* (The Social Contract) which called for a 'total renovation' of society, and its reconstruction according to a 'logical pattern'. In the eruptions that shook France at the end of the 18th century this work became the Bible of the Revolutionaries. Rousseau had affirmed that 'the fruits of the earth belong to all, but the earth itself to no one', and that 'all existing social conditions owe their origin to force and fraud; government and property are usurpations'. Basing his theories of some imagined 'primitive' society, drawn from over-romanticised accounts of travels in exotic locations, Rousseau concluded that man was by nature perfectly moral – it was simply the artificial institutions of governance that were at fault.[105] Once these constraints had been disposed of Liberty, Equality and Fraternity were bound to prevail. In effect 'The Social Contract' provided a theoretical justification for the overthrow of the entire existing order, in particular the artificial institutions of the monarchy, the aristocracy and the Church, and their replacement by a fairer, more equitable system which, Rousseau believed, would be based on rational principles. So it was that a theory that advanced the notion of the inherent purity of the human soul made a substantial contribution to the bloodstained social upheaval of the French Revolution. Most of the more violent revolutionaries owned copies of 'The Social Contract'.

---

[105] Rousseau was influenced by the ideal of the Noble Savage, a figure seen to be uncorrupted by civilisation. The associated idea of the 'innate goodness of humanity' is attributed to his predecessor the 3rd Earl of Shaftsbury

Important though they were however, Rousseau's ideas were not the only theoretical justification for radical change. In fact he was just one of a whole group of brilliant freethinking and sceptical intellectuals who, in the mid-19th century, had contributed to Diderot's *Encyclopedie*. This massive undertaking (which eventually ran to some thirty-five volumes) was intended as a summary of the whole of philosophical and scientific knowledge of the time – but it also had a sub-text of social and political reform. The *Encyclopaedists* believed that once a more rational attitude had come into play, expedited by the free exchange of knowledge and ideas (especially their own), then far reaching social changes would be bound to follow, 'promptly and reasonably'. In effect, it stoked the intellectual ferment that led to the Revolution. But although the evolution that they helped to promote was every bit as prompt as they imagined, it could scarcely be characterised as reasonable, and it progressed in ways that had not been predicted, and that many of its contributors would certainly have not approved.

Although the *Encyclopaedists*, as products of the late-Enlightenment, were united in their desire for radical reforms they actually had very different ideas on the way that these might be achieved. This is particularly evident in their differing views on the value of science and technology. The Marquis de Condorcet, for instance, one of the more prolific contributors, was a thoroughgoing 'modernist', who firmly equated social progress (and the happiness of mankind) with advances in science and the application of reason in human affairs. These views actually contrasted sharply with those of Jean Jacques Rousseau, for whom progress would be accompanied by a return to a simpler, more 'natural' state of existence, with its institutions growing organically, as it were, out of this newly-enlightened condition.

These conflicting perceptions of the potential effects of science, technology and industrialisation on human existence continued to preoccupy social theorists throughout the 19th century. In fact ever since the beginning of the Industrial Revolution there had been a divide between those who felt passionately that science had the potential to change the world for the better (sometimes for the *infinitely* better), and others who were less convinced – or indeed appalled at the miseries that rampant capitalist-inspired Industrialism had already caused. Those who advocated a return to some simpler lifestyle tended to idealise some golden era of the past – like William Morris, who was enamoured of his own blissful version of the Middle Ages (one that was miraculously free of its ignorance, cruelties and disease). The pro-science lobby, naturally, had their minds (and their fantasies) set well into the future. And this division of attitudes with respect to the value of science to human happiness is of course still very much with us.

Etzler's Paradise

During the 19th century the proponents of each side of this argument were inclined to present their forecasts in the form of tracts or utopian fantasies. The second half of the century in particular saw a huge growth in such speculative literature, much of which met with considerable popular success. The public had become very interested in the future. One of the earlier pro-science writers, J. A. Etzler, wrote a characteristically optimistic forecast, *The Paradise within reach of all Men without Labour, by Powers of Nature and Machinery* (1833), which predicted that science would change the world beyond conception. In Etzler's projection all the necessities of life would be produced in super-abundance by machinery; new plant-foods would be created, entirely original materials would be discovered and all manner of new labour-saving devices invented. Travel would be revolutionised, bringing the peoples of the world into increased contact and greater harmony and as a result of all these advances the different nations of the world would be drawn into one great society – the inevitable outcome would be universal human happiness. Etzler clearly felt that a technological Paradise was virtually within our grasp.

J. A. Etzler was American, but there were others of a similar cast of mind throughout the industrialised countries of Europe and North America. The German science writer Professor Ludwig Büchner produced a book that also promoted this optimistic mood. In his *Man in the past, present and future* (1872), he claimed that 'the guiding principles of evolution could not fail to make the world better and better'. As man left his animal condition behind him, and as a result of the efforts of his labours and intellect, strife would be replaced by 'Universal Love' leading, inevitably, to a Paradise of the future. This book, which was published in 1872, proved to be extremely popular, running to several editions and being translated into five languages. It accorded with a conviction of the future benefits of science that was common at this time, not least among philosophers and intellectuals. There were, however, notable differences of opinion as to how mankind might best be conveyed to this promised 'noble future' – projections tended to be bound up with the respective theorists' views of human nature.

Futurist projections at this period, whether in the form of tracts or Utopian fantasies, tended to assume either that people were inherently good (and were best left alone) or, that left alone they would get up to mischief of one sort or another. Following from these assumptions, it was felt that either a more libertarian, or a more authoritarian, regime was appropriate to ensure future happiness. Some (notably Rousseau and his followers) felt that too much governmental interference in people's lives simply impeded the human instinct to live in peace and harmony. Others were as equally convinced that a regulated structure was essential to maintain order within their ideal society to prevent it from being pulled apart by the selfish demands of individuals. There was a comparable division between those who saw the solution to social problems in greater material prosperity and others who felt the answer lay in the adoption of a simpler, more austere way of life. But overall the simple-lifers were in the minority. The dominant theme of 19ᵗʰ century predictive literature tended to be set by those who imagined that the world would be changed for the better by being more technologically advanced, more prosperous and more efficiently (i.e. centrally) organised. These utopian ideas proved to be very influential (many were best sellers), and some led directly to attempts to realise the fantasies of their authors

Cabet's *Voyage en Icarie*

One of the earliest of the 'scientific' socialist Utopias was proposed by the French author Etienne Cabet. Cabet had been an active revolutionary. In the early 1830s he was a member of an early Communist group, the *Carbonari*, who were dedicated to achieve total equality, by absolutely any means. As a result of his revolutionary activities he was arrested and sentenced, but managed to escape to England. Here he met Robert Owen, the pioneer socialist and philanthropist, and was converted to his methods of persuasion and non-violence as the means to attain his own ideal egalitarian society. Cabet worked in the library of the British Museum between 1834 and 1839 where he studied the ideas of other, earlier utopian authors. He came to the view that an enduring state of human happiness could only be realised in an egalitarian state that enjoyed all the benefits of advanced technology. He began to formulate his own scheme by which such a perfect social system might operate.

Cabet chose to present his ideal Communist society in the form of a visit to *Icarus*, an imaginary utopian island located somewhere in the Indian Ocean (*Voyage en Icarie*, 1840). In the wake of a revolution that has swept away the inequalities and injustice of their old society the Icarians have established a completely egalitarian system. They have discovered a new, unlimited source of energy, and this, together with their advanced technology, has enabled them to eliminate poverty. Icaria, it is revealed, has 100 provinces, each divided into six communes, every one of which contains precisely eight villages and one market town. The island is Eden-like, with an abundance of 'flowery arbours, groves and plantations'. It is picturesque and virtuous, a prosperous and exceptionally orderly society; bourgeois Heaven in fact.

But it is Icaria's social system that receives the most attention. Every aspect of life in Icaria is carefully planned by democratically elected committees (who return to their own work between times). One of these committees is responsible for the common diet; others deal with education, sanitation, furniture etc... Everyone lives in identical houses (which have identical furniture), eats the same food, and has the same education. The newspapers only print verified facts, and only good books are printed (a committee decides which sort of facts should be included, and which books are 'good') – and there is a relentless universal daily routine...

"Have you noticed the regular movement of our population? At five o'clock everyone gets up; as six approaches, all our buses and streets are full of men going to their factories; at nine the women and children appear; from nine to one, the population is in the factories or the schools; at one-thirty, the whole mass of workers leave the factories to join their families and neighbours in the people's restaurants; from two to three, everyone eats; from three till nine, the entire population goes out into the gardens, streets, terraces, promenades, popular assemblys, lecture halls, theatres and other public places; at ten, everyone goes to bed; and during the night, from ten till five o'clock in the morning the streets are deserted." There is no crime in Icaria, no drunkenness, no vandalism or adultery, and there are no loafers or spongers.

Apparently, 'Everybody is happy' in this conformist society – despite a complete lack of any form of individual expression.

Voyage en Icarie appeared in 1840, and was an immediate success. Cabet's vision completely captivated his readers. He was able to return to France quite soon after its publication, and the enormous popular response to his book encouraged him in an attempt to put his ideas into practice in some actual location. He set up an 'Icarian' movement, and this too was very successful. Within eight years he had attracted half a million followers. Their subscriptions raised an enormous sum of money to establish an experimental community, so that by 1849 the first group were able to settle on land purchased by the movement at Nauvoo in the American Mid-West.

Sadly, the real-life *Icaria* at Nauvoo, and a later commune at Cheltenham, did not achieve the sort of social harmony that was depicted in the *Voyage* – or anything like it. Cabet, it turned out, was singularly ill suited for the role of commune leader. Initially the settlements worked reasonably well but, as practical difficulties arose, Cabet's response was to become ever more dictatorial. His attempts to ban alcohol and tobacco, to introduce a special diet and a stricter sexual code met with a great deal of resistance. These quarrels soon deteriorated into a serious internal dispute, with the commune at Nauvoo finally splitting into two opposed factions, their differences culminating in a pitched battle in the commune's streets. The outcome of this eruption of violence was that Cabet himself was expelled from the community, along with 180 followers; sadly he died a week later. Both communes managed to struggle on for a few more years, their existence extended by the outbreak of the American Civil War.

Déjacque's *Humanispheres*

The ironies of a vision of an intensely bourgeois, tightly controlled Utopia by an ex barricade-storming, would-be overthrower of the social order, are even more marked in the case of another French theorist of the time, the anarchist Joseph Déjacque. Like Cabet, Déjacque had been personally involved in revolutionary activity. He took part in the Revolution of 1848 (for which he was imprisoned), and the Insurrection of 1849 (for which he received a heavy sentence, but managed to escape to America). While in exile in New York he edited an anarchist paper *Le Libertaire*, in the pages of which, in serial form, he presented his utopian ideas.

Déjacque had been an extreme advocate of revolutionary violence and his proposals for the establishment of an egalitarian society were equally extreme – religion, personal property, the family, the state, even cities as we now know them, would all be swept away. In his utopian projection, *L'humanisphere*, he portrayed a futurist fantasy that was a curious mixture of libertarian ideas and truly nightmarish regimentation. His version of an ideal society is set in the year 2858, by which time science has completely conquered Nature. Mankind has learned how to control the weather, has tapped the vast stores of energy within volcanoes, has cultivated the deserts and freed the poles of ice. People live and work in *humanispheres*, vast high-rise buildings capable of housing thousands, constructed on a radiating star plane, with separate wings for workshops and stores. The inhabitants are free to exchange apartments and workplace at will. The family has been abolished and children are raised apart from their natural parents. In the centre of each *humanisphere* there is a great assembly room where local concerns are resolved in a spirit of intellectual liberty. Each building is autonomous, and its interactions with others are conducted on the basis of universal respect and benevolence. In place of the formal structures of governance and religion Déjacque envisaged vast assemblies called *Cyclideons*, housed in monumental structures, each capable of holding a million people, which acted as 'altars of a social cult, anarchic churches of utopian humanity'. In these enormous public forums (by some unspecified means) 'the free and great voice of the public' would make itself known on all outstanding social matters – 'If a proposition can gather enough workers to put it into operation... it will be carried out'.

There is a marked contrast between Déjacques elaborate working out of the physical, structural aspects of his future society and his unrealistic expectations of human nature within it. In fact his ideal society is entirely two-dimensional, patently a vehicle for his own abstract notions, with little consideration for the complex interactions and emotional needs of real people. He was very serious about his projections, but in hindsight, along with many other of the grand social-engineering schemes of recent history, they now project a thoroughly nightmarish quality. Essentially, Déjacque's prescription for a new social order in the form of a vision of the future falls into a genre of speculative fiction that traces all the way back to Plato.

Plato presented his version of an ideal society in *The Republic*. Its constitution, by contrast with Déjacques, is strictly hierarchical, with lawmaking Rulers at the top of a social pyramid, beneath whom are the *Auxillaries* (who are the administrators and warriors). These two leisured classes constitute the aristocratic *Guardians* of Plato's imagined Republic, who govern the farmers, artisans and traders, the practitioners of the necessary (but despised) arts. Way below all of these are the slaves, who scarcely warrant a mention. It is a society in which everybody knows their role and their place. It is also perfectly obvious that Plato himself identified with the aristocratic Rulers (the class to which he belonged in real life), and that his ideal society would have a high degree of stability (that is to say, one in which aristocratic privileges were indefinitely perpetuated). Presented at a time when Athenian society itself was actually falling apart, Plato devised this persuasive format for presenting his political and philosophical ideas – and *The Republic* became the most influential of all his dialogues.

But the earliest genuinely science-based Utopia is that depicted in Francis Bacon's *New Atlantis* (1620), which was itself based on Plato's account of Atlantis in another of his dialogues, the *Critias*. In this work the imaginary island of Bensalem is ruled by a scientific elite who are attached to a Foundation that is essentially an establishment for scientific research. Bacon was the first to equate human happiness with scientific and material progress, and he and his followers clearly felt that their vision was realisable – they actively promoted the 'domination and exploitation of nature'. Bacon predicted the sort of unprecedented advances that would be made in medicine, engineering and transport, and his conviction of the improvement of the conditions of life through scientific progress was to attain a mythic power. He foresaw a time of *regnum hominis*, when a complete knowledge of 'the causes and the secret movement of things' would allow man to control the whole of nature, when all her materials and energies would be put to use for the greater benefit of mankind. Francis Bacon had an enormous influence on Enlightenment thinkers (the French *Encyclopedists* were much taken with his ideas), and he more or less established the genre of scientific futurism. The *New Atlantis* became the exemplar for many later Utopians.

Bellamy's *Looking Backwards*

In 1888 an American author, Edward Bellamy published one of the most influential of all modern utopian novels, *Looking Backwards from the year 2000*. This, like Cabet's *Icarie*, struck a chord with the public and was also an immediate bestseller. Although largely forgotten now, *Looking Backwards* was in its time the most widely read of futuristic fantasies. In common with most productions in this genre it was a vehicle for the author's ideas for improving the way society was run, and like the others discussed here, it promoted a 'scientific and systematic' and, above all, rational approach to social arrangements. By the time it appeared, at the latter end of the 19th century, technological advances were having an enormous effect on society, and notions of progress were, in the minds of many, firmly linked with science and 'scientific planning'. Bellamy's fable uses a Rip-van-Winkle formula. His hero, Julian West, is accidentally over-sedated in 1887 and is recovered from a cellar 137 years later. He awakes to an utterly transformed social order, which is essentially that of a benevolent paternalism. The nation is organised as a huge monopolistic corporation; education, welfare and a livelihood are guaranteed for all citizens. There is a centralised control of the economy, every fine detail of which is judged on a purely rational basis (to his credit Bellamy is quite aware that this would involve an extensive bureaucracy). The core institution of this society is an 'Industrial Army', to which all between the ages of 21-45 have to belong. The 'Army' carefully selects people, according to their aptitude, for the work that is most appropriate to their individual talents. Bellamy's future society is meritocratic, but it has certain checks and balances – less attractive jobs, for instances, have shorter hours. Wages are allotted in 'credit-cards', which represent an equal share of the Nations/Corporation's wealth. Since all economic problems have been solved there are no quarrels about money and, because everyone has a job that is appropriate to their skills, there is no frustration arising from unfulfilled ambitions. Many other aspects of life are collectivised; clothes are washed in public laundries, food is cooked in public kitchens; food and goods are available at company stores. People do not, however, appear to have much in the way of a private life in this regimented future world, their main pleasure seems to be listening to one or other of the music channels that are piped into everyone's home. *Looking Backwards* creates an impression of a superbly well regulated, but cloyingly conformist society; efficient, but utterly boring.

Nevertheless, it sold a quarter of a million copies in the U.S. within two years, and went on to sell a further half million (becoming the second best selling novel of the century in America, after *Uncle Tom's Cabin*). Bellamy's book was translated into most European languages and became the most widely read of all futurist fantasies. Leo Tolstoy, no less, was involved in its publication in Russia, where it was very favourably received, though later judged to be subversive and banned by the Tsar. In America the response to *Looking Backwards* was such that groups of enthusiasts formed associations to propagate its message and turn its ideas into reality. Within three years there were 163 of these clubs in the U.S. and many others in Europe.

The book and its ideas also provoked a strong critical response. Although many were attracted to the notion of a scientifically-planned, collectively mobilised society there were others who were utterly repelled by its soulless regimentation. By contrast with those who admired its solution of the problems of social conflict, and its cradle-to-grave welfare system, there were many who were suspicious of the leading role that it assigned to bureaucrats and were leery of its element of compulsion. And it has to be said that, in common with so many utopian authors, Bellamy seems to have been blind to the abuses that their 'perfect' system would offer for power-seekers and greed-heads.

Looking Backwards also came under fire from the Marxist camp. The followers of Marx and Engels were always keen to assert the superiority of their social theories over those presented in what they regarded as extravagant fantasies, and were as dismissive of Bellamy's proposals as they had been of Cabet's, and indeed of all 'Utopianism', these ideas were simply not genuinely 'scientific', unlike their own. They felt that theirs was the only practical path to an egalitarian society – but they, too, were caught up in the cult of the adoration of the machine. Marx had always recognised the power of industrial technology to transform society, although under his version of socialism it would be the instrument of peace and plenty, rather than the means of exploitation that it had become under Capitalism. In their enthusiasm for the revolutionary potential of 'the machine' Marx and his followers conveniently overlooked the fact that industrial technology had in fact been developed by enterprising capitalists in the search for profit.

The Prolekult Experiment

When, after the October Revolution, the Bolsheviks were confronted with the harsh realities of administering the vast domain that had fallen into their lap, they soon came to realise that the changes that they wanted to introduce were unlikely to bring about rapid solutions to the many and varied problems that faced them. Their thoughts turned increasingly to technological solutions to overcome their difficulties. The leaders of the Revolution were not alone in their belief of the redemptive power of technology; by 1920, with the encouragement of the Bolsheviks, the entire U.S.S.R. became positively intoxicated by the cult of the machine. Huge exhibitions were mounted in all the major cities, in which machines of every kind, from typewriters to turbines were displayed. Workers filed past these modern icons with the same mixture of awe and reverence that they had once felt in the old (and now padlocked) cathedrals – or at least, this was the idea.

But the machine-cult was far more extensive than this. Among intellectuals there was a genuine, widespread enthusiasm for things mechanical, which came to involve every aspect of the arts. Many were enlisted, in the name of *Prolekult* art, to promote and celebrate this new credo. Oratorios were commissioned in which the whirring and clanging of machinery was simulated. Ballets were devised glorifying the mysteries of the machine, with the dancers adopting jerky, mechanical movements. And painters, poets and sculptors were also caught up in this machine-worshipping frenzy. In the fine and decorative arts it became the vogue to depict the glories of heavy industry; in poetry, too, it was fashionable to eulogise the romance of railways and factories, and of the 'Electrodynamical City'. Even the theatre was touched by this craze. The function of the stage in this new era was to provide a 'social demonstration of the human mechanism', and actors were directed to act in a stilted, robotic manner.

It was at this time that Lenin proclaimed that 'Communism is Soviet power plus electrification'. In fact, he had long been enamoured not only with the West's advanced industrial technologies, but also with the 'bourgeois' concept of 'scientific management'. In his view (which was shared by other leading Bolsheviks) socialism had to appropriate and apply capitalist technology and its methods of work. It was quite characteristic, then, for him to declare that 'We must immediately introduce piece-work, and test its value'. In particular, he felt that 'The Taylor system must be tried'. F. W. Taylor was an American engineer, and the first to apply time and motion studies to industrial manufacture. His method principally involved breaking down complex tasks into simpler operations and introducing automation as far as possible. Henry Ford was a great proponent of Taylor's methods and had adopted them in his automotive factories. Both Taylor and Ford were deeply admired in Russia – to an almost cultish degree. Lenin, characteristically, imagined that Taylors notion of the 'remodelling' of the workers psyche might be extended to the whole of society: 'The socialist idea will be realised when we are able to unite the rule of the Soviets with the latest achievements of capitalism'. On a visit to Russia in 1920 Bertrand Russell noted (with approval) the Soviet regimes preoccupation with organisation and discipline: 'Everything is to be systematic.... the same education for all, the same clothes for all, the same kind of houses for all, the same books for all, and the same creed for all'.

With the sort of endorsement that they received from Lenin, the great theorist and leader of the Revolution, Taylors 'scientific methods' were given every encouragement by the Soviet bureaucracy. It fell to the President of the *Central Institute for the Scientific Study of Human Labour*, one Alexei Gastiev, to enact these theories in their most extreme (and peculiar) form. Gastiev, who was both an engineer and a poet, had conducted his own intensive research (*à la* Taylor) into the 'mechanical laws of the human organism'. He had managed to convince himself that he had discovered the 'basic laws of the human machine', and had reduced the complexity of its movements to two primary functions, 'push' and 'pull'. With this knowledge he felt (and managed to convince his superiors) that he would be able to meet the enormous demand for mechanics and engineers by applying his own idiosyncratic version of Taylorian production-line techniques. The overheated atmosphere of this period was such that it allowed all manner of crank theorists to flourish (the charlatan-biologist Lysenko being the most famous). In 1920 Gastiev's scheme was given the go-ahead; his avowed aim was to 'improve' the trainee's minds by making them as machine-like as possible.

The workers involved in these mad experiments had to wear identical overalls, and were required to march in columns to their benches. Once in position they would be ordered to their tasks by buzzers. Training was in form of direct mechanical induction. The trainees were taught to hammer correctly, for instance, by holding a hammer that was attached to a beating mechanism. They were instructed to persist with this motion until it was felt that they had internalised the machines rhythm. The procedure was repeated for other basic movements, chiselling, filing etc. The whole procedure was deliberately dehumanising. Gastiev believed that machines were superior to humans and that by making his trainees more machine-like he was engaged in a scheme that would ultimately prepare humanity for the next, obvious stage of its evolution. He looked forward to a time when all the messy, unplanned human traits (i.e. those that constituted individual personality) would disappear. 'People' would then become 'proletarian units'. They would no longer require personal names, but would be registered by cipher, by some combination of letters or numbers. He imagined a 'mechanised collectivism that would take the place of the individual personality in the psychology of the proletariat'. Human emotions would then no longer be necessary, the human soul could be measured not 'by a shout or a smile, but by a pressure gauge or speedometer'. This whole vision seems quite ludicrous now, but Gastiev himself was perfectly serious, and he was taken seriously.

In the event neither Gastiev's nor any of the other wild experiments of the early Revolutionary period solved its many problems. By 1924 Lenin had died and Stalin had taken over; idealism increasingly gave way to opportunism (and later, simply to survival). The optimistic enthusiasm of *Prolekult* faded, and the cult of the machine became subservient to the cult of Terror. Some ideas survived however. The notion of a new world in which every aspect of life was precisely calculated and centrally planned persisted, but under Stalin it was driven by an unprecedented degree of ruthlessness and brutality – and in general it was a hopeless failure. Sovietised industry was in fact horribly inefficient, and the Soviet program of collectivised agriculture led to widespread famine. The new factory-towns, the new railway and canal systems, the attempts to cultivate virgin lands led, not to the promised 'machine millennium', but to the reintroduction into the modern world of a system of slavery on a previously unimaginable scale. There was one aspect of Gastiev's vision that was adopted – those who were taken to the Gulags were deprived of their names, which were replaced by a cipher in just the way he imagined. This was appropriate. These suffering legions, the victims of Stalin's mindless, out-of-control Terror, were indeed the final, terrible product of a stream of modern ideality that was inclined to regard humans as mere ciphers in some greater ideological narrative.

14. Toxic Texts
Licence for Atrocity

'Thanks to words, we have been able to rise above the brutes;
thanks to words, we have often sunk to the level of the demons'
ALDOUS HUXLEY

'Some words cause pain, others joy, some strike fear, some stir
the audience to boldness – and some benumb and bewitch
the soul with evil persuasion'
GORGIAS (The Sophist)

Belonging and the 'Other'

One of the most deep-seated of human emotions is the feeling of belonging to a particular group, and this is always intimately bound up with our sense of personal identity. Although we come to take our own attitudes and beliefs completely for granted, group-identity of every kind is a complex business and is invariably associated with a particular set of values. In fact the process of identification with a group and its distinguishing attitudes actually gives meaning to people's lives – unfortunately, it can also lead on to this other familiar human emotion, the comparative tendency – 'We' are not like 'the Others'. There is an almost universal assumption that one's own values are the most appropriate, a feeling that the way 'we' do things is the proper way. 'Our' manners and conventions are reasonable; by comparison, 'theirs' are somehow skewed. Our language (or accent) is comprehensible; theirs is less intelligible. 'We' are straight in our dealings, 'they' are far less reliable – and to compound matters 'they' eat different sorts of food and even dress differently.

Naturally, every culture and every sub-cultural division, right down to the level of the family, has its own idea of the right way to do things, of what constitutes reasonable behaviour – although there are, of course, enormous cultural variations in this. Occasionally, the influence of the 'other' may be admitted. The modes of dress, modes of speech, culinary traditions etc. of other groups can exert a certain appeal and can sometimes be adopted, and eventually completely absorbed. But overall this is exceptional. Just as water tends to run downhill, there is a general tendency to favour the habits and values of one's own group. Unfortunately, recent psychological investigations seem to indicate that both loyalty to the group and prejudice directed towards others is a built-in instinct, intrinsic to human nature.[106] This tends to mean that group cohesion, which is the very basis of socialisation, leads all too easily to inter-group suspicion, even hostility – and history tells us there are always ill-disposed individuals who are prepared to exploit this for their own malicious reasons.

The Rage to Blame

The linkage between identity and prejudice is particularly apparent in that less than admirable human trait, hostility

---

[106] Prejudice against others seems to be particularly centred on language and accent. It seems that people associate truthfulness with ease of understanding, and that accent hampers this. See *Why don't we believe non-native speakers? The influence of accent on credibility*, Shiri Lev-Ari & Boaz Keysar, Journal of Experimental Social Psychology, 2010

towards an out-group. Here it is usually an attached minority of some kind that is the subject of vilification, but the markers of a distinctive 'otherness' can vary enormously – in fact any discrete, labelled group can become victimised. Minority religious or ethnic groups are among the more obvious targets, but the sick, the mentally ill and homosexuals have all, at different times, been the targets. Whatever it is that marks them out as different, the attitudes towards an out-group are invariably accompanied by stereotyping and quite often by a whole prejudiced mythology. An out-group can become particularly vulnerable to irrational demonisation of this sort at times of social turmoil. In the past, minorities have been held responsible for all manner of natural and man-made disasters – economic collapse, plagues, earthquakes, etc. At times there can be a certain interchangeability of scapegoats, as in 16th century Europe where witches replaced Jews and heretics as the focus of hatred (see below). Ironically, persecution, if it does not entirely destroy such groups, can create a sense of social coherence within it. Although being labelled as an outsider generally provokes unpleasant tensions, it can also strengthen a persecuted minority's sense of their own identity. In general though, being bullied and tormented in this way is obviously an unpleasant, destructive experience.

The cruel relationship that can build up between a larger and smaller group is essentially a collective phenomenon, but it has parallels on the level of individual psychology. Those suffering psychotic delusions and hallucinations are inclined to attribute malevolent thoughts and intentions to others – in this they are, of course, simply projecting their own negative feelings. In the group setting however this reaction can become far more dangerous, leading to a general perception of mendacity, the loss of empathy, and ultimately the complete dehumanisation of an alien minority. When this is coupled with a dominant group's belief in their own moral ascendancy, normal ethical scruples can be side-lined, leading to all the well documented, and unfortunately still familiar, horrors of inter-group hostility, persecution and genocide. And as in every other aspect of human activity, narratives can play a considerable, enabling role in such barbarities.

Sanctions for Evil

> *'A clever dialectic will always find a way to pretend that*
> *a meaning has been found.'*
> CLAUDE LEVI-STRAUSS

As I have emphasised throughout this book, Man possesses language, but we, in turn, can become possessed by the word, written or spoken. The power of ideological texts, in particular those bearing the stamp of pathological certainty, is enormous, and can have extremely negative consequences. The authors of the sort of texts presented below are usually deeply flawed and opportunistic characters, but the intensity of their messages were able to carry great powers of suggestion. They seem to instinctively deploy the techniques of psychological manipulation, were well aware that scapegoating provides a simple, if spurious, solution to social ills, and that illegitimate fears can always be drummed up to support prejudice. To be as successful as so many of these texts were in their intention to incite, they must not simply be understood, but be believed in. To do this a text must persuade to a narrow, closed system of belief using rhetorical methods that have much in common with the persuasive techniques of the hypnotist.

The following examples, drawn from the vast archives of these accounts, are far from exhaustive, but merely indicative of the spiteful, provocative tone of such texts – and of the immeasurable harm that they can generate. They attest to the extraordinary power of the word to persuade, but in an entirely negative way. They are also a terrible warning from history; time and time again an intemperate text has promoted and encouraged cruel behaviour.

The order of presentation here is approximately chronological. But I would caution the reader, these accounts do not make pleasant reading – in the words of Virgil, *Horresco referens*... 'I shudder as I relate'.

The *Malleus Maleficarum* (1486) and its successors

'In the name of high moral principles all the vindictiveness of derision, of torture, and of mass extinction can be employed'
ERIK ERIKSON

In 1484 Pope Innocent VIII issued a Papal Bull, *Summis Desiderantes Affectibus*, which deplored the spread of witchcraft in Germany and urged its extirpation, an appeal that was enthusiastically taken up by the Dominican Inquisitor friar Heinrich Krämer. Krämer dutifully produced the *Malleus Maleficarum* ('The Hammer of the Witches'). This must rank as one of the most odious texts ever written and was to provide an ideological framework for the persecution of many thousands of (usually poor, usually old) women in the Rhineland. The *Malleus* set out a spurious, but detailed legal and theological theory of witchcraft and indicated the ways of detecting and dealing with it. It associated this 'crime' with heresy, and recommended the use of extended torture in its investigations. When these instructions were followed they naturally (and invariably) drew 'confessions' – which in turn confirmed the Inquisitions completely fictitious assertions of an international conspiracy. After extracting confessions the victims were, as directed by the *Malleus*, burned at the stake. This was the beginning of the European Witch-Craze, whose vicious doctrines were to continue to haunt the continent for centuries to come.

Unfortunately, Krämer's work became a bestseller – worse, in the collective frenzy that followed, it was imitated in country after country. Witch encyclopaedias were published in most European languages, each trying to outdo the other in their lurid descriptions of the supposed devilish machinations of 'witches' – and in the cruelty of the punishments to be meted out on them. Eventually there were literally hundreds of examples of this grotesque genre, productions that served to institutionalise and justify the persecution, mainly of vulnerable older women. The relatively new doctrine of Protestantism was as enthusiastic in its pursuit of witches as the Catholics had been – according to Martin Luther they were the 'Whores of the Devil'. Among other justifications given for the long drawn-out Holocaust that followed was the example of Hell: 'If the All-wise God punishes his creature with tortures, infinite in cruelty and duration, why should not his ministers, as far as they can, imitate him?'. As noted earlier, rationalisations can always be found for inhumane actions. Between the 16th and 17th centuries thousands of victims were tortured and burned alive in these persecutions – and the perpetrators were always able to refer to officially sanctioned misogynistic texts to guide and justify their vile activities.

'Witches' were a characteristic out-group in that they were weak and vulnerable and could not hit back – and their fate is typical of what can happen once such a group is thoroughly demonised. In these cases maltreatment can then be felt to be fully deserved. Historically, there are few limits on this – the following example, from a later, supposedly enlightened century, involved the scapegoating and destruction of an entire town.

The *Revolutionary Decree* and the Annihilation of Lyons (1793)

> *'He who is not with the people is against the people –*
> *and must be destroyed'*
> ROBESPIERRE

Up to the time of the late 17th - 18th centuries it was generally considered that anything written down was necessarily true, that it was somehow disrespectful to subject the written word to rational analysis. This changed with the coming of the Enlightenment, when more sceptical attitudes came to the fore. European philosophers such as Descarte, Locke, Voltaire, Hume and Kant were able to think more critically and methodically about all manner of previously accepted notions – including the validity of the status quo. In fact the ideas of the *Philosophes* of the French Enlightenment (although many were of noble birth themselves) played an important part in undermining the legitimacy of the Old Regime. However, as it turned out, the optimistic hopes of these Enlightenment thinkers for a more equable, peaceful and tolerant society led directly to French Revolution – and its accompanying Terror.

The social turmoil of this period culminated, in 1793, with the establishment of a revolutionary dictatorship under the Jacobins, led by Maximilien Robespierre and Louis Antoine de Saint-Just, who regarded themselves as principled egalitarians. Ironically, both had been deeply inspired by Rousseau's gentle ideas of human perfectibility. The horrors of Robespierre's Reign of Terror, which was inflicted on the perceived enemies of the state in Paris, during which tens of thousands were summarily guillotined, is well documented and well-known. But this ruthless, bloodthirsty fanaticism was also directed against Lyons, France's second largest city, which had effectively become a rebel bastion held by the Jacobins' enemies, the

Girodins. In October of 1793, after Lyons was finally overrun, Robespierre issued a Decree that the city 'should be destroyed', declaring that 'Either these monsters must be exterminated or I perish'. Effectively, the entire city had become a scapegoat; it had to be obliterated.

The vengeful spirit of Robespierre's Decree was immediately enacted. The formality of trials was 'dispensed with'. The guillotine was soon working overtime, but this was not enough; cannons were soon being employed to execute shackled prisoners *en masse*. A collective frenzy of murder, destruction and mayhem ensued. Thousands were summarily executed – opponents and the innocent alike were butchered against a constant backdrop of explosions as the city was systematically demolished. Robespierre's agent Achard excitedly reported back: 'Still more heads and every day more heads fall. What delights you would have tasted had you seen these scoundrels brought to natural justice!'. As was usual in events of this kind, the instigator himself played no direct part in their enactment. Eventually, Robespierre himself fell foul of Revolutionary machinations and the Reign of Terror subsided. But these events, particularly the Lyons atrocities, effectively marked the beginning of unlimited, ideologically-driven, modern state-sanctioned terrorism.

Sergei Nechaev's *Revolutionary Catechism* (1869)

'Only the insane take themselves completely seriously'
MAX BEERBOHM

The seamless progression from egalitarian idealism to bloodstained intolerance that characterised the French Revolution was of course to be repeated in Russia. Here, during the mid- to late-19th century, the movements towards greater liberalism and those of Autocratic reaction were becoming increasingly polarised, with each side adopting ever more extreme positions. A turning point came with the failed assassination of the Tsar by a depressive loner, Dmitry Karakozov, in April 1866. Karakozov had himself been deeply influenced by a popular utopian novel by the literary critic Nikilay Chernyshevsky, but his actions served only to provoke a severe reaction by the authorities. The various modest reforms that had recently been enacted by the Tsarist government were rescinded, and a repressive regime was installed that ruthlessly suppressed any call for political changes, however moderate. But the atmosphere of police terrorism that followed simply raised the stakes – and it encouraged the formation of a new, far more determined, breed of revolutionaries – the Nihilists.

For these radicals the objective now became the destruction of every aspect of the social order as a prelude to some dimly conceived new order – a posture that found its most extreme expression in a group calling itself *Narodnaya Rasprava* (Popular Revenge). *Rasprava*, it later transpired, was entirely the creation of a charismatic, intense individual named Sergei Nechaev, whose methods, as laid out in his writings, reflected his essentially paranoid character. According to these, the Tsarist state and all its institutions had to be overthrown by any means possible, whatever the personal cost. To achieve this end the revolutionary had to be utterly dedicated and entirely amoral. And such were the times that within months of forming his group Nechaev had persuaded nearly a hundred of his fellow students at the St. Petersburg University to sign oaths of loyalty to his leadership.

Nechaev claimed to be in touch with a secret network that had cells throughout Russia which in reality was simply part of his own self-dramatizing fantasy. But before he or others of his group were able to put any of their plans into action they had alerted the suspicions of the police. Nechaev fled abroad, eventually making his way to Geneva, a centre of radical thought, where he connected with many of the Russian students studying there at the time. This setting proved to be fertile ground for Nechaev's revolutionary cause. He made further exaggerated claims about the power and extent of his organisation and even managed to enlist an older, more respected revolutionary theorist, Michael Bakunin (although Bakunin himself was rather given to exaggeration, claiming to be the leader of a shadowy 'World Revolutionary Alliance'). Between them they set about writing a series of propaganda pamphlets for distribution back in Russia.

It is unclear, and a matter of contention, just how much Bakunin actually contributed to these, but the murderous tone of much of the writing was unmistakably Nechaev's. One of them, *Principles of Revolution*, advocated indiscriminate destruction in the name of the revolution, declaring 'We recognise no other activity but the work of extermination'. According to this, the revolution must be pursued relentlessly, using 'poison, the knife, the rope'. These pamphlets, seven in all, are precursor's to Nechaev's later work the *Revolutionary Catechism*, in which he spells out his conspiratorial theories in greater detail – a work that must rank as one of the most chilling documents in all political history. The *Catechism* is based on the premise that a small dedicated group could destroy the state (little consideration is given to subsequent events), but it is suffused by an existential pessimism. The revolutionary is a 'doomed and dedicated man, completely amoral and devoid of human sympathy'; 'he must have only one thought, night and day, pitiless destruction'. Accordingly, 'The revolutionary must be prepared to perish himself and to destroy with his own hands everything and anyone who stands in the way of the revolution' – and so it goes on. There is a repetitive harping on the themes of destruction, turmoil and bloodshed throughout the *Catechism* – and scarcely any mention of hope for a better world. Nihilism indeed!

In the event Nechaev was arrested soon after his return to Russia in an ill-advised attempt to start the revolution. It was a disaster for the *Narodnaya Rasprava*, whose members were soon rounded up by the Tsarist police, tried, and sent to Siberia to serve very long prison sentences. Curiously, Nechaev himself was spared a death sentence on the personal orders of the Tsar – but there was a postscript to this story. After some eight years in the dungeons of the grim Peter and Paul Fortress, Nechaev managed to subvert his guards and make contact with a new terrorist organisation, *Narodnaya Volya* ('The People's Will'). They were astonished to discover that this legendary figure was still alive, and he was soon conspiring with them to assassinate the new Tsar, Alexander II. After many failed attempts the *Narodnaya* were eventually successful in this – however, it proved to be an event that was responsible for a serious intensification of the struggle between radical and reactionary forces in Russia, a conflict that was to culminate in the upheavals of the October Revolution.

Nechaev's achievement (such as it was) was to establish a new bench-mark of terrorist extremism, a recourse that seemed to offer instant action and universal solutions, in which the ends always justified the means. Unfortunately, this strategy, which was propagated throughout his writings, was to be widely imitated.

Roots of Genocide - 1. 'Scientific' Racism

'Ideas have consequences'
FYODOR DOSTOEVSKY

The years of the Nazi regime will forever be remembered as a period in which the most calculated, most horrific and most sustained crimes against mankind were perpetrated. What is far less well remembered is the origin of the sinister ideological framework on which this totalitarian movement based its depraved mandate. The Nazi belief in racial superiority, and the use of extreme violence to attain their ends, had roots in pseudo-scientific ideas that went back to the mid-19ᵗʰ century – and the authors that originated these deadly ideas must share the culpability for the immeasurable human misery that issued from them. Their contributions were the written Word at its most lethal.

Joseph Arthur de Gobineau *An Essay on the Inequality of the Human Races* (1853)

The notion of an 'Aryan' master race was the brain-child of aristocrat, Count J. A. de Gobineau. Gobineau had an early career as a diplomat and was the author of a number of light novels and travel writing before he embarked on his *chef d'oeuvre*. The *Essay on Inequality* begins with the assumption that aristocrats are patently (in his view) superior to the lower orders. Gobineau then extends this notion of the inequality of human types to a 'racial demography'. The white-skinned, Germanic 'races'– a group that he labelled 'Aryan' – could retain their natural superiority only by avoiding interbreeding with 'inferior' races (by which he meant all other peoples of the world). The 'Aryans', in his view, were the Master Race – although this was a term that he appropriated from the then current linguistic notions of archaic Indo-European peoples (long since discredited), and wove it into his reactionary theories. As an aristocrat whose family survived the French Revolution, Gobineau loathed democracy, which he viewed as a threat to both class and racial purity. Civilisations, in his view, were racially deterministic, and 'sprung only from contact with the white races'. Because of this, racial admixture could only lead to the 'downfall of civilisations'. Taken to its logical extreme (as it later was), this meant that the 'superior' 'Aryan' races had the right to dominate, and if necessary, eliminate 'inferior' breeds. Interestingly, Gobineau's predecessors had lived in Haiti for some time and he suffered a secret, abiding dread that he might have inherited some black ancestry from his mother's side.

The *Essay on Inequality* became very popular, particularly in Germany, where it was taken up by Nationalist groups who incorporated the percept of 'Aryanism' into their own distorted ideas (the book was also popular in the USA, where it continues to be republished to this day!). In Germany, Gobineau's grandiose racial theories were to provide a quasi-respectable foundation for the propaganda of hate-mongers and rabble-rousers such as Hitler – with all the well-known consequences. Curiously though, there is little mention of the Jews in his *Essay* – in fact Gobineau seems to have rather admired them and accorded them an honorary-Aryan role in his wildly speculative theories. This was, of course, a difficult aspect of 'Gobinism' for the Nazis to absorb, but they were able to ignore this and drew their pseudo-scientific anti-Semitic theories from another, equally virulent, source…

Houston Stewart Chamberlain *The Foundations of the Nineteenth Century* (1899)

Although of a later generation, H. S. Chamberlain was a great admirer of Gobineau and his racist ideas. Born in England, he spent much of his youth drifting around Europe (rather than pursuing the military career that his father had in mind for him), and ended up in Vienna, where he developed a deep fascination with all things German, particularly its more reactionary aspects, including militarism and anti-Semitism. In fact he tried to be more German than the Germans – he took to using only that language and disavowed his English background. In 1899 he wrote *The Foundations of the 19th Century*, a pseudo-scientific 'history' of humanity – in which all of its great advances were ascribed to the 'Aryan' races (a notion that he derived from Gobineau). The *Foundations* became very popular, particularly in Germany, and earned Chamberlain a fair measure of fame. Its accounts of European racial superiority – as expressed in its history of conquests, colonialism and cultural dominance – resonated particularly well with German right-wing sentiment – as did his prophecy of a new German rise to power. The book was originally intended to run to three volumes, with the later books dealing with an inevitable, apocalyptic war between the Aryan Master Race and the Jews, Blacks and Asians. These final volumes were never actually finished, to the disappointment of his Munich publisher, Hugo Bruckmann (who later commissioned Hitler's *Mein Kampf*). But Chamberlain's increasingly vehement anti-Semitism resonated with many in his milieu at the time.

In 1908 Chamberlain married the daughter of the composer Wagner (himself a fanatical racist and German nationalist), which gave him an *entrée* into the 'Bayreuth Circle' of German right-wing intellectuals. He then chose to dedicate the rest of his life to spreading the Master's message – of race-hate, anti-Semitism and German nationalism; the result was that Chamberlain's distorted ideas became an important precursor of Nazi ideology. He regarded Britain's declaration of war on Germany in 1914 as fratricidal treachery and wrote a series of propaganda pamphlets against his country of birth. Adolph Hitler was hugely influenced by Chamberlain's writings and regarded him as the 'The Prophet of the Third Reich'. Goebbels, Hitler's notorious 'Minister for Public Enlightenment and Propaganda', visited Chamberlain on his deathbed and was 'profoundly moved'.

William Delisle Hay *Three Hundred Years Hence* (1881)

Chamberlain's *Foundations of the Nineteenth Century* was translated into various European languages, including English, which ran into several editions. The book was generally well-received. In fact there were many in Britain who were as sympathetic to Chamberlain's ideas as there had been in Germany (George Bernard Shaw, for instance, described it as a 'historical masterpiece'). It seemed that Chamberlain's racially deterministic portrayal of history easily joined with existing British imperialistic, notions of superiority. The *Foundations* were not the only source of such brutally chauvinistic ideas; such sentiments were common at the time, as can be seen in particularly graphic form in the futuristic novels of William Delisle Hay.

W. D. Hay was a naturalist who wrote books on Fungi, and on New Zealand, where he lived for some time. But he was also responsible for some early sci-fi novels in which he presented his utopian ideas – aspects of which can only be described as chilling, to say the least. Hay was a white supremacist. In a letter to the Social Darwinist William Graham Sumner in 1881 he wrote: 'Looking to the world at no very distant date, what an endless number of the lesser races will have to be eliminated by the higher civilised nations throughout the world'. This premise is spelt out more clearly in his novel *Three Hundred Years Hence*, in which he envisages a whites-only future in which all other races have been eliminated – 'It was seen to be impossible to raise the Chinaman to the level of the higher race', and it was even more impossible 'to raise the Negro into a civilised and intellectual man'. Genocide, he casually indicates, is the only solution: 'The bombing planes pass over China and 1,000 million human beings are destroyed'. He then reflects that – 'We look back upon the Yellow Race with pitying contempt, for to us they are not to be regarded as belonging to the race that is summed up and glorified in United Man'. The 'Negroes' are then subjected to the same fate – and the 'Great Extermination' is completed. The white races are then able to go on to create a technological Paradise on Earth.

Hay, like Gobineau and Chamberlain, was a popular author in his time. His sinister (one might say psychopathic) forecasts would have been read by many, and would undoubtedly have contributed to the stock of paranoid racist fantasies that were to prove so destructive in the 20th century. He was a thoroughly nasty piece of work – but the persuasive power of these ideological texts, however presented, should never be underestimated.

Roots of Genocide - 2. Social Darwinism & Eugenics

There were other streams of 19th century thought that were to have serious negative ramifications in the following century – in particular Herbert Spencer's grim theory of 'Social' Darwinism, and the radical proposals of the 'Eugenics' movement.

Charles Darwin's theories of evolution, which made an enormous impact immediately after their publication in 1859, had great influence on social as well as scientific attitudes, but these were not all positive. The idea of natural selection as a driving force in nature was in fact very soon hijacked by the philosopher Herbert Spencer who misapplied the principle to the social context. It was Spencer who coined the phrase 'survival of the fittest' – and Social Darwinism became a notion that rationalised (and justified) the shocking class inequalities of Victorian Britain – ideas that naturally found favour with *laissez-faire* politicians and anti-philanthropists generally. But the Eugenics movement – dedicated as it was to 'improving' the human race – was to have a more profound, and even more deadly, outcome.

Francis Galton *Natural Inheritance* (1889)

The Eugenics movement was essentially an ideologically influenced offshoot of the legitimate sciences of genetics and evolution. It was founded by Francis Galton, (a half-cousin of Charles Darwin), who derived the term from the Greek root meaning 'noble in birth, or heredity'. Galton had a free-ranging mind which his private income allowed him to indulge. Primarily a statistician he was inclined to let his passion for measuring run away with him, attempting to apply it to such indefinable characteristics as 'beauty', 'intelligence' or 'character'. He was greatly impressed by Darwin's theories of Natural Selection when they were published – in particular, the section dealing with domesticated animals. In his own theories on the matter he transposed these ideas on selective breeding to the human sphere, with the idea of 'improving the racial stock'. As a member of the upper classes he had long been preoccupied, and disturbed by, the prospect of those with 'inferior' inherited strains (i.e. the lower classes) swamping the 'superior' classes. To him it was self-evident that the British upper classes, to which he belonged, represented an ideal racial type. He seemed peculiarly blind to the effects that poverty, poor nourishment and inadequate living conditions might have on lesser breeds – but his well-publicised ideas for a 'positive eugenics' program caught the public imagination (some sectors of it at least). Galton presented his theories in the publication *Natural Inheritance*, and gave a series of lectures both in the U.K. and the U.S., which resulted in many Eugenics societies being set up in both countries. The Eugenics movement that came out of this drive continued to gather momentum and proved to be highly influential from the turn of the 20th century on.

The notion of selective breeding as applied to humans was initially well received by those on the left- and the right- political wings, where it was seen as a means of social improvement – but it was also frequently used to reinforce existing prejudices. Eugenic solutions particularly appealed to those with other outlying social concerns (with immigration, venereal disease, crime, the feeble-minded etc.), and predictably, such ideas were used to buttress long-standing racist perceptions. These applications of Eugenic theories tended to take on a rather more persecutory tone. Notwithstanding, theory was soon being translated into practices, and the results of the Eugenics enthusiasts' drive to improve the 'genetic purity' of the general population were to have real-life consequences for many. In the U.S. 'biological unfitness' was introduced to restrict immigration by 1927, and around the same time in the U.K. the mentally deficient were being gender-segregated to avert the 'terrible danger to the race'. This scapegoating of vulnerable people by active Eugenics lobbies on both sides of the Atlantic was accompanied, as was ever the case, by the vilification of its chosen victims.

Eugenicists in general seem to have been particularly fixated on the sexual behaviour of the degenerate 'unfitted'. The early 20th century saw the U.S. enacting Eugenic measures to prevent 'unsuitable' marriages, and many States went on to introduce laws allowing sterilisation of the perceived 'eugenically unfit' sections of the community. Measures of this kind generated a great deal of interest in other parts of the world that had Eugenics lobbies. There were official visits, and reports, and recommendations were made – the outcome of which was that by the 1930s sterilisation laws were put into effect in Sweden, Denmark, Finland and Switzerland. The new German Nazi movement had also monitored the U.S. programs, and were sympathetic to them. As a direct result, as soon as they gained power in 1933, Hitler's cabinet introduced compulsory sterilisation for a whole range of afflictions (including tuberculosis, schizophrenia, epilepsy, blindness, addiction problems and physical deformities). But in the late 1930s, when war seemed inevitable, these activities were extended into a full-blown 'Euthanasia' program – the consequences of which were utterly horrific. In their comparatively short reign the Nazi's murdered some 200,000 mentally ill or disabled people – who were stigmatised as 'life unworthy of life'. They were systematically starved, gassed or had lethal injections in the very institutions that were meant to care for them. By the end of the Second World War there were no German mental or disabled patients; they had all been murdered.

Perhaps the most shocking aspect of this less well-known Holocaust is that it was made possible by the active participation of the medical and psychiatric practitioners themselves and, in many cases, with the compliance of the relatives of the victims. The relentless Nazi propaganda campaign to promote their 'Euthanasia' program, in both written and cinematic form played an enormous part in this exercise. Typical of this horrible genre was the film *Erbkrank* ('Hereditary Ill'), made in 1936, in which the mentally and physically ill are consistently portrayed as a waste of space and a burden to the healthy, with the constantly repeated message that it would be better that they should be 'delivered' from their misery. *Erbkrank* was greatly admired by Hitler, who went on to personally commission a follow-up. Many more movies of this kind were issued by the Reich's Propaganda Ministry, all of which degraded and dehumanised the afflicted in order to persuade the 'necessity' of their harsh treatment of this 'burden'. There is no question that such pitiless portrayals played a huge role in facilitating these appalling crimes.

The Protocols of The Elders of Zion (1903)

The *Protocols* was an anti-Semitic document purporting to be an account of a Zionist conspiracy for world domination. Masquerading as the minutes of a secret meeting it reveals supposed details of a secret Jewish campaign to subvert major existing institutions – of the Press, of Finance and the Church. It is a detailed, provocative and thoroughly mischievous forgery. The *Protocols* which was first published in Russia in 1903, was plagiarised from an earlier (non-racist) work, and was used as propaganda to incite the pogroms against Russian Jews in the early 20ᵗʰ century. Although exposed as a hoax as long ago as the 1920s it became a favoured document among anti-Semites everywhere – and, crude and implausible though it is, it is still in print.

It was, of course, picked up by the Nazis, who used it as part of their own anti-Semitic propaganda; under their rule it was distributed in German schools to be read as a genuine, factual account.

The Nazi culmination (1933 onwards)

As indicated above, the atrocities committed by the Nazi regime were ultimately inspired by a range of ideological, mainly pseudo-scientific, texts from the previous half-century. These poisonous ideological notions were ready-made, so to speak, for demagoguery – they merely had to be pulled together to create the supporting foundations of this vile creed, which was what Hitler did in his notorious autobiography...

Adolf Hitler's *Mein Kampf* (1925)

Written in prison after his failed *Putsch* in 1923, Hitlers's *Mein Kampf* ('My Struggle') is part autobiography, part political manifesto. In essence, it lays out his ideological program/ pathological obsessions. Turgid and prolix in style, it is wide in its scope, but there is little in it that was genuinely original. Its principle themes are the need for a German revival, a deep resentment of the German defeat in the Great War, virulent anti-Semitism (the 'Jewish peril'), and a deep hatred of both democracy and Bolshevism. There are indications in the book of his later enactments – of expansion to the East (*Lebensraum*), and of genocide ('the elimination of the Jewish corruptors').

Hitler's view of history was essentially that of a Social Darwinian struggle between races, (derived from Herbert Spencer's grim, anti-humanitarian vision); the notion of 'Aryan' racial superiority originated, as we have seen, with J.A. de Gobineau; Hitler's anti-Semitism was part of the legacy of the 'Bayreuth Circle', Wagner and H.S. Chamberlain; his enthusiasm for 'Eugenics' derived ultimately from Galton – particularly from this author's concerns that humane institutions were allowing 'inferior' humans to survive at the expense of the mentally and physically healthy. In view of the fact that there had been distinct signs of hereditable mental deficiency in his own family the appeal of this creed is a further indication of Hitler's repressive, disordered psyche.

In its essentials *Mein Kampf* is a repetitive inventory of hatred, blame and alleged conspiracy – Communists and Social Democrats were working for Jewish interests; Jews and Bolsheviks were sub-human types; Germany's defeat in the War was caused by the Weimar government, Jews and Communists; as the 'Master Race' Germany was entitled to subjugate Russian territory (Social Darwinism on a geographic scale); the weak and infirm should not be a burden on the healthy strong.

Tedious, obsessive and repetitious as it was, this malign text, with its inward-focussed system of belief, outlined the crux of Hitler's program. On attaining power, words were soon followed by actions – with all the horrific consequences of Nazi rule.

Charismatic individuals like Hitler, who are able to move others in the name of a cause or ideology, are always likely to be complex and deeply flawed personalities. Such leaders often appear when there is some disturbance to the social fabric, and there is usually a match between their personal psychic dislocation and the specific unsettling conditions. The greater the degree of national or group discontent, the greater the appeal of these extreme and unbalanced personalities who, typically, offer radical, frequently brutal, solutions to urgent but complex problems. Such is the case in these final examples of toxic texts, which have a particular contemporary relevance…

'Jihadism'

In the Islamic world in the modern period many serious-minded believers were faced with a severe case of Cognitive Dissonance, namely, how to reconcile their beliefs in Islam as the only true religion and in Islamic culture (which had in the past given rise to a series of magnificent civilisations) with the realities of the present, i.e. domination by European powers, rule by corrupt leaders, poverty, backwardness and disunity.

To reiterate… Cognitive Dissonance theory is concerned with the state of tension that arises when an individual or a group attempts to hold attitudes that are mutually inconsistent. Because this state is psychologically disagreeable people are inclined to react to it by reducing the perceived dissonance. This can be achieved in various ways – by changing one's attitude to one or both cognitions to make them seem more compatible – or by taking on new ideas/attitudes that bridge the gap between the perceived incompatibles (in other words, by rationalising or justifying the anomaly). In a modern Islamic context one solution to the dissonance between 21st century realities and traditional Islamic values has been the reactionary measure of denouncing every aspect of the modern world – including its individualistic credo, freedoms of travel and communication, and its secular, internationalist outlook. Religious revivalism is not unique to Islam; many other religious groups at different periods of the past have seen movements calling for a return to perceived fundamental principles. But since the mid-20th century Islam culture, with its mixed attitudes towards many features of modernism, has experienced something of an existential crisis.

Conflicted attitudes to those aspects of the modern world mentioned above, together with a (not unjustified) suspicion of Western intentions in particular has, for some, led to the aggressive devaluation of all the achievements of modernism and an abiding hatred of its liberal attitudes. Their response has been a militant reaffirmation of the 'original message' of the Prophet Muhammad, coupled with an ambition to restore Islam to its perceived original values and rightful position of moral leadership. This *tajdid* (regeneration) movement has given rise to a wide range of Islamic revivalist movements, and is the driving force of 'fundamentalist' Jihadism – which has drawn inspiration from various textual sources, of which the following have been the most influential...

*'From the beginning men used God to
justify the unjustifiable'*
SALMAN RUSHDIE

Sayyid Qutb *Milestones*

As was the case with Nazism, the originators of the ideological framework that justified Jihadism's campaign of atrocities are less well known than the perpetrators of those deeds. The principle figure in the construction of the doctrines of modern (Sunni) Islamic fundamentalism was an unlikely literary scholar named Sayyid Qutb. Born in a small village in Upper Egypt in 1906 Qutb's natural abilities enabled him to move to Cairo where he worked as a teacher, then as a school inspector. Later he joined the pre-war literary scene there, writing a novel and becoming a respected literary critic. However, his first real contact with the West and its values came about as a result of his gaining a scholarship to study education in the U.S. in 1948 – but this experience was to result in a profound personal crisis.

Sayyid Qutb was shocked by his encounter with America – with its easy way of life, its materialism, its prejudices against him as an Arab, but above all by its sexual laxity (as he saw it). His reaction to all this was that of withdrawal and disaffection with Western values. After two and a half unhappy years in the States, Qutb returned to Egypt with a renewed conviction of the primacy of the teachings and *Din* (Faith) of Islam; effectively he became what is now known as an Islamic fundamentalist. He joined the radical Egyptian Muslim Brotherhood movement, where his talents were soon recognised, and went on to become their head of propaganda. But the Egyptian authorities, the Nasser regime, were increasingly alarmed by the Brotherhood's advocacy of violent revolution and declared them an illegal organisation. Qutb himself was arrested in the crackdown that followed and spent 10 years in prison. However, he continued to write whilst incarcerated.

Qutb followed the classical path of the fanatic. Having formed his ideas and made his commitments, the precepts that he had adopted became impervious to criticism and resistant to change. As is usual in these cases, this led to an absolute certainty of belief, and to a polarised emotional response – for Qutb, his interpretation of Islam represented a complete, unassailable system of morality, justice and governance; by contrast, everything non-Islamic was evil and corrupt. He viewed the Western powers as decadent and intent on controlling the Islamic world with the help of local leaders. These latter, in his view, could be regarded as apostates or *Kafirs* (infidels) – which meant that it was not only legitimate, but meritorious to kill them. 'Qutbism', as his extremist jihadist ideology became known, condoned, and even encouraged, the use of physical force in the pursuit of their aims. Jihadist views and methodology were based on Qutb's interpretation of the Qur'an, and this became the source of all their thought. His dismissive, fundamentalist convictions led him to deprecate not only all non-Muslim culture, but also that of the Muslim civilisations in their entirety. The centuries of Islamic culture, learning, poetry, music and arts counted for nothing in his narrow, *Salafist* (puritanical) view. Only the (highly mythologised) 30-year reign of the first four 'Rightly Guided' Caliphs, the 7th century *Rashidun*, was worthy of imitation – he rejected all the advances of modern society, its technological achievements, the Enlightenment, Democracy etc. His outlook was characteristic of the 'All or Nothing' view of the Fanatic throughout history – and it became hugely influential.

Qutb's extensive writings (he produced twenty-four books and hundreds of articles) have had a great and lasting influence on Islamic Jihadist/terror groups throughout the Islamic world. Effectively, as a Qur'anic scholar, he bestowed religious authority on their acts of terror, whether these were directed at non-Muslims or believers. For him, there was no middle ground in the cosmic battle between those who believe in Allah (or rather Qutb's interpretation of his laws), and those on the side of Satan (i.e. everyone else). All Muslims had a duty to engage in this fight – and those who reject Qutb's interpretations were only worthy of destruction. *Jahiliyya* (Ignorance), by which he meant all other cultures and all the trappings of modernism, had to be eliminated, not only from the Islamic homeland but from the face of the Earth. This distorted philosophy, which sanctioned the merciless killing of innocent non-combatants, inspired Al-Qaeda in their attacks on the New York Twin Towers and the Bali bombings, and conferred a sense of legitimacy on the self-appointed, so-called 'Islamic State'. Both groups, and other radical jihadist movements, still follow its twisted logic.

Qutb was brought to trial by the Egyptian authorities in 1966, and executed for his alleged involvement in a plot to assassinate Nasser. He is considered a martyr by most Jihadists, and as the 'philosopher of the Islamic Revolution' continues to influence them. There are two further aspects of his tenets that he shared with the Nazis – he was a fervent anti-semite and an enthusiastic supporter of 'Eugenics'.

Abu Abdullah al-Muhajir *The Theology of Jihad* / *The Jurisprudence of Blood* - Abu Bakr Naji *The Management of Savagery*

There is a common theme in all of the accounts covered in this chapter, namely, that the possession of a mind-set that feels complete moral ascendency can allow an individual, or a group, to disregard normal ethical scruples. This is certainly the case in the modern *Salafist/Jihahdist* movement, whose shocking brutality in recent times is a terrible affirmation of the capacity of the written word to justify the unjustifiable.

The notorious Jordanian jihadist Abu Musab al-Zarqawi, the founder of 'Islamic State', (known as the 'Sheik of the Slaughterers' – and a psychopath if there ever was one) – derived the brutal methods that he applied in Iraq (2003-06) directly from the ideas espoused in the above books. Following Abu Abdullah al-Muhajir, Zarqawi introduced and personally carried out public beheadings, later declaring that 'The brutality of beheading is intended, even delightful, to God and his Prophet'. And he used the strategic theories advocated in Abu Bakr Naji's *The Management of Savagery* to justify the use of suicide bombings against not only the Western occupation forces, but to kill fellow Muslims in Iraq – effectively turning the existing insurgency into a sectarian, Sunni-Shia civil war. The killing of fellow Muslims and the act of suicide are expressly forbidden in Islam, but al-Muhajir's justifications in *The Jurisprudence of Blood* provided the necessary theological cover for both. Suicide bombing has since become an established feature of Jihadist insurgent terrorism, and anti-Shia sectarianism, including the bombing of crowded Mosques, continues.

As well as glorifying suicide-attacks and providing justifications for mass public-beheadings (of Muslims and non-Muslims), these savage writings sanction the indiscriminate killing of civilians, the use of torture, assassination, the burning of prisoners, the massacre of non-believers and the enslavement of their women – and all of these things have been put into practice. These writings give the impression that any atrocity whatsoever could, in the name of their supposedly religious *jihad*, be justified. For this reason these texts became indispensable to the so-called Islamic State. They were widely circulated among the group's provincial commanders and members, and were used as training manuals for new recruits. The vicious, brutal tone of *The Jurisprudence of Blood* and *The Management of Savagery* even extends to the notorious ISIS/Daesh videos posted on the Internet for propaganda and recruitment purposes – the 21st century digital sophistication of these productions making a bizarre contrast with the *Jihadists* 7th century aspirations. Only in the realm of the Story could the portrayal of such extreme violence, linked to a half-baked theology, be portrayed in the soft, sickly romantic tones of these postings.

*

The *Jihadist* excesses are the most recent of sustained, narrative-driven atrocities, but they are hardly unique. Because of the singular nature of human susceptibility to 'evil persuasion', abusive propaganda has more often than not been the precursor of reprehensible acts. In fact it could be said that the demonisation of a group is virtually a prerequisite for large-scale violence directed against them. In these acts the natural human instincts of empathy have to be suppressed – the target groups have to become the 'other', 'less than human', 'not like us'. All the evidence indicates that the enlightened benefits of modernity have not provided immunity from this. The 20th century saw many examples of both hate-filled propaganda and genocide – The Russian Pogroms; The Nazi Holocaust; Stalin's annihilation of the 'Kulaks' in 1930-31; the 'Killing Fields' of the Khmer Rouge 'Great Revolution' of 1975-1979; the Rwandan Civil War of 1990, in which up to a million Tutsis were killed; the Bosnian 'ethnic cleansing' campaign of 1995 – and more recently we have seen the abominable Buddhist persecution of the Rohingya in Burma. These are just some of the more serious examples of propaganda-inspired mass-persecution of the past century. The question arises: How are we as intelligent, feeling beings, peaceful for the most part, led into committing these crimes?

I have to refer back to Chapter 3... 'The narratives that we create for ourselves naturally justify all our actions, reasonable and unreasonable. They make every perception, and every action based on them, appear to be part of a consistent, seamless whole – they establish our credentials and create a responsive format with which to deal with the world. This is what humans are *really* good at; we are myth-makers and myth-believers, and for the most part we are far more concerned with maintaining the narrative matrix of our existence than with questioning any part of it. One way or another, a satisfactory story *has* to be constructed... even if it is concerned to justify the most atrocious acts imaginable.'

Postscript

*'We are accustomed to think of myths as the opposite of science. But in
fact they are a central part of it; the part that decides its significance
in our lives. Myths… are imaginative patterns, networks of powerful
symbols that suggest particular ways of interpreting the world.'*
MARY MIDGELY

*'Myths are not so much the contents of consciousness, as deep
structures that shape the contents of consciousness.'*
W. LANCE BENNETT

None of us live, or could ever live, in atomistic isolation – our
individualised, free-willing selves are, ironically, only realisable
within a cultural context. We have all been socialised into
particular, culture-based narratives and, although we are scarcely
ever aware of the fact, this is the matrix of our reality. There
is more to all of us, of course, than the mere re-enactment of
broad cultural assumptions. These 'deep' narratives are infinitely
moderated – by layers of sub-cultural narrative, by local, familial
and personal influences, and by individual interpretations of all of
the above. As a result, and despite our being thoroughly culture-
bound, we each have our own 'mythality', our own outlook that
determines the way we think, feel and interact with the greater
world. This way of living, and of relating to others of our own

kind, is uniquely human, and is almost entirely facilitated by our aptitude for language and its supporting narratives.

However, the notion that such a large part of our thoughts and feelings are comprehensively predetermined does not gain easy acceptance. In particular, the idea that we live in accordance with some common 'mythology' is particularly hard to swallow. The term 'myth' carries the sense of a collection of popular beliefs, unsupported by facts, and this is clearly not where we are at. Our realities are as factual as can be. It seems obvious to us as individuals that the objects, events and attitudes of our world are entirely consistent and plausible – more so than those of other world-views in fact. It takes a stretch of the imagination to appreciate that the ideas, beliefs, stories, customs, jokes etc. of other cultures can be anything like as convincing as the realities of our own cultural existence. In fact this feeling is exacerbated because social groups in general tend to define themselves not only by their own shared storylines, but also in contradistinction to those of others.

That our minds and brains are intimately connected is now a common assumption, but the extended notion, that our *selves* reside solely in our *brains*, is still a relatively modern concept – and it remains problematic. It is still rather difficult for most of us to take on board the fact that all the subtleties, creative powers and experiences of the human intellect (particularly of our own) somehow derive from a series of electro-chemical impulses occurring within the fatty tissue that we all carry around in our heads. Indeed, it almost defies belief that the richness of our experience, the complexities of our instincts and emotions, not to mention the extraordinary workings of our consciousness and self-awareness, can really be the product of a mere biological system, however complex. But that, for sure, is the way it is. The mundane miracle of our capacity to perceive, and essentially to recreate the world in our minds, is driven by just these electro-biomechanical processes. Ironically, a healthy functioning mind has no real sense of the existential illusion involved in this extraordinary process; generally speaking we accept our realities for what they are.

But there is of course another layer to all of this, to the multifarious ways we experience the world, because each of us has our own, very personal, outlook. Which is to say that we are not only conscious beings, we are *self*-conscious; each of us has a strong individual sense of ourselves. Moreover, we can communicate our views and needs to others in a way that no other creature can. In fact our personal narratives are the most important component of our psyche – to the extent that a serious impairment to our individual story-line can be as devastating as physical damage to our brains. To be a complete, functioning human being we *must* have a storyline, and it *must* be coherent. A completely unattached personality, free of cultural identity, is inconceivable. Narratives hold us together, individually and collectively.

By extension, any disorder of individual thoughts and feeling, and every sort of social dislocation, is likely to be accompanied by a dysfunctional narrative. The implications of this are that there are negative as well as positive aspects on our reliance on the Story – we frequently see the adoption of implausible explanations when there is no acceptable alternative for instance. Humans possess language, but we, in turn, can become possessed by narratives, written or spoken. Taken together, the power of human imagination and our susceptibility to narrative enchantment should never be underestimated – a fact that has been demonstrated many times in recent history. The persuasive power of ideological texts, particularly those seemingly possessed by pathological certainty, is enormous and can have extremely negative consequences. The power of the Story should never be underestimated.

Further Reading

1. The Ape that learned to Talk

Research into human evolution has become one of the most rapidly developing fields of contemporary science. This is partly due to the relatively recent introduction of the new technologies of scanning and DNA analysis. These, together with some extraordinary recent discoveries, have meant that paleoanthropological theories on the origins of our own and other hominid species have changed dramatically over the past two decades and are likely to be changed again as fresh discoveries are made. Unfortunately this has meant that published material can be rapidly outdated, and that the Internet can be a more reliable source of the latest thinking on the subject. Nevertheless, the following books and articles are thoroughly recommended:

- *Human Origins: 7 million years and counting*, New Scientist Instant Expert Series
- *Our Human Story*, by Louise Humphrey & Chris Stringer, Natural History Museum, London
- 'Human Origins' - National Geographic
  https://www.nationalgeographic.com/science/human-origins/

- *Human Evolution* in Wikipedia
  https://en.wikipedia.org/wiki/Human_evolution
- *How Language Began*, Daniel Everett, Profile Books, 2017
- *From Hand to Mouth: The Origins of Language*,
  Michael Corballis, Princeton Univ. Press, 2002
- *The Articulate Mammal*, Jean Aitchison, Hutchinson, 1976

2. Our Narrative Selves
- *On the Origin of Stories*, Brian Boyd, Harvard Univ. Press, 2009
- *The Literary Mind*, Mark Turner, Oxford Univ. Press, 1996
- *The Voices Within*, Charles Fernyhough, Profile Books, 2016

3. The Story-weaving Mind
- *Human: The Science behind what makes us Unique*, Michael S.
  Gazzaniga, Harper Collins, 2008
- *The Master and his Emissary: The Divided Brain and the Making
  of the Western World*, Iain McGilchrist, Yale Univ. Press, 2009
- *Memory, Identity, Community: The Idea of Narrative in the
  Human Sciences*, Ed. By Lewis P. Hinchman & Sandra K.
  Hinchman, State Univ. of New Yorl Press, 2001
- *Brain Fiction: Self-Deception and the Riddle of Confabulation*,
  William Hirstein, MIT Press, 2005

4. 'Did you hear about… ?'
- *Grooming, Gossip and the Evolution of Language*,
  Robin Dunbar, Faber & Faber, 1996
- *How Many Friends does One Person Need?*, Robin Dunbar,
  Faber & Faber, 2010
- *Thinking Big: How the Evolution of Social Life Shaped the
  Human Mind*, Clive Gamble, John Gowlett and Robin
  Dunbar, Thames & Hudson, 2014
- *Made to Stick: Why Some Ideas Survive and Others Die*, Heath
  and Heath, Random House, 2007
- *Voodoo Histories: The role of the Conspiracy Theory in shaping*

Modern History, David Aaronovitch, Random House, 2009

5. Inner Fictions: Dreams, Daydreams & Fantasies
- *The I in dreaming*, New Scientist, 12th March, 2011
- *Private life of the brain*, New Scientist, 8th November 208
- *A default mode of brain function*, Raichle et al, PNAS, 16th January, 2001
- *Lucid Dreaming: Gateway to the Inner Self*, Robert Waggoner (eBook)

6. Persuasive Narratives
- *The Age of Propaganda*, Anthony Pratkanis and Elliot Aronsem, W. H. Freeman, 1991
- *Techniques of Persuasion*, J. A. C. Brown, Penguin Books, 1963
- *A History of Hypnotism*, Alan Gauld, Cambridge University Press, 1995
- *The Hypnotic Brain*, Peter Brown, Yale Univ. Press, 1991

7. Compelling Tales
- *Why people believe Weird Things*, Michael Shermer, W.H. Freeman, 1997
- *Cults of Unreason*, Dr. Christopher Evans, Harrap, 1973

8. The Sacred Word
- *The Believing Brain*, Michael Shermer, Times Books, 2011

9. Heresy!
- *The Heretics*, Barrows Dunham, Eyre & Spottiswood, 1965

10. Cover Stories: Rationalisations & Justifications
- *Mistakes were Made (but not by Me): Why we Justify Foolish Beliefs, Bad Decisions and Hurtful Acts*, Carol Travis and Eliot Aronson, Pinter and Martin, 2007

11. 'We Shall all be Saved': Narratives of Redemption
- *The Trumpet Shall Sound*, Peter Worsley, Paladin Books, 1957
- *Magic & The Millennium*, Bryan R. Wilson, Heinemann, 1973
- *The Rush Hour of the Gods*, H. Neill McFarland, Macmillan, 1967

12. The Terrors of Hell
- *The Formation of Hell*, Alan E. Bernstein, Cornell Univ. Press, 1993
- *The Fear of Hell*, Piero Camporesi, Pennsylvania State Univ. Press, 1990

13. Versions of Utopia
- *Utopia & Anti-Utopia in Modern Times*, Krishnan Kumar, Basil Blackwell, 1987
- *The Faber Book of Utopias*, ed. John Carey, Faber & Faber, 1999

14. Toxic Texts: Licence for Atrocity
- *The European Witch-Craze of the 16th and 17th Centuries*, Hugh Trevor-Roper, Pelican Books, 1969
- *Whores of the Devil: Witch-Hunts and Witch-Trials*, Erik Durschmied. Sutton Publishing, 2005
- *Fanaticism*, Haynal, Molnar and Puymege, Schoken Books, 1983
- *Fundamentalism*, Malise Ruthven, Oxford Univ. Press, 2004
- *The True Believer*, Eric Hoffer, Harper, 1951

Postscript
- *The Myths We Live By*, Mary Midgely, Routledge, 2004
- *The Myths of Reality*, Simon Danser, Alternative Albion, 2005

Index

WITH A LOVE FOR BOOKS

With a large range of imprints, from herbalism, selfsufficiency, physical and mental wellbeing, food, memoirs and many more, Herbary Books is shaped by the passion for writing and bringing innovative ideas close to our readers.

All our authors put their hearts into their books and as publishers we just lend a helping hand to bring their creation to life.

Thank you to our authors and to you, dear reader.

Discover and purchase all our books on
WWW.HERBARYBOOKS.COM